THE SMILING MUSE

A IS Albert Edward, well-meaning but flighty,
Who invited King Arthur, the blameless and mighty,
To meet Alcibiades and Aphrodite.

B IS for Bernhardt,
Who fails to awaken
Much feeling in Bismarck,
Barabbas and Bacon.

C IS Columbus, who tries to explain
How to balance an egg, to the utter disdain
Of Carlyle, Cleopatra, Confucius and Cain.

D'S for Diogenes,
Darwin and Dante,
Who delight in the dance
Of a darling Bacchante.

Oliver Herford.

Life's "Biographical Primer," selections from which appear here and facing each chapter, are from Volume 34 of Life in the issues of 3, 10, 17, and 24 August and 7 September 1899. This was an early magazine of satire, completely different from the later and better known pictorial magazine.

THE SMILING MUSE

Victoriana in the Comic Press

Jerold Savory
and
Patricia Marks

PHILADELPHIA
THE ART ALLIANCE PRESS
LONDON AND TORONTO: ASSOCIATED UNIVERSITY PRESSES

© 1985 by Associated University Presses, Inc.

Associated University Presses
440 Forsgate Drive
Cranbury, NJ 08512

Associated University Presses
25 Sicilian Avenue
London WC1A 2QH, England

Associated University Presses
2133 Royal Windsor Drive
Unit 1
Mississauga, Ontario
Canada L5J 1K5

Library of Congress Cataloging in Publication Data

Savory, Jerold.
  The smiling muse.

  Bibliography: p.
  Includes index.
  1. Parodies. 2. Caricature—Great Britain—History—
19th century. 3. Caricature—United States—History—
19th century. 4. Great Britain—Biography—19th century
—Portraits—Caricatures and cartoons. I. Marks,
Patricia. II. Title.
NX650.P37S28   1985   741.5′0941   82-46024
ISBN 0-87982-501-4

Printed in the United States of America

If the plural of "mouse" is "mice,"
Then, the plural of "spouse" must be "spice."

We assumed that it, then, might suffice
To dedicate this volume twice:

      TO ARDIS (who's nice).
      TO DENNIS (who's nice).

Our spouses.
         Our muses.
                Our *spice*.

Contents

Acknowledgments

OUR COLLECTING FOR THIS BOOK STARTED during 1977–78 when, as Fellows of the National Endowment for the Humanities, we spent the academic year at the University of Pennsylvania under the seminar leadership of Professor David J. DeLaura. We are grateful to Professor DeLaura for his encouragement and to the staffs of the University of Pennsylvania Library, the Free Library of Philadelphia, and the Newberry Library in Chicago for help in locating material. We also appreciate assistance from reference and periodicals librarians in several other libraries, especially in Washington, D.C., Boston, and New York, as well as from numerous colleagues who have sent us examples of cartoons, caricatures, and parodies and have provided helpful leads in locating others.

Portions of this book have appeared in different forms in several publications, and we appreciate permission to reprint from the following editors: Professor Ray B. Browne for "Mrs. Wettin Meets a Chum: *Life*'s View of Victoria, 1883–1901," published in the *Journal of American Culture* 3 (1980): 80–94; Professor John M. Hill for "A Charivari to Matthew Arnold," a special issue of *The Arnoldian* 7 (Winter 1980); and Professor Jack W. Herring for "'Other Likenesses' of Robert Browning: The Poet in Caricature, Cartoon, and Comic Commentary," Baylor University Browning Interests, no. 26 (February 1981).

We appreciate the support of our own institutions, Valdosta State College, Valdosta, Georgia, and Columbia College, Columbia, South Carolina, and especially thank Helen Jordan, Head of the J. Drake Edens Library of Columbia College, for her help in researching and writing parts of the chapter on Oscar Wilde and the Aesthetes, and Vicki Pullen, Head of Columbia College's Art Department, for her help with photography.

Finally, the book's dedication says the rest. Our spouses, Dennis Marks and Ardis Savory, one an astronomer and the other a marine scientist, and both our best friends and most helpful critics, have been especially supportive of their partners' collaborative efforts to bring the Victorian era into comic focus.

THE SMILING MUSE

E IS for Edison, making believe
    He's invented a clever contrivance for Eve,
Who complained that she never could laugh in her sleeve.

F IS for Franklin, who fearfully shocks
    The feelings of
Fenelon, Faber and Fox.

1
Perspectives from the Past

The pomposity of much of Victorian life as it appears to us today is not more due to the Victorians' pompous self-image than it is to the very nature of the way that these images were immortalized. Give a man enough time to know that he is going to be recorded for posterity, and he will invariably smooth his hair, straighten his tie and assume a noble posture.[1]

WITHOUT THE EXISTENCE OF THE CARICATUR-ists, we might suspect today that nineteenth-century England was populated exclusively by frock-coated gentlemen with ramrod backbones and by straight-laced women gravely contemplating their roles as angels in the house. The artists who drew for popular magazines and society papers, however, corrected such overly formal likenesses with zest, sending dignified public figures cavorting through the pages with lopsided grins and neck-cloths askew. In fact, the exuberant printing practices of the late 1800s, coupled with major advances in photography, created a revolution in the way people saw themselves. In the 1860s the fashionable traded small *carte de visite* photographs,[2] very much as sports fans trade baseball cards; but by the 1890s, when magazines were printing elaborately engraved portraits with blank backs,[3] almost everyone engaged in the collecting mania.

Of course, not all of the "collectibles" were flat-tering portraits; *Vanity Fair* had been printing lithographed caricatures of well-known figures for years. As such caricatures show, the movement toward informality, toward depicting the individual engaged in his everyday activities, affected not just the man in the street but people in public positions as well. Perhaps such candid poses fostered the view that those in government were human beings with flaws and eccentricities rather than infallible rulers; perhaps they helped the average reader understand that literary men and women were not removed from the human condition, but immersed in it. What is certain, however, is that the caricaturists were at the forefront of the movement to informality. Aided by a growing popular press, they created an up-to-date visual commentary on current affairs, and because they made their subjects available to the public, they influenced as well as reflected popular taste. The humorists who wrote the remarks that appeared with the drawings or

13

alone as special features had a similar effect. As the nether side of serious analysis, this body of parodic material is, for the general reading public, what a review is to the scholarly. Any study of reader reaction must take caricatures and parodies into account if it is to be complete, for while no literary debate was conducted or novel written to please *Punch* or *Life*, the humorous output provides one important way to understand the popular mythology that contributes to the reputation of any public figure.

That the general readership was very much aware of noteworthy personalities and literary movements became evident as we turned the crumbling, dusty pages of some dozen late nineteenth-century periodicals. Queen Victoria, enthroned on a tuffet, graced the front cover of *Life*; the aesthetes minced through the pages of *Punch*; versifiers everywhere mimicked Gilbert's rhymes and Tennyson's meter. Clearly, an examination of selected caricatures and parodies from 1870 onward[4] would provide a key not only to reader interest on both sides of the Atlantic but to the literary character of the popular press in the latter half of the century. To limit the size of the volume, we decided to focus on the way in which certain British notables appeared to the popular imagination and, where possible, to point out the differences between American and British reactions.

Individuals were chosen for inclusion whenever the weight of periodical material allowed a reasonably detailed reading to be made, but in most cases they would have been included by reason of reputation alone. Matthew Arnold, as poet and essayist, influenced the course of critical theory, just as Robert Browning created a distinctive form of poetry; each of the two Alfreds—Tennyson and Austin—served as poet laureate and thus (presumably) as the national voice; Oscar Wilde and his devotees forced not just a change in manners and dress but a serious reconsideration of aesthetic attitudes. Where no single name dominated the publishing scene, as is true for theatrical figures and novelists, composite chapters are given. Two non-literary shapers of the age are included: Queen Victoria and Charles Darwin so affected the social, political, scientific, and ethical ideas of the time that no other figures can be viewed intelligently in isolation from them.

The material in question includes artwork ranging in complexity from the distinctive lithographs in *Vanity Fair* and the photomontages in *Life* to the simple line drawings that appear almost univer-

sally. Excerpts from the comic "biographies" that frequently accompany the caricatures are given when pertinent. Much of the humorous reaction is in the form of ephemeral anecdotes and more substantial parodic plays, poems, and essays, many of which presuppose some knowledge, not only of the original piece of literature, but also of topical events. The periodicals themselves are popular rather than literary and represent all complexions of humor,[5] from the jocularity of *Puck* to the nimble-wittedness of *Punch*. Some isolated examples are taken from such primarily newsworthy sources as the *New York Tribune*, but these are rare. What follows is a brief historical overview of some of the periodicals represented in our survey.

AMERICAN SOURCES

Three of the American periodicals examined—*Life*, *Puck*, and *Judge*—played a prominent role in entertaining their readers with the fine art of satire. Others—*Tid-Bits* and Collier's *Once a Week*—were general–interest magazines whose publication of parody was sporadic. Where the concentration of caricature and parody of British figures was highest, the periodicals were most fiercely "American," warning their readership against money-gouging British entertainers and "anglomania" and trying to bring comparable American talent to the fore. Despite such a chauvinistic stance, however, the same periodicals heaped encomiums upon "real" talent like Tennyson's and Henry Irving's and treated Victoria with affectionate regard.

Life: Founded on 4 January 1883 by John Ames Mitchell, an artist for *Our Continent*, *Life* was designed primarily as a picture paper whose goal was "getting in some painful punches upon the ribs of Melancholy and Humbug." In Mitchell's own words the line illustrations, reproduced by the sharper and more direct photoengraving process, were to be

of a style and quality unlike anything then published this side of the Atlantic. . . . Such drawings . . . must show a lightness of touch, an ease, brilliancy and force of expression . . . and a sense of humor, a playfulness and a gentle exaggeration.[6]

Mitchell attracted a host of young talent, many having served apprenticeship on the Harvard *Lampoon* and the *Acta Columbiana*. The group included the artists Francis Attwood, Charles Dana Gibson, W. A. Rogers, and Charles Kendrick, and such writers as John Kendrick Bangs, a prolific humorist; Brander Matthews, *Life*'s first drama critic; and Thomas Masson, eventually the literary editor. The magazine's motto—"Americanus Sum"—well represented its middle-class readership,[7] and its standard cover, drawn by Mitchell himself, featured the words *Society*, *Politics*, *Literature*, and *Drama*, embellished by cupids and hearts and flowers. By 1890 the circulation had reached 50,000; by 1915 it hit 150,000, a figure swelled by the Gibson Girl craze, the popularity of James Montgomery Flagg's illustrations, and editorial emphasis on the new American hobby—the automobile. Mitchell's death in 1918 began the slow decline that the Depression in the thirties completed; in 1936 *Life* was bought by Time, Inc. for a new venture that resembled it in name only. As one writer laments, "In its last decade it was a strayed reveler, having lost its way in a confused world."[8]

Puck: Unlike *Life*, which emerged full-blown in 1883, *Puck* was an offshoot of a German publication begun in September 1876 by Joseph Keppler, whose earlier yearling of the same name had failed in 1871. Keppler provided most of the illustrations for *Puck*, drawing bold, bright chromolithographed cartoons for front and back covers and centerfold, more than half of which are concerned with domestic politics. Henry C. Bunner, who assumed an editorship in 1878, provided not only the captions for the illustrations but much of the literary satire as well. He was later joined by R. K. Munkittrick, Carolyn Wells, and John Kendrick Bangs (who became the editor in 1904 after a stint at *Harper's Weekly*). Frederick Opper and Bernhard Gillam were two of the artists whose trenchant criticism of such varied social and political manifestations as divorce, Twain-ism and Blaine-ism, and women's suffrage gave the periodical a vibrancy that accounted for a circulation of 90,000 in the 1890s. The readership was certainly more politically oriented than that of *Life* and clearly enjoyed a humor that was brasher and less sophisticated. That *Puck*'s motto (" 'What fools these Mortals be!' ") was drawn from Shakespeare and that its masthead figure, an artless, chubby cupid garbed only in top-hat and tails, were anomalous to *Puck*'s political tenor scarcely seemed to bother its readers. World War I affected *Puck*'s use of color and paper stock; even a sale to Hearst

was unable to help, and it ceased publication in September 1918.[9]

Judge: Judge was founded in October 1881 by a splinter group of artists from *Puck*, with James Albert Wales as the editor. Too similar to its parent in its chromolithography and social commentary to flourish initially, *Judge* finally acquired an independent personality in 1884, when the Republican party, smarting under *Puck*'s blows, provided financial support. Both Bernhard Gillam and Eugene Zimmerman left *Puck* for the new rival. By the 1890s the circulation was in the fifty-thousand range; R. K. Munkittrick wrote for *Judge*, and the anonymous theatrical reviews were noteworthy for their severity. By 1910, when the Leslie Company replaced Republican support, other well-known humorists, among them Carolyn Wells, were attracted to the magazine. The Judge himself, a twinkling-eyed figure who loomed over the front-page cartoon, was a more fitting overseer than *Puck*'s cherub; in any case, *Judge* outlasted both of its rivals, buying *Life*'s subscription list and features in 1936.[10]

Collier's *Once a Week:* This general-interest periodical carried a variety of titles from its inception in 1888 by Peter Fenelon Collier to its demise in 1957 when the Crowell/Collier Company went out of business. In 1892, when the first editor, Nugent Robinson, retired, the magazine had a circulation of a quarter of a million subscribers. With Robinson's retirement came a shift from what was essentially a "story magazine" to a news magazine that eventually achieved fame for its halftone news pictures; nonetheless, its roster of authors included such fine writers as Henry James, Rudyard Kipling, Frank Norris, and William Sydney Porter. By the early 1900s, when the circulation had increased by another fifty thousand, *Collier's* featured such well-known illustrators as Maxfield Parrish, Frederick Remington, James Montgomery Flagg, and even Charles Dana Gibson, who by 1903 was no longer the exclusive property of *Life*.[11]

Tid-Bits: Tid-Bits, which began as an eclectic in 1884, reprinting snippets of humor and excerpts from other popular magazines, became almost entirely a humor magazine with original pieces after Wolcott Balestier assumed the editorship in 1886.

The periodical changed its name to *Time* in 1888 and ceased publication when *Time* was bought by *Munsey's* Weekly in 1890.[12]

Chic: Chic, a short-lived weekly published in New York in 1880–81, featured sophisticated wit and colored lithographs drawn by Charles Kendrick, who contributed heavily to *Life*. In format *Chic* is a cross between *Life* and *Puck*, but the lithographs are less garish than those by Opper and Gillam and by virtue of their subject matter—conditions in the theater, fashionable excesses—appealed to an audience that was on the whole more interested in society and the arts than in politics.

BRITISH SOURCES

The British publications from which the literary parodies and caricatures in this volume are drawn run the gamut from "society" papers like *Vanity Fair* to comic sheets like *Fun*. The range itself illustrates what Donald Gray sees as "a change in comic journalism" that took place during the century as a whole,

from an enterprise which at least pretended to correct political and social opinions and institutions, to one which tended to reassure its readers that what they thought about such matters was right and proper, to one which tended to take its readers' minds off such matters entirely.[13]

Vanity Fair: Founded by Thomas Gibson Bowles, *Vanity Fair* appeared in November 1868, beginning a forty-six year commentary on social and political issues. One of its best-known features is the series of caricatures of figures of the day, including politicians, scientists, sporting personalities, and literary men. The greater number of lithographs were drawn by Leslie Ward (Spy) and Carlo Pellegrini (Ape), although many other artists, including Bernard Partridge, Max Beerbohm, and James Montgomery Flagg, contributed their talents. In keeping with his idea that satire is "the unheroic representation of heroes," Bowles, as "Jehu Jr.," began the practice of providing a sardonic commentary for each of the illustrations.[14] The readership was an urbane one, of all political persuasions; according to *Deacon's Press Guide*, it was "'probably read by a larger number of official and wealthy persons than any other English weekly journal.'"[15]

Punch: The comic genius of Mr. Punch greeted the world on 17 July 1841 under the aegis of Mark Lemon, Henry Mayhew, and Stirling Coyne. Long an institution of British humor, *Punch* acquired so long a list of writers and artists that to name a few of the important—Tenniel, Du Maurier, Thackeray—is to leave many out. Like most humor magazines, *Punch* had an initially disappointing circulation, but the publication of the first supplementary *Almanac* secured its success. In 1880 Francis Cowley Burnand was the editor, followed by Owen Seaman, himself a parodist. Under Burnand *Punch* seemingly published "more about leisure and less about work, . . . more about behavior and less about action"; as R. Price, *Punch*'s historiographer, notes, Burnand changed the character of the magazine by substituting "the jovial for the humorous" and by ignoring "subtlety, tension and irony." During this period *Punch* attracted such artists as Linley Sambourne and Bernard Partridge, who complained that *Punch*'s printing methods were so out of date that detail could not be adequately reproduced.[16] In fact, *Punch* did not print the first photographic "process" block until December 1892 and waited until January 1896 to take advantage of the halftone. Nonetheless, the excellence of its artwork (due in certain measure to the skill of its engravers) and the aptness of its parodies made *Punch* the most imitated if not the most envied comic periodical of the era.[17]

Fun: The first editor of this successful rival to *Punch* was Tom Hood, who published the initial issue in September 1861. Ownership passed to the Dalziels, who made the periodical into a Liberal organ to counterbalance their conservative publication, *Judy*. *Fun* published numerous satirical poems, witty commentary of social and political interest, and a multitude of line illustrations; one of its most famous contributors was W. S. Gilbert with his Bab ballads. Ellegard estimates that its circulation in 1870 was approximately twenty thousand; he further comments that its lower- and middle-class readership was politically more liberal than that of *Punch*.[18]

The multitude of caricatures and parodies in the periodicals we examined raises the perennial—and apparently unsolvable—question of how far the popular writer or artist is influenced by the reading public and to what extent he shapes the public's taste. Clearly, a periodical that, like *Punch*, attracts an intelligent readership over a long period of time may be said to have achieved a delicate balance between leading and following its readers. Amy Cruse, for example, who uses "implications and references" in *Punch* to determine what literature its readership preferred, finds the periodical to be not only "a new social force" in its debunking of hypocrisy, but also an accurate reflector of social habit. An examination of the tone she attributes to its treatment of various literary figures illustrates both functions. In the case of Macaulay's *History of England*, she finds "kindly patronage" for its errors and "ironical praise" for its length, both adding up to a not-so-genial warning about the pitfalls in popularized history. Toward Dickens, however, she finds Mr. Punch to be as "familiar and affectionate" as the novelist's own readers.[19] Critical opinion has borne out these assessments by Mr. Punch, but other editors' opinions have not been so astute. *Life*, for example, adopted Thackeray as a novelistic model, but clearly preferred Austin Dobson and other proponents of "genteel" poetry to Whitman, Browning, and Poe.[20]

No matter how unfriendly, caricatures of literary figures do provide an index to the authors whom the reading public knew by reputation, just as satires, parodies, and imitations indicate which works were popularly read. Much of the material is, of course, topical; the humor is lost if the reader is not familiar with what is burlesqued. Even if the captions are obscure today, however, the caricatures are not. In fact, in their own day they frequently established an individual's reputation for good or ill so firmly that the real person became subsidiary to his published image. Cruse, for example, recounts what happened when a little girl met Disraeli for the first time: " 'I know you,' she said, 'I've seen you in *Punch*.' "[21] This homiletic function of caricature is especially exploited by the creators of political cartoons, who wield enormous power in baring abuses. Thomas Nast is perhaps the best-known proponent of this kind of corrective cartooning, a cartooning so effective that his victim Boss Tweed is purported to have said, " 'Stop them damn pictures. . . . I don't care so much what the papers write about me. My constituents can't read. But, damn it, they can see pictures.' "[22] The "constituents" of literary figures could, of course, both read and see; while the corrective function is primarily appropriated by serious criticism, humorous responses removed literary heroes from Parnassian heights and made them available to their readership in a witty and memorable light.

One reason for the flourishing of comic material in the late nineteenth century can be formulated inferentially; that is, the appearance of literary caricatures and parodies in periodicals that were primarily political or social (e.g., *Judge*, *Truth*, *Vanity Fair*) seems to indicate a different conception of the well-read man from the one prevalent in the twentieth century. Many of these periodicals had a very broad interest base, publishing articles ranging from political commentary to literary satire. The diversified readership initially attracted by this broad base not only remained, but grew in size, as is attested by the economic stability and long lives of many of the publications. With very few exceptions, the potpourri of political, social, theatrical, and literary features offered to the nineteenth-century audience in the periodicals we have studied simply does not exist in the more specialized magazines available today; when it does, the literary "news" is more often than not confined to a book-review column rather than spread throughout.

The primary reason for the outpouring of parody and caricature may, however, be ascribed to the tremendous growth of the popular press, for which numerous causes, other than the rise of literacy, may be cited.[23] In England alone, between 1864 and 1884 the number of periodicals more than doubled, going from 126 to 276;[24] in the United States, a five-year analysis of publication figures shows that between 1870 and 1880 the number of magazines published increased by 92%.[25] As one analyst points out somewhat facetiously: "Apart from the lecture platform the most serious competitor, both inexpensive and readily available, was liquor."[26] According to R. W. Gilder, editor of the *Century* in the late 1800s, dailies, weeklies, and monthlies outstripped quarterlies in popularity because of the reader's insatiable thirst for news and entertainment.[27] That the reader's curiosity could be easily and cheaply satisfied is not the only answer, however. Clarence Gohdes cites increasing Anglo-American cooperation as one of the reasons for the press's growth; by 1870 "editorial policies" and "superiority of American methods of illustration" had attracted a wide British readership, and by 1890 the proliferation of American magazines in Britain had made simultaneous publication unprofitable for American authors.[28] Such transatlantic overlapping of serious periodicals in which new works of fiction and poetry were published created a cosmopolitan readership familiar with both American and British works; this sort of familiarity made British parody and caricature intelligible to Americans, and vice versa.

Importantly, technological advances in all phases of printing were the handmaiden to experimentation; in fact, even a superficial comparison of two publications, *Punchinello* (1870) and *Life* (1883–1936), shows not just that the latter had better-trained artists but that it had more sophisticated printing capabilities. Nonetheless, some editors who admired the Cruikshank tradition of expressive pen work found the inevitable stylistic changes unattractive. Gilder, for example, directly blamed the development of photography for the factual and "prosaic" content of much magazine art, complaining that contemporary illustration was too formalistic.[29] To be sure, a number of artists whose work appeared in turn-of-the-century issues of *Life* seemed to be imitating the photograph by relying on delineation rather than on suggestion, but no one will disagree that some of the best illustrations were the result of improvements in the printing process. The evolution from woodblock to halftone had at least two far-reaching effects: the artist, no longer dependent on the engraver, could have his work reproduced exactly as it appeared in the original; moreover, he could create delicate tonal shades by means of washes, a technique impossible when cross-hatching was the only way to produce a semblance of shading on wood.

What facilitated the development of the new printing processes was, of course, Louis Daguerre's accidental discovery in 1839 that an image on an iodized silver plate could be developed by mercury fumes. Once the process was perfected, a number of applications resulted.[30] One of the simplest, pasting the photograph directly onto the wood block to foster accurate hand engraving, saved many priceless drawings from being similarly destroyed, as was the case in the *Punch* offices between 1841 and 1880.[31] Another, more advanced application was developed by Walter Bently Woodbury in 1866. While woodburytype and analogous intaglio methods created fine photographic reproductions, none could be used in conjunction with ordinary press runs because the contours of the images could not be inked in conformity with the contours of the type. It was Fox Talbot's 1852 "photoglyptic engraving" that prepared the way for the halftone, a revolutionary process that entailed breaking up a photographic image into dots or points and then bathing the plate in acid to produce a mechanically reproducible photograph. The popular press took immediate advantage of the development: on 4 March 1880 the *New York Daily Graphic* published the first such picture.[32] Magazines seem to have been slower than newspapers to retool their presses; the 1884 *Century* was apparently the first to print such an illustration.[33]

Given the remarkable changes taking place both in the readership and in printing processes, research in nineteenth-century periodicals has been surprisingly meager. For information about American sources Frank Luther Mott's five-volume *History of American Magazines, 1741 to 1930* (1930–68) is indispensable, but unfortunately no up-to-date bibliographical compilation exists. Researchers can go, however, to the "Newspapers and Periodicals" division of Lewis Leary's *Articles on American Literature, 1900–1950* (1954) and *1950–1967* (1970), or to the "Periodicals" subsection of the yearly MLA *International Bibliography*. Some information can be gleaned from *Poole's Index to Periodical Literature* and the *Nineteenth-Century Reader's Guide*. Those who investigate the histories of British publications are more fortunate: not only does the Research Society for Victorian Periodicals publish a journal, the *Victorian Periodicals Review*, but Lionel Madden and Diana Dixon have compiled *The Nineteenth-Century Periodical Press in Britain: A Bibliography of Modern Studies, 1901–1971* (1975). In addition J. Don Vann and Rosemary T. VanArsdel have edited *Victorian Periodicals: A Guide to Research* (1978), and Donald Gray has written a valuable introduction to his "List of Comic Periodicals Published in Great Britain, 1800–1900" (*VPN*, 1972). A bibliography appears at the end of this volume.

What remains to be examined, then, is the collection of caricatures and parodies that link us directly to the popular mythologies about literature and culture in the late nineteenth century. To open a copy of *Fun* or *Life* to the Bab illustrations as Gilbert drew them or the diminutive, cherubic Victoria that Attwood created is to participate, if only briefly, in a bygone era. Compiling such a collection of parodies and caricatures is thus not only to take pleasure in fine artwork or in clever turns of phrase, but to become acquainted with the nineteenth-century imagination itself.

1. William Sansom, "The Fabric of Life," in *Victorian Life in Photographs* (London: Thames and Hudson, 1974), p. 29.

2. Brian Coe, *The Birth of Photography: The Story of the Formative Years, 1800–1900* (New York: Taplinger, 1977), p. 35.

3. Frank Luther Mott, *A History of American Magazines*, 5 vols. (Cambridge, Mass.: Harvard University Press, 1938–68), 4:152.

4. The collection begins with 1870, the year of Dickens's death, and ends with the First World War. While some of the material may appear incidentally in more specialized sources, such as biographies, we do not duplicate other studies such as Graham Everitt's *English Caricaturists and Graphic Humorists of the Nineteenth Century* (London: Swan Sonnenschein, 1893), a book whose focus is on caricatures published before 1864. One of the more complete collections of nineteenth-century parodies is Walter Hamilton's *Parodies of the Works of English and American Authors*, 6 vols. (London: Reeves & Turner, 1884–89); again, we include much material either not noticed by him or published after 1889.

5. One of the best descriptions of the comic press is given by Donald Gray in "A List of Comic Periodicals Published in Great Britain, 1800–1900, with a Prefatory Essay," *Victorian Periodicals Newsletter*, no. 15 (1972): 2–39. He notes a number of characteristics: such periodicals are inexpensive and published frequently; they are illustrated, the drawings running the gamut from small cuts to large double-page cartoons; they are "highly topical," treating contemporary matters in "puns, squibs, parodies, versions of theatrical burlesque and pantomime, and . . . continuing features."

6. John Ames Mitchell, "How *Life* Began," *Life* (Jubilee Number), January 1883, pp. 17–18.

7. John Flautz, *Life: The Gentle Satirist* (Bowling Green, Ohio: Bowling Green University Popular Press, 1972), pp. 3–4.

8. Mott, *History*, 4:556–68, gives a reliable sketch of *Life's* history.

9. For a sketch of *Puck's* history, see Mott, *History*, 3:518–32.

10. *Judge's* history appears in Mott, *History*, 3:553–56.

11. *Collier's* history appears in Mott, *History*, 4:453–79.

12. *Tid-Bits* is mentioned in Mott, *History*, 3:268.

13. Gray, "A List," p. 7.

14. The history of *Vanity Fair* is given in Jerold J. Savory's *The Vanity Fair Gallery: A Collector's Guide to the Caricatures* (South Brunswick and New York: A. S. Barnes, 1979).

15. Alvar Ellegard, "The Readership of the Periodical Press in Mid-Victorian Britain, Part II," *Victorian Periodicals Newsletter*, no. 13 (1971): 22.

16. Such archaic printing methods were one reason British magazines had lost ground to their American rivals by 1870; see Clarence Gohdes, *American Literature in Nineteenth-Century England* (Carbondale: Southern Illinois University Press, 1944), p. 67.

17. For a complete history of *Punch*, see M. H. Spielmann, *The History of Punch* (London: Cassell, 1895); R. G. G. Price, *A History of Punch* (London: Collins, 1957); and Arthur Prager, *The Mahogany Tree: An Informal History of Punch* (New York: Hawthorn Books, 1979).

18. Ellegard, "Readership," p. 22.

19. Amy Cruse, *The Victorians and Their Reading* (Boston: Houghton Mifflin, 1935), pp. 391, 394, and 399–400.

20. Flautz, *Gentle Satirist*, p. 123.

21. Cruse, *The Victorians*, p. 394.

22. Stephen Hess and Milton Kaplan, *The Ungentlemanly Art: A History of American Political Cartoons*, rev. ed. (New York: Macmillan, 1974), p. 13.

23. John S. North, "The Rationale—Why Read Victorian Periodicals?" in *Victorian Periodicals: A Guide to Research*, ed. J. Don Vann and Rosemary T. VanArsdel (New York: Modern Language Assoc., 1978), p. 4.

24. Ibid., p. 5.

25. Gohdes, *American Literature*, p. 67, n. 58, gives the number of periodicals published in each decade. The increase between 1840 and 1880 is an astounding 1,263%!

26. North, *Rationale*, p. 5.

27. Richard Watson Gilder, "Newspaper, the Magazine, and the Public," *Outlook*, 4 February 1899, pp. 316–21.

28. Gohdes, *American Literature*, pp. 56–57.

29. Gilder, "Newspaper," p. 320. Two contemporary writers would agree with Gilder. In *The History of the Nineteenth Century in Caricature*, Arthur Bartlett Maurice and Frederic Taber Cooper suggest that the movement from individual artistic expression to standardized editorial policy caused cartoonists to violate their own principles and that the rise of quick printing processes sacrificed care to haste and wasted talent on producing "mediocre" ideas (New York: Cooper Square, 1970), pp. 281–84.

30. Texts that deal with the connection between photograpy and printing abound. Two helpful ones are Brian Coe's The *Birth of Photography: The Story of the Formative Years, 1800–1900* (New York: Taplinger, 1977) and Beaumont Newhall's *The History of Photography from 1838 to the Present Day* (New York: The Museum of Modern Art, 1964). An authoritative text is Helmut Gernsheim's *The History of Photography* (New York: McGraw-Hill, 1969); Gernsheim also prepared *Masterpieces of Victorian Photography* (London: Phaidon, 1951).

31. Kenneth Bird, "Drawing and Reproduction," in *The History of Punch*, by R. G. G. Price (London: Collins, 1957), pp. 358–39.

32. Coe, *Birth of Photography*, p. 176.

33. Mott, *History*, 4:153.

G IS Godiva, whose great bareback feat
    She kindly but firmly declines to repeat,
Though Gounod and Goldsmith implore and entreat.

H IS for Handel, invoking deep tones
    On the organ for Hamlet and Howells and Holmes,
Who kindly consent to assist on trombones.

Oliver Herford.

2

The Many Faces of Victoria

I mourn the safe and motherly old middle-class queen, who held the nation warm under the fold of her big, hideous Scotch-plaid shawl and whose duration had been so extraordinarily convenient and beneficent.[1]

SO WROTE HENRY JAMES TO WENDELL HOLMES several days after viewing Queen Victoria's funeral procession, expressing with characteristic precision an opinion shared by many of his contemporaries on both sides of the Atlantic. That the expatriate was a spokesman not only for his own, limited readership but also for the general public becomes quite clear when we examine a number of popular periodicals. The myths that the humorists created about the Queen in fact reflected the tastes of the readership; thus to examine the parodies and caricatures in a detailed way is to examine the readers' preconceptions, preconceptions that determined how other major figures of the age were seen. While the differences between the American and British views cannot be ignored, Victoria indisputably influenced the social mores of the day, just as Matthew Arnold affected the critical viewpoint and Darwin the scientific. Some humorists, of course, objected to the "old hen and her sixty-three chickens" (figure 1), but most practiced the kind of "gentle satire" that made *Life* famous.[2] In anecdote, pun,

parody, and caricature Victoria was depicted as mother not just to her royal brood but to the British nation as well; she was chaffed for her literary attempts, her relationship with John Brown, and her refusal to give up the throne to the Prince of Wales. To be sure, the casual tone adopted by the American comic press was an outgrowth of its insistently democratic stance. British writers, for whom royalty was a political reality, were more formally witty. As a rule, then, the Americans enjoyed the broad, pun-filled anecdote, while the British preferred metrical commentary and elaborate lithographs, such as those published in *Vanity Fair*, *Punch*, and *Truth*.[3] No matter what their national bias, however, readers were frequently reminded of the queen's very ordinary tastes, a facet of her personality well symbolized by the "big, hideous Scotch-plaid shawl" which James uses as an emblem of her double role as protector and comforter.

While we shall highlight the large body of satirical material that grew up around the queen during the latter part of her reign, the reactions of the

Figure 1. "Fifty Years of Queen Victoria," Judge, *25 June 1887.*

popular press at her death illustrate some of the fundamental differences between the American and British views. In keeping with their democratic stance, the Americans emphasized personal, rather than royal status. For example, *Life* laid Victoria to rest on the cover of its 7 February 1901 issue (figure 2) with a sober drawing by William Walker, in which attention is focused not so much on the shadowy figure on the bier as on the jointly sorrowing figures of Columbia and Britannia. The very human tone of the picture, as if two sisters were weeping for a dead mother, exemplifies the position *Life* adopted from its earliest years, when it found Victoria's "safe and motherly" nature to be a touchstone for the domestic humor that appealed to its middle-class audience. The caption—"'She wrought her people lasting good'"—is from "To the Queen," the dedicatory poem with which Tennyson opened his 1851 volume of verses. While the poem as a whole stresses rulership, *Life* draws its caption from two stanzas that demonstrate Victoria's other roles:

> . . . May children of our children say,
> "She wrought her people lasting good";

Figure 2. "She wrought her people lasting good," Life, *7 February 1901.*

Figure 3. "The Roll of Great Monarchs: History adds Another Name," Punch, 30 January 1901.

"Her court was pure; her life serene;
   God gave her peace; her land reposed;
   A thousand claims to reference closed
In her as Mother, Wife, and Queen. . . ."

Likewise, *Puck*'s obituary, while noting the "love that all classes and parties bore her," played down her statesmanship:[4]

Victoria wielded the influence of a lovable woman, as maid, wife, mother and widow; a high-minded, thrifty, middle-class British house-keeper. . . . Unofficially, her staunch woman's rectitude sweetened her times beyond calculation. Reigning in a time of transition, when a

Queen every day became less and a good woman more, it was her fortune to be very much a woman and very little a Queen.

In contrast, the dignified tribute published in *Punch* is classical in its restraint (figure 3). A comparison with George Gilbert Scott's ornate Albert Memorial in Kensington Gardens shows how far aesthetic taste has shifted; Victoria is mourned in terms that she herself might not have appreciated. A simple memorial is shown, rather than the bier itself, and a wreath replaces tears as an expression of grief. In this example, Britannia is a visual demonstration of *Punch*'s comment that "Grief asks for words, yet

Characteristic of the American emphasis on personality are the satiric biographies published in *Life*, which introduced its readers to the "facts" not once but three times. In each case Victoria is treated as a "remarkable old lady" whose royalty is an unfortunate accident but whose matchmaking talents deserve admiration. She first appears in this way in Charles Kendrick's 1883 sketch of the "Widow Guelph" (figure 5), an uncomplimentary study that nonetheless pictures her in a domestic capacity, knitting (like Dickens's Mme. DeFarge) amidst a troupe of squalling children. An excerpt from the accompanying "biographette" indicates how thoroughly she has been Americanized into a working woman with a son in the "advertising" business:

Figure 4. Victoria, Vanity Fair, *31 January 1901.*

silent grief were well" (30 January 1901, p. 92). *Vanity Fair*'s memorial lithograph, a black-and-white version of an earlier caricature by Jean Baptiste Guth, is restrained in like manner (figure 4). While such reprinting ingeniously solved the immediate difficulty of publishing an illustration (preparing a new lithograph would have involved a lengthy process), the queen's unchanged pose seems to emphasize the continuity of the British Empire in the face of death; moreover, the solitary figure again evokes grief rather than depicting it as *Life*'s cover does. Unlike the Americans, the British did not subsume Victoria's political role to her personal role; rather, they equated the two. For *Vanity Fair*, "the sentiment of protecting tenderness . . . was not only a national feeling, it was a personal and individual romance. The soldiers and sailors of the Queen were not only fighting for an Empire, they were the defenders of a Woman."

Figure 5. "The Widow Guelph," Life, *5 April 1883.*

a reputation as a womanizer by his support of such actresses and "professional beauties" as Lily Langtry[6] and Mary Anderson.

The illustrations for *Life*'s other two series, the "Gallery of Beauties" (1889) and the "Growth of Greatness" (1895) are more technically complex photomontages, or collages of photographs and paintings. In one example the seventy-year-old Victoria is shown (figure 6) as a saintly "Beauty" hovering over a platter full of children half hidden under a large hat labeled "Bundestag" ("Federal Diet"). This visual pun on the English translation of the word for the representative assembly of the German Confederacy reflects *Life*'s comic amazement at Victoria's growing number of grandchildren. The marriage of Princess Victoria to Frederick III of Germany produced a constant "diet" of newly arrived offspring whom the Germans were expected

Figure 6. "Gallery of Beauties," Life, *17 October 1889.*

Mrs. Guelph is now tolerably well known throughout England and its neighborhood. She founded the most prosperous Royal Matrimonial Agency in Europe, which had patrons in every kingdom. Lately, however, her stock has run short, and it is probable she will soon retire from business, and leave her interests to her son Al, who at present earns a precarious livelihood by writing puffs for professional beauties. (5 April 1883, p. 166)

Life frequently used both "Mrs. Guelph" and "Mrs. Wettin" as cognomens for the queen as a witty way to deemphasize her royal title. The names in themselves describe her lineage: her grandfather, George III, was descended from one branch of the Guelph family who owned the duchy of Brunswick; the prince consort, as a Saxe-Coburg-Gotha, was of the Wettin family.[5] By 1883, when the "biographette" was published, Victoria had considerably strengthened her influence by the marriage of her children, and "her son Al"—later Edward VII—had acquired

Figure 7a. "Vicky Guelph. From a photograph taken when six years of age." From "The Growth of Greatness," Life, *28 February 1895.*

Figure 7b. "*Miss Victoria Guelph. A view taken in 1851.*" *From "The Growth of Greatness," Life, 28 February 1895.*

to support;[7] moreover, one of them—Wilhelm II—had, by the 1889 caricature, celebrated his first anniversary as emperor. As usual, however, *Life* refused to be awed by titles and in its commentary presented the queen as an ordinary British housewife with "few of the vices of women"; even the prince consort, *Life* claims, never complained "that her doughnuts were not up to his mother's standard of doughnut architecture" (17 October 1889, p. 217). Six years later in the "Growth of Greatness" the emphasis shifts from her domestic attributes to her queenly ones, but the democratizing effect is the same, since her eccentricities and hobbies are elevated to royal duties: she is occupied chiefly with "keeping the moths out of her extensive collection of India shawls," a fitting pastime for the empress of India, and with writing books "which patriotic English people read when they are afflicted with insomnia" (28 February

1895, p. 135). Similarly, in putative photographs from the royal family album, she devotes great seriousness to her tasks of swinging and boating; then, in royal regalia, she is ironically portrayed as a child in costume (figures 7a, 7b, and 7c).

Quite another sort of record—at once more dignified and nostalgic—may be found in the British caricatures and parodies that celebrate the signal events of Victoria's reign. At her death in 1901 *Punch* reprinted a representative selection of early drawings, all (in contrast to the American view) emphasizing queenliness and political involvement. An 1860 cartoon in which the "best rest for the Queen's rifle" is the top of Mr. Punch's head (figure 8) illustrates the periodical's attitude of respectfulness touched, at times, by whimsy. Other sketches included are more documentary, like those

Figure 7c. "*Mrs. Victoria Wettin. The queen of Great Britain and empress of India, as she appears when receiving company.*" *From "The Growth of Greatness," Life, 28 February 1895.*

Figure 8. "Best Rest for the Queen's Rifle," Punch, *7 July 1860.*

of the young queen reluctantly accepting a letter of introduction from Sir Robert Peel (1841), who had toppled the government of the queen's first and favorite prime minister, Lord Melbourne, and of Lord John Russell receiving his mandate for a ministry in 1846 (figure 9). The most nostalgic, however, was reprinted twice before, first on 4 February 1845 and then on 18 June 1897 for the Diamond Jubilee. Victoria is shown enthroned amid her political friends and adversaries, including Sir James Graham, who opposed Peel's free-trade measures; Lord Henry Goulburn, Peel's Home Secretary in 1834; Lord Henry Peter Brougham, who opposed Melbourne; Daniel O'Connel, leader of the Irish independence movement, who wanted to "repeal the union"; and Benjamin Disraeli, who became prime minister in 1868. As this excerpt from the accompanying poem suggests, Victoria's youth and promise evoked early support from many political factions:

The opening of Parliament, by our young
    QUEEN in person!
A theme which *Punch*'s loyal Muse failed not to
    turn a verse on!
   . . . .
All cluster around the sweet girl QUEEN who
    holds in fingers taper
A memorable Royal Speech, that wondrous
    "Scrap of Paper,"
Whilst down below, in a wild rush the "loyal
    Commons" troop,
Headed by Mr. SPEAKER. PEEL and
    RUSSELL lead the group.
GRAHAM and GOULBURN follow; there is
    BROUGHAM'S colossal beak;
O'CONNEL, with "Repeal," intent Ould
    Oireland's wrath to wreak
Upon the haughty Saxon, whilst behind him
    swift "BEN DIZZY,"
Intent on "smashing everyone," is making very
    busy.
             (30 January 1901, p. 76)

One of the much-discussed issues during Victoria's lifetime was that of British imperialism. It is hardly surprising that the American view was generally antagonistic; for the British, of course, colonizing was a way of increasing national wealth, although the economic advantage was often disguised as heroism or protectionism. *Punch*'s metrical version of a speech given by Sir George Ferguson Bowen, governor of Victoria, Australia, illustrates this point. The punning refrain, "Victoria," shows the equation between the "imperial instinct" and honoring the queen:

> Hail far colonial Commonwealth,
> Where a young giant, full of health,

> Sprung from the loins of England, grows
> To greatness in a calm repose. . . .
> Shame to the dullards who desire
> To quench our colonising fire,
> To keep the imperial instinct down,
> And make a fool's cap of the Crown.
> It shall not be: while ocean rolls,
> And Englishmen have gallant souls,
> And court the strong heroic hour,
> While Freedom is a word of power,
> While great colonial nations rise
> In alien seas, 'neath unseen skies,
> We do not dread that servile
> day—VICTORIA!

(15 May 1875, p. 205)

According to the original speech reported in the London *Times*, Bowen refers to the English as "the true *Gens togata* of modern times" (30 April 1875, p. 5, col. 5). Like the Romans, they were, to be sure, a civilizing force, yet the financial importance of colonizing cannot be overestimated; while the poem points out with patriotic fervor that the "wealth that comes from crowded mart / Is spent on Letters and on Art," the proceeds from Australian gold, for example (the first strike was made in the 1850s), helped swell England's treasury for nonaesthetic purposes as well. Again, protectionism, according to *Punch*, prevents Famine from entering the Indian Empire (figure 10), but, according to *Life*, is a euphemism for slavery (figure 11).

Some American caricatures reveal an interesting tension between the republican ideal and colonialist actions, particularly during the Spanish-American War and the annexation of the Philippine Islands. In this regard *Life*'s William Walker draws Victoria as a little girl with her arms full of dolls from the colonies; Uncle Sam, staring wistfully at his Philippines doll, complains, "Saint Nick gave me that doll last Christmas, but I haven't had any fun with it. Guess I'll give it to a little girl I know who has a collection of them" (2 December 1889, p. 461). *Judge*, however, takes a uniformly dim view of all colonialist activities: vignettes in figure 1 show the British lion devouring the earth and a monument to "a reign of civilization" listing wars undertaken in the name of protectionism. The other of *Judge*'s 1887 Jubilee drawings suggests that such protection had, for the Irish, its human toll. The magazine's sympathy for the worker and for democracy is drawn as a contrast between the haughty, bejeweled queen and the impoverished Irish family

Figure 9. "The Queen, Prince Consort, Lord John Russell, and Sir Robert Peel. 1846," Punch, *30 January 1901.*

(figure 12). While the cartoon suggests that starving Irish tenants who are evicted by British agents for nonpayment of rent will get no redress from a regent who spends money on lavish state celebrations, *Judge*'s attitude changes when the matter is brought home; staunchly supportive of the Irish laborer on his own ground, *Judge* is bitterly resentful of the waves of Irish immigrants in the 1880s that changed the complexion of the labor force. In contrast, perhaps because of its ambiguous attitude about colonialism, *Life* can afford to be humorous about the Irish question. After Wales visited Ireland in 1885, Francis Attwood shows not starving farmers, but Victoria and her son's chagrin at receiving various state gifts, including "specimen brick-bats spontaneously presented by the people of Mallow" and a dead cat—none exactly indicating

the "enthusiastic and loyal" reception that one early biography maintains.[8]

In the final analysis *Life* and its sister magazines probably welcomed such signs of unrest as indications of the break-up of British hegemony not only by the "Republican Idea" (figure 13) but also by other forces. *Puck*, for example, pictures a crowd of crowned heads (including Alexander III, Alphonso, Humbert, and Franz Joseph) fleeing in panic from such assorted threats as "communism," "nihilism" and "Peter's pence" (the Pope's interference). The accompanying commentary is blunt:

The truth is that kings and queens have had their day and have now become a nuisance and a bore. We have shown the world pretty well that we can do without them, and it is about time that other nations followed our example. . . . It is a very fine thing, no doubt, to be born

Figure 10. "Disputed Empire," Punch, *1 September 1887.*

Figure 11. "For Sale, British Subjects," Life, *24 July 1890.*

Figure 12. "The Queen's Jubilee," Judge, *4 June 1887.*

Figure 13. "The Republican Idea," Life, *9 January 1890.*

to receive in perpetuity a big salary from the people for doing nothing, and to be brought up with the idea that one is the wisest, best, and most respectable of mortals, when in reality you are the most vulgar, most ignorant, most ignoble and stupidest person in existence. . . . But a change must come—and a change has come. . . .

Let them come here; . . . they may be quite sure that they will be safe from daggers, pistols and bombs. . . . Come along, Mrs. Victoria! Never mind your large family and Mr. Albert Edward's shady record. (30 March 1881, p. 56)

The tone is crude and the chauvinism obvious, but *Puck*'s welcome—not to the tired and poor but to the persecuted and wealthy—incorporates a number of beliefs common to the popular press: that republicanism is better than monarchism, that one's class depends on inner qualities and not on birth, and that America is a safe haven for those of different persuasions. All of these beliefs contributed not only toward *Life*'s amused tolerance for what it considered an ineffective institution but toward *Judge*'s and *Puck*'s exacerbation with corrupt government.

Political issues where not, of course, the only facet of Victoria's reign of interest to the reading public; the large amount of material devoted to the queen's family, literary output, and habits indicates that what particularly interested readers was a glimpse—however exaggerated—into the way in which her personal life influenced her public image. *Punch* and *Life*, for example, found humor in the conflict between Victoria's family relationships and political imbroglios, particularly those occasioned by her status as "Grandmama of Europe." Her first and most troublesome grandchild was Wilhelm II of Germany, whose stature is considerably diminished when he is upbraided by his famous relative. On Attwood's cover for *Life* (23 January 1896) Wilhelm's interference in Rhodesia is reduced to a domestic quarrel. Victoria, chiding her grandson for endorsing President Kruger's "independence" during the Jameson Raid, is given a line that parodies the German use of the familiar "du" as well as German sentence structure: "O William, fie! I scarcely could believe that thou would'st thus thy anxious Grandma grieve!" (figure 14). Earlier, *Punch* shows the Kaiser playing childish war-games during his visit to England in the summer of 1889 (figure 15). Wilhelm, permitted to wear the uniform of a British admiral for his first state appearance in Britain, was impressed by the honor, reportedly saying, "Fancy wearing the same uniform as St. Vincent and Nelson; it is enough to make one quite

giddy."[9] The two cartoons differ in an important respect: *Life*'s humor is directed at Victoria, whose diminutive size and fussy manner are no threat to her towering grandson. *Punch*'s humor, on the other hand, is intended to minimize Wilhelm's power; as a small boy sailing a boat on a lake, he is clearly under the control of his larger-than-life grandmother. The American magazine reacts as an observer; the British magazine, as a participant whose political fortunes are directly affected by her continental neighbor.

Unlike Wilhelm, Victoria's youngest daughter, Beatrice, appealed to popular sympathies. She was overprotected and shy; when she finally decided to marry Prince Henry of Battenberg, the queen was so distraught with "horror" at the idea of losing her closest companion that the couple agreed to remain part of the royal household.[10] *Fun*'s wedding tribute makes reference to Beatrice's double role of wife and daughter—she is "Fair, filial, fond, elate, / Glad bride and daughter loyal" (1 August 1885, p. 53)— while *Punch* celebrates the event by showing Beatrice and Battenberg in a scene from *Much Ado About Nothing* and slyly comments, "This knits the golden circle up, / And brims with joy the Royal Mother's Cup" (10 January 1885, p. 22). The most entertaining report of the royal ménage, however, comes from *Life*'s Carlyle Smith, who commented on the queen's activities in his column, "From Foreign Fields." Writing as the "Chum to Potentates," he treats Victoria as if she were his next-door neighbor and uses Beatrice's marriage not only as an excuse for a long series of mother-in-law jokes but as an opportunity to portray a "potentate" in a purely dometic situation. Like other contributors to *Life*, the republican Chum is unimpressed by titles. Visiting Windsor on New Year's Day in 1886, he finds that Beatrice's husband "has been appointed Deputy Earl of Her Majesty's Front Stoop" (in fact, Battenberg was given the title *His Royal Highness* by the queen to make up for his morganatic birth[11]); he asks for Victoria as "Y. M. I. L., Mrs. Saxe-Coburg of Guelphtown" and as "Your Mother-In-Law, old H. R. H., the Lordess of the Earth and Grand High Teetotum of Calcutta" (21 January 1886, pp. 53–54).

Thoroughly domesticated as a royal "ma-in-law," Victoria provided entertainment for years to come. The birth of Beatrice's first child, Alexander, on 23 November 1886, was given precious treatment by *Punch* in "Babydom: A Contribution to the Poetry of Pap (Not by Mr. Algernon Charles Swinburne),"

Figure 14. "Mischievous Willie," Life, *23 January 1896.*

England; for this middle-class publication, "the hand that rocks the cradle rules the nation" applies both literally and figuratively. The columns can be taken, moreover, as a parodic response not just to Victoria but to the exposé popular in yellow journalism. To be sure, *Life* never published stories of the sort that Robert Bonner's New York *Ledger* delighted in, but the Chum's confidential style satisfied in an imaginative way the same sense of curiosity about intimate details that was manifested by the *Ledger*'s readers.

This sort of restraint is well exemplified by *Life*'s treatment of the Prince of Wales, popularly dubbed "Edward the Caresser" for his notorous liaisons with "professional beauties." Dedicated to publishing nothing that would bring a blush to the cheek of the all-American girl, the editors preferred innuendo to overt statement. Typical of this approach is a double-page cartoon appearing in January 1883 to protest the influx of British performers; Lily Langtry's reputation is authenticated by a tag—"This is a Lily / signed Albert Edward." Similarly,

a set of satirical verses in which derision is reserved for the artistic excesses committed in the name of the royal event. Typically, the Chum directs his humor at Victoria, who prepares the "Imperial Granum" for the new despot in the throne room:

> The crown encircled his waist. The bauble, broken into four pieces, was strewn about the floor. The Magna Charta, brought at his command from the British Museum, was torn to shreds in the usurper's efforts to absorb the red paint on the seals.
> Premier Salisbury sat on the first step of the dais, with his necktie untied, and his hair gripped by the strong right hand of the new King.
> The Queen's collection of crowns adorned the ankles and wrists of the new monarch, and the members of the Royal Family were standing around the room with salvers in their hands, tears in their eyes, and wrath generally depicted on their other features.
> "There," said Wales, "that's what we've come to. Mother has abdicated in favor of that! If we take the crown from him he yells the roof off the castle, and we can't afford to pay the repair bills, and, as it's put up or shut up, we have to shut up." (30 December 1886, pp. 421–22)

Life's Chum columns exemplify the magazine's view of woman's place, comically applied to the Queen of

Figure 15. "Visiting Grandmamma," Punch, *3 August 1889.*

Figure 16. "Gallery of Beauties," Life, *24 January 1889.*

The commentary that appears along with an elaborate "Gallery of Beauties" caricature (figure 16) demonstrates a different facet of *Life*'s restraint: its preference for finding humor in Edward's anomalous position as king-in-waiting and for making serious comments about the dangers of anglomania. Depicted as a child dressing up in his mother's regalia, Edward is further trivialized by a list of his responsibilities:

The duties of Mr. Guelph's position at present consist in the laying of cornerstones, the booming of actresses, the extension of courtesies to visiting prize-fighters, the holding of levees when Mrs. Guelph is indisposed, and the bestowing of the precious boon of an interview upon American public men.

Importantly, the columnist turns his humor into a warning against the anglicization of American manners and dress by raising an objection to court etiquette, an objection reflecting the same kind of republicanism displayed by *Puck* in its welcome to the crowned heads of Europe.

Nine-tenths of the persons who participate in this ceremony at this advanced stage of human development are higher moral types than the man they abase themselves before; three-fourths of them are his intellectual superiors, and two-thirds are better men from a physical point of view—all of which goes to prove what a great man Mr. Guelph is. (24 January 1889, p. 49)

American magazines were not, however, totally uncognizant that democratic behavior might border on rudeness and hence were particularly sensitive to the way in which republican ideals were represented abroad. Consequently, John L. Sullivan's boxing match with the English Charley Mitchell provoked criticism of America's representative as well as of "Bertie's" taste. Harvard *Lampoon*'s scenario illustrating what might happen were the "charming widow and America's pet" to shake hands places the onus on the "ugly American":

"Glad to meet you, Mrs. Guelph. Excuse me for not taking off my hat sooner, but I remove it instantly for no woman except my wife. I have heard of you a good deal too," added Mr. Sullivan; "seen your name in the papers once in a while. Bertie wanted to bring me up to see you last evening, but I was rather tired, and didn't care about climbing two flights of stairs, and as he said you didn't sport an elevator, I thought I might just as well wait till this morning." (6 April 1888, pp. 20–21)

the response to Edward's involvement in the baccarat scandal is couched in terms understandable only to those already familiar with the details of the case. Each of the entries in "The Rules of Baccarat Compiled for American Players by H. R. H. the P----e of W----s" (23 July 1891, p. 38) alludes to some aspect of the affair, in which Edward was called as a witness in a court suit brought by Sir William Cumming, a lieutenant-colonel in the Scots Guards accused of cheating at a private game of baccarat. Rule #3, for example—"There should be a lawyer convenient to put any necessary agreements in legal form"—refers to a virtual admission of guilt signed by Cumming and witnessed by Edward and other participants in the game; likewise, Rule #9—"If there should be any cheating, don't be fool enough to go and tell a woman about it"— refers to Edward's breaking a gentleman's agreement to preserve secrecy.[12]

That the *Lampoon*'s criticism may be motivated by snobbishness is suggested by the slangy diction and boorish address attributed to Sullivan; clearly, however, the *Lampoon* associates the Prince of Wales with an unbecoming form of entertainment, and while the boxer actually won the match, Queen Victoria won the putative social confrontation.

A more complex satire on a different incident proves, however, to camouflage a complaint about anglomania. When E. J. Phelps sailed to England to replace James Russell Lowell as U.S. minister, *Puck*, parodying the flamboyant style of the New York *World*, published "Minister Phelps Interviews the Queen, and an Effete Despotism Trembles." In this "news item," the American statesman is invited to Windsor for dinner, but

True to the dear banner he represents, Mr. Phelps paid no attention whatsoever to the request for an answer, but made up his mind to show Her Majesty that the American eagle still possessed lung enough to scream a Dutch despot deaf, and not half try.

After the American envoy distinguishes himself by his rudeness, *Puck* concludes,

Thus ended one of the proudest and most memorable scenes in the history of American diplomacy, and our representative has shown himself to be not only worthy of the post he occupies, but also a true Jeffersonian gentleman and Democrat. (22 July 1885, p. 324)

In fact, the report obscures the facts: when Phelps arrived, he was given an enthusiastic welcome by all but Lowell, who had been summoned to dine with Victoria on the same evening. On 18 May, two days after Phelps's arrival, Lowell introduced him to the queen; on 4 June Phelps made a complimentary speech as guest of honor at the lord mayor's banquet.[13] *Puck*'s heavy irony seems to imply that Phelps is not the Jeffersonian he should be and that in his official appearances he is less overtly loyal to his "dear banner" than expected.

Such "insights" into the Queen's political and domestic relationships eventually bear reference, for the American publications, to the question of the logic of birth. On the one hand, to democratize the queen by emphasizing her role as "mother" or "mother-in-law" is to ask why she, rather than any other woman, should be queen; on the other hand, to use her as a foil for American behavior is frequently to justify republican integrity. An important example of this kind of questioning is the material relating to her authorship of *Leaves from the Journal of Our Life in the Highlands* (1868) and *More Leaves* (1884),[14] records of the queen's holidays at Balmoral Castle. The satires and parodies seem to be humorous accounts of the very human habits of the queen; in a larger context, however, to discuss her commonplace tastes is to illustrate "what might have been" had she not been of royal parentage (figure 17). One of *Life*'s longer essays, an account of the queen's supposed excursion to Wales, has the multiple effect of humanizing her, burlesquing the reports commonly found in periodicals like the *Illustrated London News*, and satirizing the "adventures" she records in her journals. Her temper, her parsimony, and her stoutness are all matters for humor:

After breakfast Her Majesty drives a spirited Electioneer colt to the post-office for her mail, very often telling the post master what she thinks of him if he happens to have no letters for her.

After luncheon Her Majesty takes a nap. The doors and windows are carefully plugged with cotton so that the royal slumbers shall not be disturbed, and to keep the neighbors from complaining to the Board of Health

Figure 17. "What might have been," Life, *14 December 1899.*

about the royal snoring. During the evening two maids read LIFE aloud to Her Majesty, and after an hour or two of penny-ante, straights barred, Her Majesty retires. Out of deference to her Welsh subjects Her Majesty eats nothing but Welsh rarebits.

During her visit Her Majesty has become greatly interested in the copper-mining industries of Wales, and in her walks about has picked up numerous specimens of refuse ore. These she will have mounted as scarfpins and brooches to be used for wedding gifts and rewards of valor. She has also been pleased to manifest her interest in local commerce by purchasing a pair of white cotton hose from a leading firm in the haberdashery line.

Her Majesty has paid considerable attention to field sports during her stay and is becoming quite an expert player at mumbletypeg. She laughs as heartily as anyone when she has to remove her crown and get down on her face and pay the usual penalty. . . .

The climate of Wales seems to agree with Her Majesty. She is gaining in weight and her last summer's gowns have had to be let out several inches around the waist and back of the shoulder. With the exception of a slight indisposition caused by an unfortunate combination of broiled lobster and buttermilk, she has enjoyed the best of health. (13 October 1892, pp. 205–6)

Like this account of a fictitious journey, which focuses on the prosaic nature of the queen's activities, her authorial style came in for attack on the same grounds. The comic press was quick to point out that Victoria would not qualify as one of the Immortals, even though she had given her journal manuscript to Sir Arthur Helps for editing.[15] Her "happy faculty of putting things" is facetiously extolled by *Life*, which pictures her as a new staff writer (figure 18). More pointed is *Life*'s parody of her journal, "Mystic Meanderings by her Royal Nibs." Although the piece shows the prime minister William Ewart Gladstone and the poet laureate Alfred Tennyson upset by the contents—or the length—of her book, one biographer notes, "Everyone was kind about the Queen's book except, as before, the Queen's family."[16] Nonetheless, the staccato style of the parody is representative of the original, as is the queen's innocent egotism. Alert readers no doubt appreciated the suggestion that the queen was blind to the sly irony of her favorite Highland servant, John Brown:

April 10th.—I sent for Brown, and read him this journal for a year. He sat with closed eyes, nodding his head whenever I came to a favorite passage. He then said that he did not think any distinguished woman had ever writ-

Figure 18. "Mrs. W. at Work," Life, *13 August 1896.*

ten anything like it. I chided Brown for flattery, but he assured me it was honest truth. I will read it to Mr. Gladstone.

April 12th.—Mr. Gladstone called. I read it to him.

April 13th.—Mr. Gladstone is very ill.

April 14th.—I wanted to read nineteen more chapters of my journal to Brown, but he said he really could not think of letting me tire myself. Said he would take the book and read it in his study. . . .

May 7th.—Mr. Tennyson called. . . . I read him some of my journal.

May 8th.—Brown says Mr. Tennyson is quite ill. I wanted to read some of my journal to Brown, but he said it was very enervating for an author to read her own work. I find this literary life indeed wearisome, and I sometimes wonder how Mr. Tennyson stands it. It killed poor Mr. Disraeli. I suppose it will kill me too some day.

May 9th.—I spoke to Brown about publishing the journal. He said if I did it would create a sensation. To know the working of the sovereign's heart, and see just how much interest she takes in the affairs of the nation, which is so spendthrift in her honor, is a boon for the people. Brown says it will show them just what kind of ruler they have. Brown is right. I will publish the book. (24 March 1884, p. 161)

Whether *Life*'s editors were aware of what might have been a real "sensation," Victoria's proposed memoir of Brown, is unclear; before the parody appeared, the manuscript of the memoir had been read by Sir Henry Ponsonby, Lord Rowton, and the dean of Windsor between 23 February and 6 March. All gingerly hinted that even private publication would be unwise.[17] Rumors of Victoria's involvement in Brown's spiritualist seances, however, probably reached *Life*, as is evidenced by the title of the parody, yet the contrast between the supposedly "mystic meanderings" and the very matter-of-fact style effectively—if not intentionally—undercuts the rumors.

In dealing with the journal, *Puck* agrees with *Life:* the queen is unsophisticated, and the honors she distributes gratuitously are worthless. *Puck*'s parody, however, which shows her enjoying "a glorious luncheon of Limburger cheese and pretzels, washed down with Islay whiskey and Milwaukee lager," satirizes the tastes of its own readers as well as those of the queen. She makes Brown a K. C. B. for frolicking with her in a wheelbarrow, then an earl to celebrate his recuperation from a minor skating injury. Finally, while she is in the kitchen boiling potatoes, he asks for "a wee bit of a jamboree":

I was so charmed at the frankness of his query that I felt inclined to give him a dukedom on the spot; but that would not suit old Billy Gladstone. So with great difficulty I suppressed my feelings. Scarcely had I finished suppressing them, when thirty-five of the servants and a few spare noblemen and countesses who were about the establishment rushed in and began dancing reels and drinking whiskey toddy. Brown told me that he wanted to surprise me. How good and considerate of him! The Marquis of Salisbury insisted on my waltzing, and refused to allow me to finish cooking the potatos. All of us had an awfully good time, and we danced until the "wee sma' hours." Brown and the rest of the boys drank large quantities of toddy; but then we don't have a surprise-party every day. I did not see him in the morning. Perhaps his poor shin pained him again. Dare I make him a duke? (20 February 1884, p. 388)

Puck's comic account mirrors the popular conception that Brown took advantage of Victoria's kindness and that she herself was willfully blind to his faults. In England, however, his familiarity with

the sovereign was a serious matter, especially since her disinclination to appear publicly after the death of the Prince Consort in 1861 gave rise to gossip. As her biographer notes, "she might have been excused John Brown if her drives round London had been more frequent. The people needed to see more of Brown sitting on the box not less. All the Queen's troubles went back to the same source: her seclusion."[18]

The queen's isolation from the people she ruled was, for the average American reader, one of the major flaws of the monarchical system. *Tid-Bits* implicitly condemns the humor of its contemporaries by suggesting that to make much of Victoria's middle-class tastes is to lose sight of how out of touch she was with her subjects' unemployment and poverty, an idea illustrated on the 5 November 1887 cover where she is shown offering "sympathetic Cook-Books" and "Guides to the Poorhouse" to the starving crowd that gathered in Trafalgar Square and rioted when refused the right of assembly (figure 19). A mock-sympathetic letter appearing later in the month pursues the same theme:

Figure 19. "Rags and Royalty," Tid-Bits, 5 November 1887.

I hasten to condole with you over the disturbances of yesterday at Trafalgar Square. Such pernicious activity on the part of a mob must be very discouraging to a peaceable old lady like yourself. . . . Such an occurrence must be a serious interruption to your study of the Hindoostanee language, and to keeping tally of Princess Beatrice's progeny.

I can imagine you sitting quietly by the kitchen stove, combing the hair of one of Trixy's children, and thinking that a few million pounds rent is almost due (your crown and the cares of state having been temporarily thrown on the bed) only to be interrupted by the wild rush of a mob, asking in large, dark red tones, for bread. . . .

If I may venture to advise, the most effectual mode you can choose to disperse the next mob will be for you to appear before them, clad in your royal robes and an air of superiority, and read aloud some extracts from your own writings. This would act as an anesthetic, and, after the mob had been put to sleep, the bayonet could be introduced with great effect. (26 November 1887, p. 7)

Unlike *Tid-Bits*, which found a scapegoat in Victoria, the British *Fun* and *Punch* shift the blame to general governmental corruption and the selfishness of the average citizen. While *Fun* is not uniformly friendly to Victoria, in much of its treatment of the Trafalgar Square riot it protests a "guns, not bread" mentality and inveighs against those who joined the riot "for fun." The magazine consistently sides with "'The Martyrs of Civilization'" who are being thrown "'To the Lions'":

> But these of latter time are driven thus
> By poverty, not persecution, there;
> Nor are their lions fierce and ravenous,
> But Landseer's lions in Trafalgar Square.
>
> Night after night, crouch'd close beneath their feet,
> Lie hungry, wretched creatures, pale and wan,
> Sleeping; and the policeman on his beat
> Can scarcely find the heart to say, "Move on!"
>
> (26 October 1887, p. 177)

Like *Fun*, *Punch* decries the middlemen who steal food from John Bull's helping hand. In "''Arry on Law and Order" *Punch*'s readers were given the viewpoint of the conservative man in the street, one who stands for "Horder" until it interferes with "*my* larks, or *my* lush, or *my* gal." 'Arry objects to the "Socherlist lot" that wants an equal distribution of wealth:

> I 'ate 'em, . . . I 'ate 'em! They wants to stop piling the pelf,
> Wen that is wot every dashed one of us wants to be piling hisself.
> No, Wealth is wot *must* be kep up and perfected, whoever goes wrong;
> And to talk of abolishing Millionnaires, . . . *is* coming it strong.
>
> They are like prize Chrysanthemums, . . . for, if you want *them*, don'tcherssee,
> You must nip off some thousands of buds to let one or two swell and grow free.
> Jest you turn a lot loose in yer garden, and *that* ain't the way as they'll grow;
> But if 'undreds weren't sacrificed daily to one, you would not get no Show.
>
> (20 November 1887, p. 249)

For *Punch*, then, much blame can be placed on the entrepreneurs whose own avarice frustrates the workings of a beneficent government.

While it is hardly surprising that the British readership should be well acquainted with the queen's political and personal problems, the parodies in the American popular press suggest that the Americans themselves must have followed news of Victoria with great eagerness if they were to understand the purport of the humor (which, of course, in itself supplied some of the innuendo—about Brown's flattery, for example—that would not have appeared in a straight news article). The connection between the comic papers and legitimate news sources was thus for the Americans a complementary one, breaking down only in the case of a completely fictive account, such as the reports that appeared from time to time of the queen's planned visit to America. That these reports were continually surfacing seems to attest not just to the Americans' desire to see the queen but to their humorous appreciation of the contrast between a monarch and the citizens of a republic. Perhaps such scenarios were ways to test the strength of the New World against an incursion from the Old, a way to validate American manners in the face of elitism; but whatever the case, the American press warmly "welcomed" Mrs. Wettin on innumerable occasions.

In one instance she was reported to have abandoned the throne to become an actress. In "Startling Intelligence" *Puck* learns that she has sent John Brown to America as her advance agent and that, having shown continual interest in Lily Langtry's career, the queen is determined to outdo her in playing both Juliet and Roslind. The satire is a highly topical gallimaufry of references to Victoria's reluctance to let the Prince of Wales have the throne, her concern with his liaison with Lily Langtry, her petulance at sharing power with Gladstone, and her acting ability in reading her speeches to Parliament. The whole is accompanied by Frederick Opper's sketch of Victoria as she appears on her American tour—preceded by Uncle Sam, she histrionically waves a handkerchief in one hand and clutches a small, dismayed British lion in the other (22 November 1882, p. 180). *Life's* readers were likewise regaled with the spectacle of the queen participating in a number of American celebrations. She is depicted, for example, at Grover Cleveland's 1885 inauguration ball in a double-page cartoon by W. A. Rogers; with her ermine cape tossed jauntily over her shoulders, she dances a jig with O'Donovan Rossa, who has a bomb wired to his coattails. Such a partner would of course, be no laughing matter to the average British reader. Rossa, the American Fenian leader, represented the threat of violence that the royal party continually feared (5 May 1885, pp. 134–35).[19]

One long "news" item about the British performance of Bill Cody's "Wild West Show" ends with speculation about a royal visit. The queen, a performer herself, may use the same agent as Matthew Arnold and Oscar Wilde during their earlier tours of America:

Her Majesty's desire to see these untutored savages in their native lair may induce her to visit New York next season, in which case she will probably be under the management of D'Oyly Carte.

What is important about this particular satire is not so much that it suggests such a visit, but rather that it presents the American conception of British *mis*conceptions about American manners. Carlyle Smith (the pseudonym of *Life's* writer John Kendrick Bangs)[20] gives a parodic reconstruction of what the London *Times* reports as a private command performance for the queen on 11 May 1887 (p. 7, col. 6). Reacting to the kind of comment made by one British reporter that "the Wild West Show represents after an effectively realistic fashion one very prominent phase of American life,"[21] Smith presents New York as if it were a provincial cow town:

Several cow-ladies were then introduced, giving the British aristocracy a fair imitation of high life in New York city. The Queen was much surprised at the refined way in which American ladies do their shopping on bucking ponies, and when one of the young ladies with auburn hair showed with what facility American girls use their firearms when their young gentleman friends decline to take them to the opera, the royal family was nearly carried away with delight.

The show featured an Indian attack on the Denver stagecoach. In Smith's hands the performance becomes a statement about cultural disparity:

as the carriage neared Fourteenth Street, the low, ominous war-cry of the Sioux Indians was heard, and the faithful picture of New York life that then followed, with its awful butchery and bellowing of buffaloes on Union Square, needs no description for your readers who have grown so familiar with it in the daily round of life. Suffice it to say that the British aristocracy fairly yelled with joy as Mr. Vanastorbilt slew file after file of the attacking party, losing only his scalp and four children in the melee. (28 May 1887, p. 290)

To be sure, the queen is presented as being both childlike and gullible, but the fact remains that "wild west" tales received an enthusiastic reception in England. As Amy Cruse points out, the Western mania began when James Fenimore Cooper's novels were transported across the Atlantic.[22] Cody's show was simply a later manifestation, as *Fun's* "Intelligent Foreigner at the Wild West" points out: "[this is] ze life all of vich I have read in ze books of ze much read Mayne Reid, Fenimore Ze Cooper, Mark Hart and Bret Twain" (18 May 1887, p. 208). Minor references, in which "Bill Cody" is given as a contributor's name and politicians are drawn wearing blankets and headdresses, are numerous.

Punch's record of the command performance is a parody of Longfellow's "Hiawatha," entitled "The Queen at the Wild West: The Song of Punchiwatha."

> Would you hear how Colonel Cody
> Gave his wondrous exhibition
> Of his Indians on the war-path,
> In the sight of Queen VICTORIA:
> Listen to this simple story
> From the mouth of PUNCHIWATHA.
>
> When she reached the Exhibition,
> Lo! a box near the arena
> Was prepared for her reception.
> . . . .

Then the Indians and the Cowboys,
And the wonderful Vanqueros,
Raced and charged and whirled before her,
Stopped the coach, and wheeled and circled,
Like some birds of brilliant plumage
Round a carcase on the mountains.
Balls of glass were thrown and shattered
By the clever Colonel Cody,[23]
Like WABE-NO the magician;
Ladies, too, there wielded rifles
Even as the strong man KWA-SIND.

The poem ends with the hope that the "squaws and their papooses" will go back on the "Home-Wind o'er the water,"

Singing gaily all the praises
Of the gentle Queen and Empress,
And the wonders of the North Land.

(21 May 1887)

On the whole *Punch*'s poem is serious; there is less hint than in the satire in *Life* of anything anomalous in the confrontation between a very old culture and a new.

The "untutored savages" were not fortunate enough to see Victoria on the soil of "their native lair" except in the pages of the popular press.[24] They nonetheless joined—wholeheartedly, in the case of *Life*—in offering congratulations in the Jubilee years 1887 and 1897. Many of the offerings are characterized by an affectionate regard that is more pervasive than the bitter commentary published in *Judge*. In the British *Punch* and *Fun*, however, the congratulations are more restrained, more in keeping with the solemnity of the occasion. The difference between the British and American views is, in fact, similar to that demonstrated at Victoria's death.

One of the best humorous reports for the 1887 Jubilee appears in *Life*, whose reporter "travels" by special invitation to sit beside the queen during the ceremony. A number of long-standing themes are touched on, including Edward's long wait for the throne. *Life*'s reporter tries to console the prince, who bursts into tears when the "Imperial Band" plays "'What is Home Without a Mother?'" To the assurance that "'all things come to him who waits,'" Wales returns a complaint that runs the gamut from the Parliamentary debate on the Peace Preservation Act to control Irish agitators to poorly staged plays at Lester Wallack's New York theater:

"Waits? Well, my dear Chum, I've watched the Coercion bill for fourteen long months; I've watched for a new joke in *Punch* since Thackeray died; and when I was in New York, I went to Wallack's Theatre and sat in my seat between the acts—but never, never have I waited so wearily for anything as I have for the solution of the problem, 'What is home without a mother?'"

Life takes the opportunity to inveigh against the overtaxed and oversubjugated state of the average Britisher:

Then your correspondent enjoyed the supreme bliss of driving through fourteen miles of London mob, who had the honor to be bulldozed by the soldiery for the privilege of viewing Her Majesty ride by them, with her nose at an angle of forty-five degrees with the vest pockets of the taxpayers. There was more pomp and vanity between the Palace and Westminster Abbey than the most devout churchman could renounce in a century.

The political satire resolves itself into comedy, however: small boys cry "'Ail to the Chief!" and the "crimson draperies" are arranged in the pew at Westminster to permit the queen to nap in private during the ceremony. As the Chum leaves, he is presented with a bill of £28 for such amenities as the "Use of the Throne Room," "1 Bottle of Imperial Fizz," and a "First-class Carriage to Westminster." He returns Victoria's parsimony in kind, however, pinning to her throne an equivalent bill, which includes "Consolation to the Prince," "Wear and Tear on Digestion at Jubilee Banquet," and "Cash to Battenberg for Expenses of Beatrice and Baby" (23 June 1887, p. 349).

The British reaction, as seen in *Fun* and *Punch*, was certainly less humorous, befitting those who were most directly affected by the queen's policies. *Fun*, in fact, was clearly less laudatory than *Punch*. Its sketches—of Victoria reflected in a mirror as a youthful queen and dancing a minuet with John Bull—were toned down, perhaps in consonance with what Ellegard calls its more liberal, less educated readership.[25] *Punch*, on the other hand, published a Jubilee issue that included much ephemera, like mock advertisements for "Jubilee Boarders" and "Royal Anniversary Soap" as well as a number of attractive sketches. One is of the British lion attired in tights emblazoned with the Union Jack: "Leo Britannicus" prepares to enjoy the day, because "there's a something that we owe / To impulses born of the heart." In contrast to *Judge*'s complaint that money should be spent to solve the Irish problem and not wasted on court extravaganzas, Leo complains that the celebrations are not grand enough:

> But to-day I'm not stern, nay, nor thrifty.
>   My motto is, "Oh! what a larks!"
> They come only one year in fifty,
>   These scenes in our streets and our parks.
> One thing, though, my bosom to ire works,—
>   The job seems imperfectly done.
> Why could not the people have fireworks
>   To finish the fun?
>
> There's a dash of the dowdy and dingy
>   About Metropolitan plans;
> Even poor GEORGE THE THIRD was less stingy.
>   Roast oxen and loud rataplans
> May not be entirely in keeping
>   With these high aesthetical times,
> But rocket-rains whirling and weeping
>   Are surely not crimes.
>
>   (18 June 1887, p. 294)

In fact, the fireworks did take place; what restraint there was in the ceremony came from Victoria herself, who had stubbornly refused to wear her crown and state robes since the death of the Prince Consort.[26] Because it exhibits Mr. Punch's long-standing support for the queen, a more typical reaction than "Leo Britannicus" is the drawing for the 1887 Almanac. Entitled "The Victorian Era, 1867–87," it shows a realistic Victoria surrounded by some of the events of the two decades, including the finished Royal Albert Hall; Wales, accompanied by Edward Bulwer Lytton (Viceroy of India), shooting tigers; and a personification of India, presenting the crown that made Victoria empress in 1876 (6 December 1886). *Judge*'s bitter reaction (figure 1), which details the more devastating effects of her reign, seems, in fact, to be a burlesque of this type of genre drawing, a burlesque that shows Victoria's achievements from a radically republican point of view.

Fun's tributes for the Diamond Jubilee were generally warmer than ten years before, perhaps in recognition that the queen's long reign was undoubtedly drawing to a close. Nonetheless, its formal portrait, a somber, majestic Victoria surrounded by embodiments of Empire and Peace, carries an undercurrent of criticism, for the accompanying poem, while stressing that she is "strong in all her people's love," emphasizes the enslaved nature of her subjects:

Figure 20. Punch, *19 June 1897.*

Figure 21. "Vivat Victoria Regina et Imperatrix," Life, 24 June 1897.

Captives beside her, doubtless stride,
Brought from Her Empire great and wide,
Dragged by chains of love and pride
    From lands across the sea.
Across the sea, that's her domain,
Chained, but with the self-wrought chain,
That binds the brave and free.
               (22 June 1897, pp. 226–27)

While *Fun* seems to echo *Life*'s comment about the overburdened state of the populace, *Punch* again published a special issue, including a sketch of prehistoric man enjoying a prehistoric Jubilee! Victoria was portrayed as one of the "Great Queens of History," and Thomas Hood's "Song of the Shirt" was rewritten as "Song of the Jubilee." Linley Sambourne's tribute was a "Victorian Shield" crowded with the "gentler conquests" of art, "science's victor course," "images of Peace, and types of War," and "Triumphs of Health, sweet ministries of Light," all

   . . . showing plain how Power and Wealth,
Culture and Cultivation, Taste and Health,
Growths of her sixty years, their honours yield
To deck the disc of the VICTORIAN
      SHIELD!
               (19 June 1897, p. 300)

Punch's emphasis is in all respects positive; in fact, its complex celebratory spread, which portrays Victoria as an emblem of the empire (figure 20), is very much in consonance with the restrained, classically complimentary presentation offered in the British obituary drawings. Enthroned on a dais, she is both regal and expressionless, a telling contrast to Francis Attwood's charming and personal cover for *Life*, in which the plump, diminutive queen sits on a tuffet amid a cascade of roses, a gallant British lion offering her his paw (figure 21). Two months later the Americans went even further: Victoria, wearing a polka-dotted travelling dress and carrying her own umbrella and valise, is shown perched on a

Figure 22. "An Inexpensive Outing," Life, 5 August 1897.

dock piling in preparation for "an inexpensive outing" (figure 22) to make up for the financial drain of the celebrations.

Each of the two views—American and British, domestic and political—tells only half of the story. Together, they show us not what the queen was really like but how she was perceived by the reading public. That the queen herself was not immune to humor, gentle or otherwise, gave license for other well-known and seemingly untouchable figures to be caricatured. Certainly one effect of such constant appearance of the giants of the age was that they were made accessible to readers whose social circles were far removed. Another was to provide a running commentary on the news of the day, a commentary that allowed the reader to imagine that he had a voice, that "his" periodical was not afraid to utter his private, iconoclastic thoughts publicly. In short, the caricatures and parodies created figures that the reader could imagine he knew. Victoria, in truth, had many faces, not the least of which was the one revealed by the popular press.

NOTES

1. Quoted in Leon Edel, *Henry James*, 5 vols. (Philadelphia: Lippincott, 1953–72), 5:90.

2. John Flautz, *Gentle Satirist*, gives *Life*'s history.

3. *Truth* published elaborate Christmas numbers in which the year's events were reviewed in verse and illustration. In 1891, for example, a double caricature lampooned modern taste: "Society's Idol, 1841" shows the young Victoria accompanied by such "poets and prophets" as Tennyson and Darwin, while "Society's Idol, 1891" features the Prince of Wales and Lily Langtry.

4. Accompanying the obituary (13 February 1901, p. 7) was a picture of "Lachrymae"—a sorrowing woman leaning on the tomb of Victoria—that seems to be an American version of a drawing that appeared two weeks earlier in *Punch* (see figure 3).

5. The Wettin name was dropped in favor of Windsor when George V relinquished all German titles for himself and his descendants in a proclamation on 17 July 1917. See Peter Townend, ed., *Burke's Genealogical and Heraldic History of the Peerage, Baronetage and Knightage*, 103d ed. (London: Burke's Peerage Ltd. on Shaw Publishing Co., 1963). Flautz, who traces Thackeray's influence on *Life*, attributes the Guelph cognomen to the novelist's "Four Georges" lecture (p. 59) without mentioning the genealogical import.

6. Both James Brough, *The Prince and the Lily* (New York: Coward, McCann, & Geoghegan, 1975) and John Pearson, *Edward the Rake* (New York and London: Har-

court, 1975) explore the more sensational aspects of Wales's career. Philip Magnus, *King Edward the Seventh* (New York: E. P. Dutton, 1964) gives a reliable, full-length biography.

7. For a discussion of Victoria's offspring, see Theo Aronson, *Grandmama of Europe: The Crowned Descendants of Queen Victoria* (Indianapolis and New York: Bobbs-Merrill, 1973).

8. Edgar Sanderson and Lewis Melville, *King Edward VII*, 6 vols. (London: Gresham, 1910), 4:48.

9. Elizabeth Longford, *Queen Victoria: Born to Succeed* (New York: Harper and Row, 1964), p. 508.

10. Ibid., p. 478.

11. Ibid., p. 479.

12. A complete account of the affair may be found in the London *Times* from 2 June 1891, when the trial began, to 10 June 1891, when a verdict for the defendants was declared. Sidney Lee, in *King Edward VII, A Biography*, 2 vols. (New York: Macmillan, 1925), 1:586–88, discusses Wales's resentment at public opinion that judged him unfit for the throne because of his involvement in the scandal.

13. For the newspaper record of the incident, see the *New York Times*, 10 April 1885, p. 5, col. 4; 16 May 1885, p. 1, col. 4; and 19 June 1885, p. 5, col. 3.

14. An introduction to the circumstances surrounding the publication of Victoria's books may be found in David Duff, ed., *Victoria in the Highlands* (London: Frederick Muller, 1968), pp. 11–16.

15. Longford, *Queen Victoria*, p. 347.

16. Ibid., p. 453.

17. Ibid., pp. 454–55.

18. Ibid., p. 345.

19. *Life* was well aware of the possibility of the queen's assassination. When she suffered a "slight accident" (reported in the London *Times*, 20 March 1883, p. 10, col. 1), the magazine published a news "extra" entitled "Attempted Assassination! Fiendish Attempt on the Life of Her Majesty the Queen" (29 March 1883, pp. 145–46). The account attributes the accident to "Soap Secretly Set by Irish Servants on the Staircase." The burlesque may have been motivated partly by an attack on Lady Florence Dixie, which took place a day earlier; the London *Times* suggested that Irish revolutionaries, incited by Rossa, were to blame (19 March 1883, p. 9, cols. 2–3).

20. While Flautz, *Gentle Satirist*, contends that Smith is a "regular contributor" about whom "nothing is known" (p. 72), Frank Luther Mott, *History*, 4:560, identifies him as John Kendrick Bangs, who joined *Life* as literary editor in 1884.

21. The reporter's comment appears in the London *Times*, 10 May 1887, p. 10, col. 1, as part of a news item that describes the Wild West Show and its adjunct, the American Exhibition, a commercial fair including gardens, a tobogganing slide, an art show, and manufacturing samples. The reporter professes wonder at "the shooting of the frontier girls Miss Annie Oakley and Miss Lillia Smith, the latter only 16 years of age."

22. Amy Cruse, *The Victorians*, pp. 236–59, discusses Cooper's reception in England.

23. According to *Life*'s version, "Buffalo Bill shot the Koh-i-noor out of the Queen's Spring crown seven times running, much to the delight of her Majesty" (28 May 1887, pp. 290–91).

24. David Duff's *Victoria Travels* (London: Frederick Muller, 1970) gives details of Victoria's twice-yearly circuit of Osborne, Windsor, and Balmoral.

25. Ellegard, "Readership," p. 21.

26. Longford, *Queen Victoria*, pp. 500–501.

I IS for Ibsen, reciting a play,
While Irving and Ingersoll hasten away.

J IS for Johnson, who only says "Pish!"
To Jonah, who tells him his tale of a fish.

3
Darwin and Darwiniana

BECAUSE OF THE IMMEDIATE AND LASTING IMpact of Charles Darwin's *Origin of Species* (1859) upon nearly every aspect of Western life and thought, it is hardly surprising to discover Darwin and his writings frequent subjects of satire in Victorian comic periodicals. The theory of evolution did not originate with Darwin, and even his ideas of natural selection and survival of the fittest had been reached independently by his contemporary, Alfred Russell Wallace; but Darwin's was the first widely read English book on the ideas, and he soon became the center of a controversy that was to remain lively for well over a century.

In 1861 *Punch* offered a poem "Monkeyana" by "Gorilla," illustrated by a cartoon of a great ape with a sign around its neck, "Am I a Man and a Brother?" (figure 23). The accompanying poem is largely a comic commentary on the rival views of Thomas Huxley and Richard Owen, the two scientists most in the forefront of the Victorian evolution debate; but a prominent place is given to the one whose book started it all:

> Then Darwin set forth,
> In a book of much worth,
> The importance of "Nature's selection;"
> How the struggle for life
> Is a laudable strife,
> And results in "specific distinction."
> Let pigeons and doves

> Select their own loves,
> And grant them a million of ages,
> Then doubtless you'll find
> They've altered their kind,
> And changed into prophets and sages.
> (*Punch*, 18 May 1861, p. 206)

If *Origin of Species* prompted chiding comments on birds becoming prophets and sages, Darwin's second book, *The Descent of Man* (1871), led the satirists' imaginations in the opposite direction. In *Origin*, Darwin seemed careful to avoid the logical step of saying that man, like lower forms of life, was also the product of natural selection. *Descent* proclaimed it clearly, suggesting the likelihood that his ancestors were the anthropoid apes. If the first book inspired visions of manlike birds and beasts, the second stimulated visions of beastlike men. Indeed, Darwin himself was frequently caricatured as an ape (figure 24), and one *Punch* cartoon by Linley Sambourne shows him as a pipe-smoking monkey in a tree contemplating the habits of his horticultural environment (figure 25). *Punch*'s caption suggests the cartoon as an illustration for Darwin's work on the movements and habits of climbing plants. Another tree-sitter is a monkey with an open Darwin book in hand, lecturing to passers-by (figure 26). This cartoon is accompanied by a little note called "Piety and Parallel":

AM. I A MAN AND A BROTHER?

AM I satyr or man ?
Pray tell me who can,
And settle my place in the scale.
A man in ape's shape,
An anthropoid ape,
Or monkey deprived of his tail ?

Figure 23. "Monkeyana," Punch, 18 May 1861.

Some of *Punch*'s better comic verses from 1871 include two on Darwin that are worth quoting. The first is entitled "A Darwinian Ballad":

> O, many have told
> Of the Monkeys of old
> What a pleasant race they were,
> And it seems most true
> That I and you
> Are derived from an Apish pair.
> They all had nails
> And some had tails,
> And some—no "accounts in arrear,"
> They climbed up the trees
> And they scratched out the _____ these
> Of course I will *not* mention here.

> They slept in a wood
> Or wherever they could,
> For they didn't know how to make beds,
> They hadn't got huts,
> They dined upon nuts,
> Which they cracked upon each other's heads.
> They hadn't much scope
> For a comb, brush, or soap,
> Or towels, or kettle, or fire.

The celebrated Nonconformist Divine who flourished under the Commonwealth and Restoration, and wrote the *Saints' Everlasting Rest*, the *Call to the Unconverted*, and another awakening appeal addressed to Christian backsliders, is said to have been accustomed, whenever he saw a criminal on his way to the gallows, to exclaim, "There, but for divine grace, goes Richard Baxter." A distinguished Naturalist, author of the recently published work on the *Expression of the Emotions in Man and Animals*, a sequel to his famous treatise on the *Descent of Man*, may be imagined occasionally giving utterance to a corresponding though different reflection. At the sight of a monkey scratching himself in the Zoological Gardens, that philosopher might with much propriety observe, "There, but for National Selection and the Struggle for Existence, sits Charles Darwin."

Figure 24. Darwin is "aped" in this cartoon of ridicule from a London Sketch Book *of the 1860s.*

Figure 25. Caricature by Sambourne in Punch, *11 December 1875.*

They had *no* coats, nor capes,
  For ne'er did these apes
Invent what they didn't require.

  The sharpest baboon
  Never used fork or spoon,
Nor made any boots for his toes,
  Nor could any thief
  Steal a silk handkerchief,
For no ape thought much of his nose;
  They had cold collations,
  They ate poor relations;
Provided for thus, by the bye.
  No Ou-rang-ou-tang
  A song ever sang—
He couldn't—and so, didn't try.

  From these though descended,
  Our manners are mended,
Though still we can grin and back-*bite*;

  We cut up each other,
  Be *he* friend or brother,
And tails are the fashion—at night.
  This origination
  Is all speculation—
We gamble in various shapes;
  So MR. DARWIN
  May specualte *in*
Our Ancestors having been Apes.
                    (*Punch*, 10 June 1871, p. 234)

The second, "A Darwinian Development," is suggested as lyrics to the song, "My Lodging is on the Cold Ground":

  Your law of Development, Darwin, were that
    As true as some deem it absurd,
  Would make certain causes develop a Bat;
    Like causes develop a Bird.

47

Figure 26. *"There, but for Natural Selection and the Struggle for Existence, sits Charles Darwin,"* reads the commentary to this Punch *cartoon of 30 November 1873.*

As varied effects they would further produce,
  And there would be more living things,
From trying to fly, by continual use,
  In like manner furnished with wings.

Some monkeys, from trees ever leaping to
    trees,
  If use o'er formation presides,
Through ages, would webs have acquired by
    degrees,
  Connecting their arms with their sides.

In aeons, the flying arboreal Ape,
  His trees having happened to fail,
Might, under conditions, which modify shape,
  Have got hoofs and horns, with a tail.

Tradition, preserving those features, combined,
  Whose type Time had come to exhaust,
Might with them have limned, to the popular
    mind,
  The Hero of *Paradise Lost*.

Figure 27. Punch, *4 April 1874.*

Conceive a Gorilla, developed, in hue,
  And form, like one needless to name,
Whose image Development moulding, if true,
  Would fully account for the same.
            (*Punch*, 16 September 1871, p. 110)

Probably Darwin, through the publicity of the popular press, did almost as much as P. T. Barnum to feed public craving for unusual and exotic creatures. If Barnum managed to create a personality for the elephant—Jumbo—Darwin at least assisted in the personification of chimpanzees and gorillas. In response to the news of the death of a chimpanzee in the British Zoological Gardens, *Punch* offered a cartoon of a talking ape conversing with a well-dressed Englishman (figure 27). Along with the cartoon is the following:

In Memoriam

"The Chimpanzee of the Zoological Gardens is dead!"
—*Times*, March 21, 1874.

Lament our poor brother departed!—
    From anthropoid anthropos began—
And DARWIN deep mourning has started,
    For this *"Princeps editio"* of man!

It seems as if Nature had matched him
    And his visitors, man against brute;
But those who most closely have watched him,
    On the rivalry choose to be mute.

Look at him—thus peacefully lying,
    Manhood hid quadru-manhood within!
If developed, he might have feared dying,
    As it is, what a 'scape of our sin!

Had selection made *him* man of monkey,
    And taught him to cringe, cheat, and lie—
À la mode of my lord and his flunkey,—
    He had found it less easy to die.

No monkey speaks ill of a brother;
    Chimpanzees hand o'er slander to man:
But could apes sit to cut up each other,
    There he lies, let them say all they can!

He was *not* paid to slaughter and plunder,
    He was not paid to lie in a wig;
He ne'er out-roared Truth with Press-thunder,
    Milked a horse, or ran Stock Exchange rig!

He ne'er lived to be husband or father,
    Or a model of both we had seen;
So much from his conduct we gather,
    Since his home with the Zooloos has been.

Brother men, Chimpanzees though too plainly,
    You ne'er, do your utmost, can be,
Yet aspire—may it not be all vainly—
    As good as poor JOEY to be!

(*Punch*, 4 April 1874, p. 141)

The passing of the Zoological Garden's chimpanzee continued to provide cartoonists with material, such as the drawing of young "Jack" being questioned on his biblical knowledge by his elder sister (figure 28). Young Jack's claiming that Adam lived in the "Z'logical Gardens" may have amused *Punch* readers, but Victorian religious controversies over evolution were seldom as good-humored as comic cartoons. Along the same line is the cartoon entitled "Misapprehension" (figure 29), which shows a stern-faced mother calling her daughter from staring at a billboard of a gorilla at the Royal Aquarium

DARWINIAN.

Elder Sister (wishing to show off her small Brother's Accomplishments). "Now, Jack, who was the First Man?"
Jack. "Adam!"   *Elder Sister*. "Quite right! And where did he Live?"
Jack (who has notions of his own about an earthly Paradise). "In the Z'logical Gardens!"

Figure 28. "Darwinian" conversation depicted in Punch, *25 November 1876.*

MISAPREHENSION.

Mary Jane (*indignant*). "COME ALONG, 'LIZA. DON'T STAND LOOKING AT THAT—WHICH I CALL IT SHAMEFUL O' THEM PREFANE DARWINITES! I DON'T BELIEVE IT'S A BIT LIKE HER!"
[*Dedicated to Hanging Committees*

Figure 29. "Misapprehension," from Punch, *4 May 1878.*

Squat of figure,
Like a Nigger,
In the eyes and face and colour;
Grave and gentle,
Dull in mental
Aptitudes and getting duller.

Young chimpanzee
One might fancy
Turning out a man and brother;
Full of frolic,
Melancholic,
If one moment, gay another.

High-rope swinging,
Cross-bar clinging,

because she has failed to note that the sign "Adam and Eve" is for another advertisement. The cartoon's reference is to Pongo, a gorilla that had been brought to London's Aquarium, an event that had led to a cartoon (figure 30) accompanied by a *Punch* poem, "Reflections on the Gorilla":

Master Pongo,
From the Congo,
Or, more strictly, the Gaboon-stream—
Sole Gorilla
That doth fill a
Place beneath pale Europe's moon-stream—

Figure 30. "Master Pongo," from Punch, *4 August 1877.*

THE DESCENT OF MAN.

Figurative Party. "So long as *I* am a Man, Sorr, what does it matther to me whether me *Great-Grandfather* was an Anthropoid Ape or not, Sorr!"

Literal Party. "Haw! wather disagweeable for your *Gwate Gwand-mother*, wasn't it!"

Figure 31. "The Descent of Man," from Punch, *24 May 1873.*

Hand-o'er-hand, Jack-tarlike, climbing.
  Hugging, snatching,
  Kissing, scratching,
Much like Man, his baby-time in.

  Not so Pongo:
  You may long go
Ere you'll meet a sadder creature,
  Duller, drearier,
  Travel-wearier,—
Babe as 'tis,—in air and feature.

  Springs his glumness
  From his dumbness,
That he can't return our greeting,
  Tell each brother,
  "You're another!"
Or drink "Our next merry meeting"?

  Or is't sadness
  At Man's badness,

In two capitals detected,
  That can fill a
  Babe Gorilla
With a gloom so deep-dejected?

  Though at dinner,
  For a sinner,
He enjoys his beef and beeà,
  Sad and testy,
  Oft his breast he
Beats, as who'd say, *"Culpa mea!"*

  Or is't owing
  To his knowing
Science threatens rank quadrùman?
  That to-morrow—
  Shame and sorrow!—
Darwin may proclaim him human!

(*Punch*, 4 August 1877, p. 41)

51

A YOUNG DARWINIAN.

Jack (to his Married Sister). "Hi'! Polly!! Look!!! Here's your Baby trying to walk on its Hind Legs!!!!"

Figure 32. "A Young Darwinian," Punch, 1 May 1880.

So numerous were cartoons relating to Darwin's *Origin of Species* and *Descent of Man* that a few selections will have to represent the many. *Descent* is obviously responsible for the conversation between "Figurative Party" and "Literal Party" (figure 31) in which one gentleman is clearly drawn with apelike features to accentuate the satire. Another, by Du Maurier, shows "a young Darwinian" (figure 32) proving his evolutionary knowledge to his married sister! A third, representative of numerous *Punch* playful speculations on stages of human evolution, is the "Darwinian Ancestor" (figure 33) composing the song, "For O it is such a Norrible Tail!" The insectlike creature is based on Darwin's comment to Lyell, "Our ancestor was an animal which breathed water, had a swim-bladder, a great swimming tail, and an imperfect skull." One amusing series called "Evolutionary Assimilation" featured various types of persons in different vocations in the process of metamorphosis into the objects of their callings (figures 34 and 35).

Among several amusing comic magazine verses on Darwinism are the following three, included for different reasons. The first, "Joca Darwiniana," suggests the rhythmic influence of Gilbert and Sullivan:

> I contend the explanation
> Of a jester's inspiration
> Is no momentary brilliance of the brain,
> But a steady evolution
> From idea to execution,
> And a word or two will make the matter plain.
> First there comes a tiny spasm
> Which I think is Protoplasm,

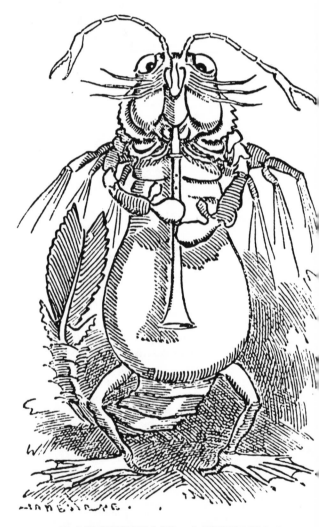

DARWINIAN ANCESTOR

Composing the Song, " For O it is such a Norrible Tai

"Our ancestor was an animal which breathed wate swim-bladder, a great swimming tail, and an imperfect s *Darwin to Lyell.*

Figure 33. "Darwinian Ancestor," Punch, 10 December 1887.

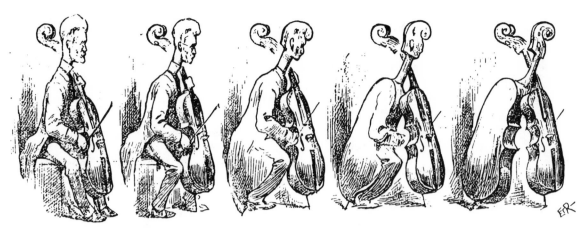

Figure 34. The cellist evolves into his cello in Punch, *12 July 1890.*

For it may denote a poem or a pun,
    And amorphous Protozoa
    Of the best of jokes must grow a
Certain size before they're obviously fun.
    But when matter gets in motion
    Quite a complicated notion
May evolve itself from just a simple cell,
    For a joke that's told with unction
    Is organic in its function,
And the function of an organ is to "swell."
    Thus it rises by gradation
    In the scale of recreation
To a jest'ng after dining without stint,
    Till it breaks its final trammel
    And declares itself a mammal,
Which is vertebrate enough to "go" in print.
    Braving dangers of rejection,
    By a natural selection
It survives amid the fittest of the fit;
    In the process of evolving
    Very fortunately solving
That great difficulty—specie to wit.
            (*Punch*, 20 June 1900, p. 438)

The American satire magazine *Judge* provided its readers a "Darwinian Alphabet," which took them from "A" to "M" (Ape to Man):

A is an ape, the forerunner of man,
According to Darwin's magnificent plan.

B his next brother's got up in the scale
Of creation, since he has discarded his tail.

C is a creature, a live one, I think,
But Darwin don't know, he's the one missing link.

D is for Darwin, I wish, I must own,

He would trace his own line, and let our line alone.

E is an Exquisite pinched into shape,
The most perfect of monkeys, the best style of ape.

F is his fur, which good Dame Nature gave,
But he scrapes it all off when he learns how to shave.

G is gorilla, a monkey, you know,
But you'll see men just like him wherever you go.

H is the head, and it ought to contain,
Both monkey and man, some proportion of brain.

I is just I—you may guess, if you can,
If I'm nearest akin to the monkey or man.

J is *The Judge*, who is wondrously blest,
For *both* species in him are displayed at their best.

K's for our kindred. It's rather a bother,
I confess, that an ape is "a man and a brother."

L's for the ladies, but they must escape,
Even Darwin daren't call Mrs. Darwin an ape.

M is a man, that's the best I can say,
But he winds up the matter, at least for to-day.

One of the most heated Victorian debates was over the influence of scientific discovery on religious dogma. Darwin's publications fanned the flame, and *Punch* could not resist getting in on the act. An 1878 issue carried a bit of philosophical verse suggesting that Darwin, like earlier scientific "heretics," would eventually work his way into the ranks of the defenders of the faith:

Darwinism and Dogma
(Song for the "Anthropological Section")

'Twas the Sun that stood still, GALILEO
    declared,
    And the Earth that around him was moving;
And we know how at Rome the Philosopher
    fared,
    Fact, but heresy likewise, for proving.

Astronomy threw Mother Church into fits
    By what seemed to her lore contradiction.
Now it chimes so with chapter and verse, she
    admits,
    That 'tis taught free from priestly restriction.

Then Geology made out this Earth's age more
    vast
    Than a Sunday School teacher supposes;
And divines, for the most part, awhile stood
    aghast
    At apparent discordance with Moses.

But when Saurians extinct could no more be
    denied,
    Nor the "flint in the drift"'s proof confuted,
They found truth scientific and text coincide
    Both chronologies rightly computed.

By-and-by, if we find our first parents were
    apes
    That 'tis proved to each soul's satisfaction,
Word received in new senses, things taking
    new shapes,
    Will be squared with man's simious
        extraction.

And 'twill then be thought only a bit of bad
    taste
    To inquire if as apes die so men die?
Faith and Science, at odds howsoe'er they seem
    placed,
    Will aye find out a *modus vivendi*.
            (*Punch*, 31 August 1878, p. 85)

Turning next to a series of caricatures of Darwin
himself, we begin with what is probably the finest
to have appeared in any of the comic periodicals. It
is the colorful chromolithograph from the 30 September 1871 issue of *Vanity Fair* (figure 36), showing the sixty-two year old scientist during the year
of the publication of *The Descent of Man*. The almost
skeletal figure with deep-set eyes, wearing what appears to be a glove on his right hand, is seated on
the thick-cushioned chair with the rollers that allowed him to move from place to place without
having to stand and walk as he did his work. While
the drawing seems a caricature, it is actually a rea-

sonably good likeness, a semi-caricature at best. Accompanying each *Vanity Fair* "cartoon" was a biographical sketch by "Jehu Junior," the pen name for
the founding editor, Thomas Gibson Bowles. A
paragraph is worth quoting.

Among these theories [of human origins] one of the most
striking is that which Mr. Darwin has given to the world
with reference to the Origin of Species by means of
Natural Selection. Mr. Darwin, who was born sixty-two
years ago, has spent the whole of a most laborious life in
close converse with the material world in which we live,
and the beings that it has from time to time seen upon its

*Figure 35. "A Darwinian Student's After-Dinner
Dream" shows wish fulfillment in panoramic evolution in*
Harper's Weekly, *23 December 1871.*

development simply from individual aberrations. Nevertheless, so unknown to us are our fellow-beings that even for ordinary men his writings have all the charm of romances; while they will remain to all time, if nothing else, at least a record of earnest and honest devotion to the solution of the most momentous of the problems by which mankind are surrounded.

Another fine caricature, certainly more fitting that label than the *Vanity Fair* drawing, is one by Frederick Waddy from the 8 June 1872 issue of *Once a Week* (figure 37). The naturalist is in a subtropical setting, emerging from the jungle and walking with stick in hand. Although the accentuated beard and the enlarged head with deep-set eyes suggest a

Figure 36. Captioned "Natural Selection," this cartoon of Darwin, signed "Coide," appeared in Vanity Fair, *30 September 1871.*

surface. He has thus become one of the most accomplished naturalists now in existence, and any theoretical structure that he builds upon his researches must be regarded with great respect. His books are written to a large extent for an appeal to ordinary men. This, indeed, it is which gives them their great importance. This, however, makes it also allowable to say that to ordinary men the chain of inferences seems to be very loosely hung together by which he seeks to establish that the various species of animals now existing on the earth inherit all their immense dissimilarities from a common ancestor, and that they have acquired their wide differences of

Figure 37. Another cartoon captioned "Natural Selection" is by Frederick Waddy in Once a Week, *8 June 1872.*

Figure 38. Darwin's "Fancy Portrait" by Sambourne in
Punch, *22 October 1881.*

duced a more earnest or more able student than the author of the theory of Natural Selection.

From *Punch* comes one in a series of well-known Victorians called "*Punch*'s Fancy Portraits," all of which were drawn by Linley Sambourne. Sambourne shows Darwin, in the 22 October 1881 issue, as "Charles Robert Darwin, LL.D., F.R.S." (figure 38) and adds

In his *Descent of Man* he brought his own species down as low as possible—i.e., to "a hairy quadruped furnished with a tail and pointed ears, and probably arboreal in its habits"—which is a reason for the very general interest in a "family tree." He has lately been turning his attention to the "politic worm."

Accompanying the caricature, which shows Darwin contemplating an enlarged earthworm in the form of a question mark (with a book entitled "Diet of Worms" lying open on the grass!), is a short poem:

The Worm Turns

I've despised you, old Worm, for I think you'll
    admit
    That you never were beautiful even in youth;
I've impaled you on hooks, and not felt it a bit;
    But all's changed now that DARWIN has told
    us the truth
Of your diligent life, and endowed you with
    fame—
    You begin to inspire me with kindly regard:
I have friends of my own, clever Worm, I
    could name,
    Who have ne'er in their lives been at work
    half so hard.

It appears that we owe you our acres of soil,
    That the garden could never exist without
    you,
That from ages gone by you were patient in
    toil,
    Till a DARWIN revealed all the good that you
    do.
Now you've turned with a vengeance, and all
    must confess
    Your behaviour should make poor humanity
    squirm,
For there's many a man on this planet, I guess,
    Who is not half so useful as you, Mister
    Worm!

(*Punch*, 22 October 1881, p. 190)

touch of "aping" the famed scientist, Waddy's biographical sketch is clearly complimentary. Surveying Darwin's life and works, Waddy notes his most recent *Descent of Man* as "long-expected" and adds,

The conclusion to which the author came was that, "at a remote period, Man, the wonder and glory of the Universe," and the monkey, had the same parental relations. This theory is at first a little shocking, and has been attacked as violently as it has been stoutly defended. Whatever there is of truth in this startling new theory of Natural Selection, whether it be almost of equal weight with a revelation or completely false in its assumptions, time may prove. Men of eminence, of great learning and great sagacity, can be catalogued both for and against it.

We have no space to enter into the abstruse discussion; but it is a simple duty to record here, that for close observation of the various phenomena of natural history, unflagging energy and perseverance in the search after truth, and great intellectual power, no country has pro-

Figure 39. Thomas Nast's cartoon in Harper's Weekly, *19 August 1871.*

In quiet sanctums few descry,
Still trimmed and tended patiently
  By unobstrusive sages.

And when that light begin to show
Its keen but unfamiliar glow
  To poor be-muddled mortals,
The dullards blink, the quidnuncs croak,
The zealots fain would Heaven invoke
  To bar those perilous portals.

In vain; that clear and conquering light
Wins as it widens, calms affright,
  Dull souls from dread delivers;
Till they who came to curse make shift
To give a welcome to the gift
  And honour to the givers.

So comes my Darwin's turn of phrase
And the green honours of their bays
  The men who banned you offer;
The smile, of such occasion born,
Might well have had a touch of scorn,
  Could wisdom be a scoffer.

Although the present study focuses primarily upon British periodicals, a drawing by the American artist Thomas Nast in an 1884 issue of *Harper's Weekly* deserves note. Captioned "Mr. Bergh to the Rescue," it shows Mr. Bergh and Darwin (*Origin of Species* tucked under his arm) next to a gorilla in front of the Society for the Prevention of Cruelty to Animals, of which Bergh was then president (figure 39). The "defrauded" gorilla points to Darwin and says, "That *Man* wants to claim my Pedigree. He says he is one of my Descendants." Mr. Bergh replies, "Now, Mr. Darwin, how could you insult him so?"

While it is obvious that most of the comic periodicals, both English and American, had frequent fun at Darwin's expense, *Punch* could also take a serious turn toward the distinguished scientist. An 1877 tribute cartoon, "*Punch* to Dr. Darwin" (figure 40), is accompanied by the following explanatory poem:

> Our world's stage footlights flare and fume.
> While the clear light that shall illume
>   The Future's farthest ages,

Figure 40. "Punch to Dr. Darwin," Punch, *1 December 1877.*

Figure 41. Carlo Pellegrini's ("Ape") caricature of Thomas Huxley in Vanity Fair, 28 January 1871.

As free from rashness as from dread,
    You follow without swerving.
Fame meets you fairly on the way,
And where's the duffer who to-day
    Dare question your deserving?

Punch cracks his jokes at you *sans* ruth;
His honest fun wars not with Truth,
    But rather serves to test her;
And, serious now, he bows respect,

But only shallow smartness mocks,
The antics of the orthodox,
    The dogmatist's wild capers,
Smile, but ne'er lift the heel to spurn;
Trust Truth's *asbestos* to outburn
    Delusion's glimmering tapers.

Science would be the last to claim
Infallibility's false fame,
    Which only Folly urges.
The truth to seek with patient guest
Is hers, content to leave the rest
    To blatant *Boanerges*.

So have *you* done; the road you tread,

Figure 42. "Spy's" first cartoon for Vanity Fair, Professor Richard Owen appeared as "old Bones" in the issue of 1 March 1873.

58

Figure 43. Huxley by Waddy, Once a Week, *31 August 1872.*

Figure 44. Owen by Waddy, Once a Week, *6 July 1872.*

Sure that the Sage will not reject
    The tribute of the Jester.
             (*Punch*, 1 December 1877, p. 241)

Five years later, when Darwin died in 1882, *Punch*'s obituary tribute was brief in its recognition that the world had lost a prophet:

Charles Robert Darwin
Born, February 12, 1809   Died, April 19, 1882

A studious porer over Nature's plan,
    Calm tracker of her steps, keen, watchful,
        wise;
Recorder of the long Descent of Man,

And a most living witness of his rise:
Long o'er his life-work may the fight be fought,
Yet leave him still a leading light of Thought.

During Darwin's lifetime two Victorian scientists most prominent in the evolution debate were pro-Darwinian Thomas Huxley and anti-evolutionist Richard Owen, both of whom were frequently caricatured in the popular press. In an 1862 issue *Punch* offered a nine-stanza poem, "The Gorilla's Dilemma," dedicated to the opposing professors in the great debate. The theme is set in the first stanza:

Say am I a man and a brother,
    Or only an anthropoid ape?
Your judgment, be't one way or 'tother,
    Do put into positive shape.
Must I humbly take rạnk as quadruman
    As OWEN maintains that I ought;
Or rise into brotherhood human,
    As HUXLEY has flatt'ringly taught?
              (*Punch*, 18 October, 1862, p. 164)

Both Huxley and Owen appeared in caricature in *Vanity Fair*, Huxley featured as "the inventor of protoplasm" in an excellent 1871 cartoon by Carlo Pellegrini (figure 41) and Owen presented as "Old Bones" in the magazine's first offering from the famous Leslie Ward as "Spy" (figure 42). The two were also subjects of the clever Frederick Waddy in his 1872 *Once a Week* series. Huxley is shown in professorial posture, lecturing on "bones and stones and such-like things" (figure 43). Owen is more comically portrayed in sporting clothes on the back of a prehistoric skeleton with the caption "Riding His Hobby" (figure 44). Both men appear in one of *Punch*'s "Fancy Portraits" in 1884 (figure 45). In the center, as a poodle lecturing to a circle of attentive dogs, is Owen, described as "A Knowin' Professor." In the background and to Owen's right crouches Huxley, doglike, with a package in his mouth, apparently as if to bring an offering to his "master," an implied relationship that would hardly have met with Huxley's approval! Beneath the cartoon, however, a couple of sentences poke equal fun at Owen:

It is said of him that "from the sponge to Man, he has thrown light over every subject he has touched." To have thrown light from a sponge must be a marvellous a scientific achievement as extracting sun's rays from cucumbers, and the Professor deserves to be considered one of the greatest scientists of his time.

Although Darwinianism itself was often the subject of satire and caricature, it was also used as a weapon for satiric attacks on other Victorian movements that provided periodical artists with material for visual comedy. One such movement, aestheticism, is the subject of a later chapter because of the widespread publicity given it by its prominent apostle Oscar Wilde, who, during the 1880s and early 1890s, appeared regularly in British and American magazines and papers. "How Far is it from This to This?" asked an 1882 *Washington Post* cartoon comparing a "wild" man of Borneo to the "Wilde" man from Britain on his American lecture tour (figure 46). The *Post* comments:

We present in close juxtaposition the pictures of Mr. Wilde of England and a citizen of Borneo, who, so far as we have any record of him, is also Wild, and judging from the resemblance in feature, pose and occupation, undoubtedly akin. If Mr. Darwin is right in his theory, has not the climax of evolution been reached and are we not tending down the hill toward the aboriginal starting point again? Certainly, a more inane object than Mr. Wilde, of England, has never challenged our attention, whose picture, as given herewith is a scrupulously correct copy of a photograph put out with his sanction and which may be seen in all public windows. Mr. Wild of Borneo doesn't lecture, however, and that much should be remembered to his credit.

Figure 45. Owen by Sambourne in Punch*'s "Fancy Portrait" of 5 January 1884.*

THIS

TO

THIS?

Figure 46. "Mr. Wild of Borneo" in The Washington Post, *22 January 1882.*

Somewhat related to the *Post* cartoon is W. H. Beard's "The Aesthetic Monkey" (figure 47) appearing as an engraving in the 28 January 1882 issue of *Harper's Weekly*, just a fortnight following Oscar Wilde's departure from England for his American tour. Quite obviously, Wilde is the intended victim of the satire; readers of *Harper's Weekly* would recognize immediately the symbolic sunflower, lily, and open book of poems. A decade earlier, *Harper's* had "eclipsed" Darwin (figure 48); however, he continued to "shine" through the century.

However incongruous evolution and aestheticism may seem to us in the 1980s, it is clear that the comic press of the 1880s saw relationships that amused readers. That there were more serious connections between science and poetry in the Victorian period is clear from numerous poems by the era's most outstanding laureate, Alfred Tennyson. Thus, while most of the remainder of this book will deal with Tennyson and other poets of the day, we have, as noted in the introduction, started with Victoria and Darwin because one gives the period its name and the other gives the period one of its most pervasive ideas. The Victorians enjoyed poking fun at their prominent parliamentarians, prime ministers, and socialites, as well as at their royalty and their most controversial spokesmen on issues scientific, religious, and educational; the comic periodicals rarely missed a chance to deal with these in caricature or cartoon. Some of the most amusing and often most witty and imaginative visual and

Figure 47. "The Aesthetic Monkey," from Harper's Weekly, *28 January 1882.*

61

Figure 48. "Darwin Eclipsed," Harper's Weekly, *23 September 1871.*

verbal satire, however, resulted from their efforts to parody their poets, novelists, and theatrical personalities. Thus we turn next to the poets laureate, Alfred Tennyson and Alfred Austin, working our way through several of the period's major poets and writers, concluding with a curtain call of playwrights and performers who dominated the Victorian stage and consequently found their way into the popular comic commentaries of their time.

K IS the Kaiser, who kindly repeats
　　Some original verses to Kipling and Keats.

L IS Lafontaine, who finds he's unable
　　　To interest Luther and Lizst in his fable
While Loie continues to dance on the table.

4

The Laureates Alfred: Tennyson and Austin

DURING THE PERIOD WE ARE SURVEYING, EN-
gland's two poets laureate were Alfred Tennyson,
from 1850 to 1892, and Alfred Austin, from 1896 to
1913. While Austin (or "Alfred the Little," as *Punch*
called him!) was hardly competition for his distinguished predecessors, Wordsworth and Tennyson,
he was, as laureate, frequently caricatured and
parodied in comic periodicals during the.1890s and
early twentieth century. Indeed, the fact that his
actual appearance was close to caricature and his
poems often less skillful than the ones that parodied
or mocked them made him a vulnerable victim of
the satirist's pen. We give him, therefore, in this
chapter a corner of the spotlight otherwise focused
on the far superior talent, Alfred Tennyson.

As one might expect, Tennyson appeared frequently in comic periodicals during the last half of
the nineteenth century. From 1850, when he succeeded Wordsworth as poet laureate, until his death
in 1892—and well into the twentieth century—
Tennyson appeared with predictable frequency in
such popular magazines as the British *Punch*, *Vanity
Fair*, *Fun*, and *Once a Week*, and the American *Judge*,
Life, and *Puck*. Dozens of the parodies have been
collected by Walter Hamilton, Jelle Postma, Walter
Jerrold, and R. M. Leonard, and, more recently, by
George O. Marshall, Jr.[1] Although caricatures of
Tennyson and cartoons on Tennysoniana are occa-
sionally reprinted to illustrate books and articles on

the poet, published collections of these drawings
are either rare or nonexistent. While it is beyond
our present scope to attempt anything like an exhaustive collection, our representative selection
contains what we believe to be some of the best
examples from the more popular British and American press.

Even before Tennyson became poet laureate, he
was the victim of parody in an 1843 issue of *Tait's
Edinburgh Magazine*. Parodying "The Merman," the
fairly well-known verse concludes

> 'T is I would be
>   The Laureate bold,
> With my butt of sherry
> To keep me merry,
> And nothing to do but pocket my gold!

Tennyson would have to wait, however; it was
Wordsworth who was made poet laureate in 1843,
following the reign of Robert Southey. But the idea
that accepting the laureate's robes meant giving up
the muse for money and popular conformity was
soon expressed by Robert Browning in "The Lost
Leader," his poetic regret for Wordsworth's selling
out to the establishment, and later by such magazines as *Punch* with its periodic jabs at Tennyson.
By the time that Austin was appointed Laureate,
the salary sack and sherry keg, along with lines
from "The Merman" parody, were standard favor-

Figure 49. "Re-engaged" *shows Austin celebrating his laureateship with a song:*

> *Tis I would be the Laureate bold*
> *With a Butt of Sherry*
> *To keep me merry*
> *And nothing to do but pocket the gold!*

From Punch, *31 July 1901.*

ites for caricaturists and satirists to include in drawings, such as Bernard Partridge's 1901 *Punch* rendition of the Pegasus-perched Parnassian Circus-rider (figure 49) when Austin was reappointed laureate and the 1902 cartoon of Austin standing on his sherry keg while offering his "Official Cornation Ode" for the ascendency of Edward VII (figure 50). Enough for the moment, however, on the *second* laureate Alfred, and back to the *first*, Alfred Tennyson.

In his essay "Tennyson in Parody and Jest," George O. Marshall, Jr., points out that while Tennyson possessed a sense of humor rarely recognized or acknowledged by even his more perceptive critics, his hypersensitivity to criticism of any kind made him particularly resentful of parodies of his work. Although Tennyson was parodied, sometimes with remarkable skill, during the period between his becoming poet laureate in 1850 and his acceptance of the peerage in 1883,[2] he received more than his share after this. Marshall cites the *Pall Mall Gazette*'s anonymously written "Baron Alfred Vere De Vere" as one of the better-written parodies reflecting the disappointment of many who would have preferred their bard's remaining a commoner.

Figure 50. Austin sings his "Official Coronation Ode" in Punch, *25 June 1902.*

We hail the genius—not the lord;
    We love the poet's truer charms.
A simple singer with his dreams
    Is worth a hundred coats-of-arms.

Punch offers a full-page cartoon in its issue of 22 December 1883 with "Mr. Punch" presenting the peerage crown to Tennyson and commenting, "Glad, My Lord, you have been tempted to change your hat." (figure 51). All seems complimentary enough in Linley Sambourne's drawing, until we scrutinize the background to discover the poetic muse on her pedestal and two hats, tossed in the air by their owners Alfred Austin and Algernon Swinburne, one of whom is seen in an apparent dance. Subtle satire may be intended by visual ambiguity.

Figure 51. Punch *presents the peerage crown to Tennyson in the issue of 22 December 1883.*

Are Austin and Swinburne dancing for joy over the honor given to a fellow poet? Or, are they running to offer their *own* poet's hats in exchange for a crown, thus leaving Mr. Punch glad that it was Tennyson, rather than one of the other two, who received the honor? Is the muse with her upraised arm hailing a favorite son, or is she waving goodbye to him? While *Punch* was not unusually cruel to Tennyson during the 1880s and 1890s, occasional cartoons seem to have combined compliment with criticism. Another good example is Sambourne's "*Punch*'s Fancy Portrait" (figure 52) from an 1882 issue in which "Alfred the Great" lounges regally on his throne while holding the symbols of his recent plays, *The Cup* and *The Falcon*. Beneath are the lines by "Halfred Minor":

What we call our Bard's our Best,
    And may his poetry never be Werse!

One of the earliest and certainly one of the finest caricatures of Tennyson is by "Ape" (Carlo Pelleg-

Figure 52. Punch's "Fancy Portrait" by Sambourne in the issue of 22 March 1882.

rini) in the 22 July 1871 issue of *Vanity Fair* (figure 53). Accompanying the drawing is the letterpress biographical sketch by "Jehu, Junior" (the founding editor, Thomas Gibson Bowles), which is worth quoting:

There has arisen of late with regard to the Poet Laureate that reaction which seems fatally destined to overtake all men who are famous in their own lifetime; and it has become a fashion to doubt his genius and to depreciate his works. In spite of all, however, he remains unquestionably what the public voice has long pronounced him, the first poet of our day, and he will endure as one of the first that all time has produced. The greatest living master, for certain purposes, of the English language, he has revealed to the most refined all its unsuspected treasures of richness and delicacy, and has yet poured them out in such simple and sober channels that his songs go straight to the hearts of the most homely. The mere mention of his name awakens in every Englishman an echo of sweet sounds gently rippled into flowing verse, which lies about the chambers of the memory like the low hum of a

summer afternoon, and which harmonises as nothing else can with the spirit of a sentimental and peaceful generation.

Nevertheless, Mr. Tennyson is perhaps the poet who has done the most to teach us that there is after all no use in poetry. He lacks the blind driving passion and the fierce faith of the very greatest poets. The beautiful and the true seem to act upon him, but never to enter into him. He seeks to be both teacher and singer; he weaves the most delicious web of fancies; but will never let us go without pointing out that, after all, his intention is only to provide good strong homespun for the making of warm raiment. "Oh! teach the orphan-boy to read, or teach the orphan-girl to sew," is the conclusion to which he continually points as sufficient and satisfying for men and poets here below, and to this he brings us ever from the highest flights of fancy with something of the sensation of a fall and a bruise. "The glorious Devil, large in heart and brain, that did love Beauty only," appears to him a shocking example altogether unlovely, and if it can ever be said of him, as he has said of himself, that "he saw through his own soul," he must see that he is not to the full "dowered with the hate of hate, the scorn of scorn, the love of love," which he holds to be the attributes of the true poet.

Tennyson evidently feels that were he to cut loose the bonds that thus bind him to earth, he would be perhaps a greater, but certainly a more dangerous poet. He soars up continually to the great problems that lie above and about us all, but he never dares to touch them, and after doubting and wondering for a space, always turns off awed and in another direction, leaving us only confused and confounded. He is then greatest when he sinks the mystic and shows us the materialist, for there are few who more strongly feel, and none who have so tenderly displayed, a full and many-toned sympathy with this fair earth and the creatures that therein inhabit.

Although several of Tennyson's appearances through parody in *Once a Week* have been reprinted,[3] the magazine's delightful caricature by Frederick Waddy has not received the attention it deserves. Captioned simply "Poet Laureate," the cartoon (figure 54) appeared in the 13 April 1872 issue as one in the series of several dozen literary personalities contributed by Waddy during that year. Tennyson is shown swinging on his "popularity" and "name" in a starry night sky of "poetic fancy." Waddy's treatment of the laureate may seem less unflattering if one compares it to the artist's depiction of Browning as a pied piper (see figure 3 of chapter 5 on Browning) and to his caricature of Arnold as a trapeze artist coasting in mid-air between poetry and criticism (see figure 4 of chapter 6 on Arnold).

While the Waddy cartoons themselves were sometimes unflattering, the biographical and critical comments accompanying them were generally appreciative. Such was the case with Tennyson. Although he is found to have less "manly vigour" than Browning and Swinburne, he is, according to *Once a Week*, "a worthy successor of Wordsworth in the Laureateship" and one who "may well claim the first place among living bards." Among the "salient characteristics" of Tennyson's poetry that *Once a Week* lauds are the "objective rather than subjective" treatments of nature and things of beauty, the "calm, pensive, and retrospective" voice used to prophesy "the lessons which depend upon the present for the benefit of the unborn future," and the "exquisite grace and beauty" of the poet's narrative and lyric styles. After lauding *Idylls of the King* as characteristic of Tennyson's "merits at their highest," the magazine concludes:

To compare him with, or to gauge him by, the standard of any of his famous predecessors, as has been sometimes done, would be idle. Like all great artists, he has learnt and adapted from the finest models before him. Beyond this, he is a poet *per se*, and this is his greatest praise. (13 April 1882)

During the 1880s and 1890s, cartoons of Tennyson and parodies and puns on his poems were to be found in nearly every issue of *Punch*. Most provided commentaries on current political events and social issues. "Bake, Bake, Bake" lamented the polluted stink of the Thames on its "way to the sea"! "Bike, Bike, Bike" lamented the loss of "girlish grace" as

Figure 53. Tennyson by Carlo Pellegrini in Vanity Fair, *22 January 1872.*

Figure 54. "Poet Laureate" by Frederick Waddy, Once a Week, *13 April 1872.*

women took to riding bicycles. "Peers, Idle Peers!" is the "wail of the eldest sons of peers" on the parliamentary event of prospective banishment from the Commons and burial in the Lords. "Jeers, Idle Jeers" is the wishful versing of a would-be laureate whose shunned poems seem to him *at least* equal to the likes of Alfred Austin's! "Wring out the clouds in that damp sky" offers a "New Christmas Song" after *In Memoriam* for English weather-watchers hoping for a new year to "bring some dryer weather in!" And, alas, *In Memoriam* also bears the burden of some typical *Punch* puns. In one cartoon, a secre-

tary is at her typewriter, and in another, a printer is in his shop; the Tennysonian captions are, predictably, "So careful of the type she (he) seems." Or, what could be worse than the Tennysonian "Motto for Dyspeptics":

Our little systems have their day,
They have their day, and cease to be.

It was almost inevitable that parodists would see the verbal kinship between Tennyson's name and the increasingly popular sport of tennis to create the likes of "The Lay of Lawn Tennis." Equally inevitable was that Tennyson would find his way into one of countless periodical poems attacking the new fashion for women to smoke cigarettes. Hence, the following offers a quotable example of the kind of anti-smoking verses that saturated the popular press of the period:

TO A FAIR NICOTIAN.
(WITH A WHIFF OF LORD TENNYSON.)

DEAR Lady CLARA, let me, pray,
  Remonstrate. It's beyond a joke,
When your flirtations, so you say,
  Begin, as oft they end, in smoke.
You're beautiful, but fairer far
  You'd be, if only you would let—
Your male friends smoke that big cigar,
  And yield them too that cigarette.

You smoke because you think it's fast.
  How sad the day when you began
To bridge the difference—so vast—
  Between a woman and a man.
The heroine of idle tales,
  Of scorn, of slander, and dispraise;
Your womanhood is lost 'mid veils
  Of smoke, your foolish lips upraise.

And, Lady CLARA, though mayhap
  These words may never reach your ear;
Young LAURENCE was a decent chap,
  And his old mother held him dear.
Why did you teach the hapless boy
  To smoke?—'twas quite against his will;
Tobacco, you so much enjoy,
  Made him, we know, extremely ill.

Oh, trust me, CLARA, though I like,
  Myself, my yard-long Brosely clay,
Your lovers all will go on strike,
  If you smoke in this awful way.
Howe'er it be, it seems, my girl,
  Your ladyship too oft forgets
A maiden's lips were meant to curl
  And kiss, and not smoke cigarettes.

Dear Lady CLARA, as I've said,
  If time be heavy, work and play;
Try going earlier to bed,
  With some lawn-tennis every day.
Don't give the orphan boy bird's-eye,
  The orphan boy a pipe, You know
How ill they made you first. Good-bye!
  Remember ALFRED told you so.
                (26 October 1889)

Visually, as well as verbally, Tennyson "graced" *Punch*'s pages in his role as laureate. In an 1883 issue he is on board the ship of state harping a tune while the Grand Old Man, Prime Minister Gladstone, dances his "supposed latest performance" on the deck (figure 55). The cartoon is accompanied by the following poem:

ON THE SKYE-LARK.

A Song of High Jinks among High Personages in High Latitudes, dedicated in a holiday humour, but with profound respect, to whom it may concern.

             AIR—*"Jack Robinson."*

THE perils and the pothers of the Session past,
The *Pembroke Castle* Northward ho! was bound
  at last,
And WILLIAM to the winds all his longshore
  troubles cast;

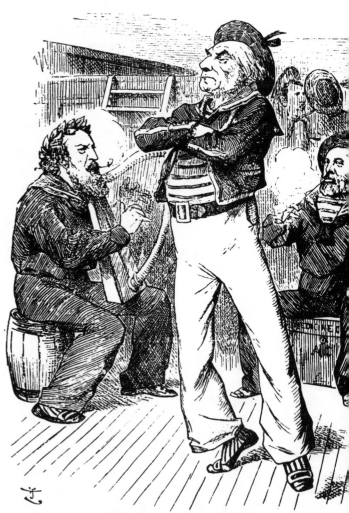

Figure 55. Gladstone dances to Tennyson's music in Punch, *22 September 1883.*

70

And chief among his messmates was ALF
    TEN-NY-SON.
For ALFRED had a tenor voice, and songs could
    sing galore,
And he twangled "like an angel" on a harp he
    always bore,
And along with the crew he had come away
    from shore,
    As Minstrel for the voyage—ALFRED
        TEN-NY-SON!
        Singing toddi-oddi-iddi-iddi-
            um-tum-tay! &c.

For WILLIAM he had met with him, and cried,
    "I say,
Mayhap you'd not object that harp to twangle
    and to play,
Like the old Sirens, out at sea?" The Minstrel
    answered, "Nay,
    I shouldn't,—not a morsel," says ALF
        TEN-NY-SON.
Says WILLIAM to him "I have joined this here
    ship,
And my shore-going comrades I have given all
    the slip,
So mayhap you will partake our cruise and join
    us for the trip."
    "You're a right good sort of fellow," says ALF
        TEN-NY-SON.
        Singing toddi-oddi, &c.

So upon the *Pembroke Castle's* poop they both
    sat down,
A-talking of great statesmen and of bards of
    high renown;
And they drank as much—say nectar—as
    might come to half-a-crown.
    "This is really very jolly!" says ALF
        TEN-NY-SON.
As WILLIAM was about another long yarn to
    out-pay,
A Sawbones party came abaft—in nautical
    array.
"Why, shiver me!" says WILLIAM, "if here isn't
    that Sir A——."
    "Who'd ha' thought of seeing *you* here?" says
        ALF TEN-NY-SON.
        Singing toddi-oddi, &c.

The Sawbones he seemed staggered. "Eh!" says
    he, "the talk called 'tall'?
And grog? and pipes? Oh! WILLIAM, such high
    jinks won't do at all!"

"On, never mind!" says ALFRED; "don't *you* go
    and raise a squall.
    Confound it, don't you know *me*?—I'm ALF
        TEN-NY-SON!"

Says WILLIAM, "Pray remember the advice *you*
    gave to me.
'Tis now three years ago or more since first I
    tried the sea,
I find these frolics set me up, and so I'm sure
    will *he!*"
    "Upon my word, he hits it," says ALF
        TEN-NY-SON.
        Singing toddi-oddi, &c.

Says the Sawbones, says he, "Well, it *may* be as
    you state,
But you do not mean to say you've got *this* Idyll
    chap as mate?
You know you promised me to keep jaw-tackle
    taut." "Just wait,
    And you'll find we're on the 'Skyelark,'"
        says ALF TEN-NY-SON.
So he plumped down on a barrel, and the
    laurels round his head
Took a Bacchanalian rake, and on his harp he
    twan-gle-ed,
Whilst WILLIAM danced a hornpipe, with a light
    elastic trend.
    "There, *that* doesn't look like doldrums," says ALF TEN-NY-SON.
        Singing toddi-oddi, &c.

Then the Sawbones hitched his trousers and
    he—measured out a glass—
Which *wasn't* homœopathic—and he cried,
    "Well, let it pass!"
Then he lit his pipe and listened. "Why, a man
    must be an ass
    To play the owl for ever!" says ALF
        TEN-NY-SON.
"To fret and stew about things much is all in
    vain.
We are off to Skye and Orkney, and 'to
    Norroway o'er the main'—
As to WILLIAM, when to Westminster he *does*
    come back again—"
    Then they *were* off ere one could say, "ALF
        TEN-NY-SON!"
        Singing toddi-oddi-iddi-iddi-
            um-tum-tay! &c.

                                    (22 September 1883)

Tennyson also assisted "Mr. Punch" in ushering
in new years through *Punch's* prefaces, cleverly illustrated by Charles Keene. In one, the poet
laureate carries his play *Becket* into the year 1885
(figure 56) with the following dialogue:

SCENE—MR. PUNCH'S *Sanctum*. MR. PUNCH *and the* POET
LAUREATE *discovered in confidential confabulation.*

71

Figure 56. Preface to Punch, *27 December 1884.*

Mr. Punch. When bard meets bard, then comes the—pipe of peace!

Poet Laureate. "I pipe but as the linnets sing," you know,
"And do but sing"—and smoke—"because I must."

Mr. Punch. Refill, my Lord! Could RALEIGH make a third,
(Defiant here of JAMES's *Counterblast,*)
The spacious times of great ELIZABETH
Might seen returned—almost.

Poet Laureate.   Well qualified!
Shall "days that deal in *ana*" deal with aught
In the large-thoughted free Shakspearian style?
Leviathan may not be aped—or judged—
By "literary leeches."

Mr. Punch.   Humph! There peeps
A glint of green from out that pocket.

Poet Laureate (*flushing slightly*).   Oh!
My play—my poem—say my poem-play;

No theatre-thing, in present trim at least
But SELBORNE likes it; you, I thought, might care
To scan—appraise—

Mr. Punch.   Mellifluous ALFRED mine,
From green to green, of cover, know I it.

Poet Laureate. And think?

Mr. Punch.   A large-schemed work wakes *many* thoughts,
Scarce summable in the smart young critic's phrase
Of cynical cocksureness.   Stately-sweet,
High-souled, and unhysteric, like all verse
From lips that satyr-froth has never stained,
Nor Cockney spasm vulgarised.

Poet Laureate.   Such praise
From PUNCH's lips is present pledge of Fame.

Mr. Punch. Well buttered, both!—would sneer the Twopenny
Timon; Eh, Tony?

Poet Laureate.   *He*'s no Tenant of the Tub,

	No Cynosarges prompt at snap and snarl.
Mr. Punch.	But has a bite in him for Humbug's heels,
	Or Folly's calves. He'll not touch yours, my Lord!
Poet Laureate.	"Beggar that I am, I am even poor in thanks."
Mr. Punch.	Talking of Beggars, what would BURNS, I wonder,
	Have said to *yours?*
Poet Laureate.	Why, what say you?
Mr. Punch.	BURNS painted

With more than CALLOT power of graphic coarseness
And biting humour; put his "Jolly Beggars"
Beside your Mediæval Mendicants,
My Poet, and perpend! Shakspearian grasp
Of many-coloured wide humanity,
With more than lovely faint-limned lyric shadows,
Mellifluous-tongued abstractions, strained conceits,
And gross grotesqueries our Stage would furnish.

Poet Laureate. I fain would serve it.
Mr. Punch. "All the World's a Stage,"
And *that* you've served with sweetness many a year,
With pure unpoisoned charm of such Art-honey
As you alone can hive. Your home's on Hybla,
But in Thalia's haunt you need a hand
Of practised guidance. One good turn, my Lord,
Deserves another. Book for Book! Behold!
"That is the humour o 't," as *Nym* would say.
The humour! Here you'll find what, 'faith, you lack,
The art of midriff-moving,—*Walter Map*
And *Margery* miss your "Northern Farmer's" touch
Of true *vis comica,*—will find much else
That *Israfel* might learn from *Yorick.* Take

From your friend PUNCH's hand
   Wit's beacon-light,
True Humour's fount,
   Humanity's map and chart,
His Gift of Gifts, his
   EIGHTY-SEVENTH
   VOLUME!
      27 December 1884

In another preface the scene is an olive glade under the Heliconian Ridge, with interlocutors Tennyson, Mr. Punch, and the blind Theban prophet Tiresias (figure 57):

Punch.	The olive-glade, my Theban, and the peak!
	But from the watery hollow, clear and cool,
	Pallas Athene climbs not.
Tiresias.	Better so.
	Your blindness were the eclipse of Britain's sun,
	In days when darkness dominates o'ermuch
	Her "men of light and leading."
Punch.	Never fear!
	Not "gazing on divinity disrobed"
	Will dull my patriot vision. Eh, my Bard?
	Like green in winter, music midst the storn,
	Comes, over vernal in despite of time,
	Melodious still through Faction's fiercest roar,
	Your Muse's latest gift!
Tiresias.	The Golden Bough
	Bare never mellower fruit since SAPPHO sang.
Tennyson.	Thanks! Yet I loathe the Lydian flute,
	That tootles an effeminate song,
	With sickly sweetness making mute
	Firm manhood's clarion clear and strong.
	I would that through my dainties Art
	Should thrill, with true Tylæan might,
	"The song that nerves a Nation's heart,"
	And fires the patriot plumed for fight.
Punch.	Fear not, my mellifluous Alfred, we Englishmen know you of old,

Figure 57. Preface to Punch, *26 December 1885.*

With the true knightly steel in your
    temper, for all that your lips are
    of gold,
A patriot valiant and wise as that
    other great ALFRED, who smote
The Danes, flew the Dragon-flag
    sea-ward, and silenced the
    Raven's hoarse throat.
A Story *your* lips should have sung,
    as they sung the Arthurian lay.
But, Baron, your ballads have dropt
    on a barren and bellicose day
Of angry and heady word-warfare.
    When Christmas has softened
    their souls,
And sweetened their tempers, who
    lately went frantic and fierce at
    the Polls,
Like Manna in Party's bare desert,
    will light their melodious lilt,
As sweet as the music, TIRESIAS, to
    which your loved city was
    built.
Tiresias. Will they *then* hear him, the mad
    multiude,
To whom wise words, if cast against
    the wind

Of their wild wishes and vain hopes,
    are vain,
    Here, as in Thebes?
Punch (cheerily).   At last they *must* hear ME!
Tiresias (admiringly). Happy your lot, not blind
    nor unbelieved!
Tennyson. Thrice happy, to no faction thrall,
    With Fairness and gay Fun,
    Flouting the tyranny of All,
    As well as that of One!
Punch. Why certainly, my Laureate. And
    the Nation's Do-well follows
    My Think-well, as your Ancient
    Sage would say. Our new
    Apollos,
    Gods of the *Long* Bow most of them,
    lack light as well as lightness;
    But through the medium of Mirth
    Punch manifests *his* brightness.
Tennyson. And now your Genial Power
    Breaks forth anew,
    Thaws Winter's cold, and fills
    Eyes with glad dew;
    Your Artists have their wills,
    Your Poets too.
Punch. Precisely, Sir. Your hour will come,
    but after Row confusing,

Figure 58. Tennyson with Browning and Swinburne,
Punch, *27 December 1884.*

The world wants something gay and
    bright and genial and amusing,
To soothe and smooth and sweeten
    it. Bring it along, my Toby—
There! I'll remove his muzzle!
    So,—no fear of hydrophoby!—
There!—that's the Party febrifuge,
    demulcent, tonic pick-up.
'Twill beat Pasteur for *rabies,* still
    the wild spasmodic kick-up
Of Faction's *tetanus!* Take it! There
    is joy in every line.
Take, read to friend Tiresias, my
    VOLUME EIGHTY-NINE!
        (26 December 1885)

In one 1884 *Punch* cartoon Tennyson, Browning,
and Swinburne are shown as "Christmas Waits"
(figure 58) with Tennyson reading from his *Becket.*
The caption-verse beneath suggests the fairly common critique that the better-known poets were inspired at least as much by money as by the muse:

    Oh, bless you, Gentlemen, whose looks
        Are very far from frowning,
    Pay cash, and buy the latest books
        Of Tennyson, Swinburne, Browning!

Since there are several other amusing things about
this cartoon, we shall discuss it at greater length in
the chapter on Browning.

Several *Punch* drawings during Tennyson's late
years reflect the poet's social and political involve-
ments. In one for 1885 he is about to play Guy
Fawkes by blowing up the Admiralty through his
Pall Mall Gazette contributions which, as the cartoon suggests, will ignite public opinion (figure 59).
The accompanying pair of poems narrate the situation:

TENNYSON TACKLED.
I.
THE FLIGHT!
Companion Poem to "The Fleet," A Rejoinder.

You—you—*if* you have failed to understand
    How ships are built on paper at Whitehall,
Have picked up from the *Pall Mall,*
        second-hand,
    Facts which but after all
        Make circulation great—

Your Isle,—where you possess the snuggest
    berth,

*Figure 59. "Guy Fawkes Tennyson Blowing Up The Au-
thorities of the Admiralty," Punch, 2 May 1885.*

75

The tangled lanes, clear stretches of the
    sea,—
Might feed your Muse; of matter you've no
    dearth
So why this unprovoked attack on me,—
    This—regular slate?

You—you who, I admit, *can* write,
    If you have talked of "kicking" to my face:—
Well, pr'aps I ought to seek the Isle of Wight,
    And kick you at your place;
        And may—though late, though late.

II.
THE BARD
Another Companion Poem. A Reply.

YUM-YUM,*if I have failed to understand
    The tons, and guns, and "ends," whereof
        they brawl,
At me, at least, can no man point the hand.
    For hypothetical
        Purely, is all I state.

YUM-YUM, *if* any man has starved the Fleet,
    If any man has his head punched for this,
Kicked by a million boots along the street,
    That sight I would not miss,
        Nay, nor arrive too late!

And what, *if* flying collars and a face
    Familiar once in Highland tour with me,
I saw thus pelted in the market-place?
    Well, well, so might it be;
        And, *if* deserved, First-rate!

                            (2 May 1885)

*YUM-YUM, believed to be Japanese Muse of Hypothetical Poetry,
corresponding to "You, you."

In another from 1885, Tennyson is present to help
Punch comment on the fall of Gladstone and the rise
of Lord Salisbury as prime minister (figure 60). The
poet invites Gladstone to "Come into the garden,
Will," and the recently defeated Gladstone replies,
"No thank you, Alfred, I prefer (sings) to paddle
my own canoe." Again, the accompanying verses
narrate:

COME into the garden, WILL.
    For the black bat, Place, has flown,
Come into the garden, WILL,
    I'm going it all alone;
And the Woolsack's spices are not half bad,
    Though they may be the least bit blown.

But the breeze of Faction moves,
    And SALISBURY's carried on high.

Figure 60. Gladstone and Tennyson, Punch, *27 June
1885.*

Already half swamped by the Party he loves,
    As he'll find to his cost by-and-by;
Most thoroughly swamped by the Party he
        loves,—
    Come,—I'll give him till Christmas to die.

So grace this gay garden of elegant Earls,
    Step in, all your labours are done;
I *should* like to see how you look in your pearls!
    Come along, do—it will be such fun
To see your grand head capped with
        gingerbread pearls;
    If there e'er was a swell—you'll be one!

What! You're going? Won't try the retreat!
    You think to march over my head?
Well you may. Still I've found the place sweet,
    And I've ever so airy a tread!
Titled dust you would shake from your feet,
    Whereas I, though a century dead,
Shall my gew-gaw existence repeat,
    And still blossom in tinsel and red.

                            (27 June 1885)

"Have we Forgotten Gordon?" is the caption for another of *Punch*'s cartoon commentaries on Tennyson's social activities (figure 61). Again, the circumstances are described by *Punch*'s poet:

"HAVE WE FORGOTTEN GORDON?"

[Lord TENNYSON, under this heading, writes appealing to Englishmen for subscriptions to the funds of the "Gordon Boys' Home" at Woking, which is in want of £40,000. Contributions should be sent to the Treasurer, General Sir DIGHTON PROBYN, V.C., Marlborough House, Pall Mall.]

ARE we sleeping? "*Have* we forgotten?" Like
    the thrust of an Arab spear
Comes that conscience-piercing question from
    the Singer of Haslemere.
Have we indeed forgotten the hero we so
    be-sang,

Figure 61. "Have We Forgotten Gordon?" Punch, *5 August 1891.*

When across the far south sand-wastes the
    news of his murder rang?

Forgotten? So it had seemed to him, as alone
    afar he lay,
With the Nile to watch for laggard friends,
    fierce foes to hold at bay;
Though the tired red lines toiled onward up the
    Cataracts, and we
Dreamed of the shout of the rescuing host *his*
    eyes should never see.

When chivalrous BURNABY lay slain, with a
    smile in the face of death,
And for happy news from the hungry wastes
    men yearned with bated breath;
When WILSON pushed his eager way past
    torrent-swirl and crag,
Till they saw o'er GORDON's citadel wave
    high—the MAHDI's flag.

That shame was surely enough, enough, that
    sorrow had a sting
Our England should not court again. The
    Laureate's accents ring
With scorn suppressed, a scorn deserved
    indeed, if still our part,
Is to forget a purpose high that was dear to
    GORDON's heart.

"This earth has borne no simpler, nobler man."
    So then sang he
Who sounds a keen reveille now. "Can you
    help us?" What say we?
Oh, out on words, that come like WOLSELEY's
    host too late—too late!
Do—*do*, in the simple silent way that made lost
    GORDON great.

Surely these Boys that GORDON loved in the
    Home with GORDON's name
Should speak to every English heart that cares
    for our England's fame;

And what be forty thousand pounds as an
    offering made to him
Who held so high that same bright fame some
    do their worst to dim!

Fit task for patriot poet, this! TYRTÆUS never
    stood
More worthily for heroic hearts or his
    home-land's highest good.
Give! give! and with free hands! His spirit's
    poor, his soul is hard,
Who heeds not our noblest Hero's appeal
    through the lips of our noblest Bard!
               (5 August 1881)

Figure 62. "Crossing the Bar," Punch's *memorial cartoon, 15 October 1892.*

One of *Punch*'s more memorable cartoons was occasioned by the poet's death in early October 1892. Captioned "Crossing the Bar," the illustration shows the laurel-crowned bard in the boat, prepared to meet his Pilot "face to face" (figure 62), and the laudatory poem alludes to several of the Laureate's best-loved poems.

"CROSSING THE BAR."
IN MEMORIAM.
Alfred Lord Tennyson
BORN, AUGUST 5, 1809. DIED, OCTOBER 6, 1892.
"TALIESSEN is our fullest throat of song."
The Holy Grail.

OUR fullest throat of song is silent, hushed
    In Autumn, when the songless woods are
        still,
And with October's boding hectic flushed
    Slowly the year disrobes. A passionate thrill

Of strange proud sorrow pulses through the
        land,
    His land, his England, which he loved so
        well:
And brows bend low, as slow from strand to
        strand
        The Poet's passing bell
Sends forth its solemn note, and every heart
Chills, and sad tears to many an eyelid start.
Sad tears in sooth! And yet not wholly so.
    Exquisite echoes of his own swan-song
Forbid mere murmuring mournfulness; the
        glow
    Of its great hope illumes us. Sleep, thou
        strong
Full tide, as over the unmoaning bar
    Fares this unfaltering darer of the deep,
Beaconed by a Great Light, the pilot-star
        Of valiant souls, who keep
Through the long strife of thought-life free
        from scathe
The luminous guidance of the larger faith.
No sadness of farewell? Great Singer, crowned
    With lustrous laurel, facing that far light.
In whose white radiance dark seems whelmed
        and drowned,
    And death a passing shade, of meaning
        slight;
Sunset, and evening star, and that clear call,
    The twilight shadow, and the evening bell,
Bring naught of gloom for thee. Whate'er befall
        Thou must indeed fare well.
But we—we have but memories now, and love
The plaint of fond regret will scarce reprove.

Great singer, he, and great among the great,
    Or greatness hath no sure abiding test.
The poet's splendid pomp, the shining state
    Of royal singing robes, were his, confest,
By slowly growing certitude of fame,
    Since first, a youth, he found fresh-opening
        portals
To Beauty's Pleasure-House. Ranked with
        acclaim
        Amidst the true Immortals,
The amaranth fields with native ease be trod,
Authentic son of the lyre-bearing god.
Fresh portals, untrod pleasaunces, new ways
    In Art's great Palace, shrine in Nature's
        heart,
Sought the young singer, and his limpid lays,
    O'er sweet, perchance, yet made the quick
        blood start
To many a cheek mere glittering rhymes left
        cold.
    But through the gates of Ivory or of Horn

Figure 63. Bards' Battle, Punch, *22 October 1892.*

Its manly harmonies, as sane as strong;
    So that the captious few
Found sickliness in pure Elysian balm,
And coldness in such high Olympian calm.
Impassioned purity, high minister
    Of spirit's joys, was his, reserved, restrained.
His song was like the sword Excalibur
    Of his symbolic knight; trenchant,
        unstained,
It shook the world of worldly baseness, smote
    The Christless heathendom of huckstering
        days.

                    (15 October 1892)

The week following *Punch*'s memorial to Tennyson, the magazine attended immediately to new business—speculation about his successor as poet laureate:

    The laurels vacant from the brows of him
    In whose fine light all lesser lustres dim.

Five of the "lesser lustres" appear in "The Battle of the Bards; Or, The Lists for the Laurels" in the 22 October 1892 issue (figure 63). Gathered around the enthroned Mr. Punch, from left to right they are: Edwin Arnold, William Ernest Henley, Lewis Morris, Alfred Austin, and Algernon Swinburne. While *Punch* seems to suggest the prospects for the more conspicuous foreground figures of Edwin Arnold and Algernon Swinburne, the accompanying "proem" is noncommittal. It begins

    Tan-ta-ra-ra-ra-ra! The trumpets blare!
    The rival Bards, wild-eyed, with wind-blown
        hair,
    And close-hugged harps, advance with
        fire-winged feet
    For the green Laureate Laurels to compete;
    The laurels vacant from the brows of him
    In whose fine light all lesser lustres dim.
    Tourney of Troubadours! The laurels lie
    On crimson velvet cushion couched on high,
    Whilst *Punch*, Lord-Warden of his country's
        fame,
    Attends the strains to hear, the victor-bard to
        name.

                    (22 October 1892)

The first to sing is Swinburne, "a brief bard! (in stature, *not* in song!)," who twangs his lyre in praise of his own poetic accomplishments and concludes by turning to "these jingling jays with plume-plucked wings" who are about to compete with him:

His vivid vision flocked, and who so bold
    As to repulse with scorn
The shining troop because of shadowy birth,
Of bodiless passion, or light tinkling mirth?
But the true god-gift grows. Sweet, sweet, still
    sweet
    As great Apollo's lyre, or Pan's plain reed,
His music flowed, but slowly he out-beat
    His song to finer issues. Fingers fleet,
That trifled with the pipe-stops, shook grand
    sound
    From the great organ's golden mouths anon.
A mellow-measured might, a beauty bound
    (As Venus with her zone)
By that which shaped from chaos Earth, Air,
    Sky,
The unhampering restraint of Harmony.
Hysteric ecstasy, now fierce, now faint,
    But ever fever-sick, shook not his lyre
With epileptic fervours. Sensual taint
    Of satyr heat, or bacchanal desire,
Polluted not the passion of his song;
    No corybantic clangor clamoured through

Beshrew the blatant bleating of sheep-voiced
    mimes!
True thunder shall strike dumb their chirping
    chimes.
If there *be* laureate laurels, or bays, or palms,
In these red, Radical, revelling, riotous times,
They should be the true bard's, though
    mid-age calms
His revolutionary fierce rolling rhymes,
Filfilled with clamour and clangour and storm
    of—psalms!

Next in line is Lewis Morris, "trim, tittivated, tin-tinnabulant".

Some bards pipe from Parnassus, some from
    Hermon;
Room for the singer of the Sunday Sermon!
His stimulant tepid tea, his theme a text,
Carmarthen's cultured caroller comes next!

Singing to the tune "The Birth of Verse," the moralistic Morris claims that what he may lack in poetic inspiration, he makes up in his ability to "moralize my song." Referring to his 1871 volume of verse, *Epic of Hades*, he claims, "And I am he who opened Hades,/To harmless parsons and to ladies!" Recalling his former praise of Tennyson, Morris concludes,

If these be not sufficient claims,
The worth of Verse is vastly small.
I've called him various pretty names,
The honoured Master of us all;
"His place is with the Immortals." Yes!
But I could fill it *here*, I guess!

His "chaste white Muse" could not object,
For mine is white, and awfully chaste.
Now Algernon has no respect
For purity and public taste.
Edwin is given to allegory,
Whilst Alfred is a wicked Tory!!!

The narrator for "The Battle of the Bards" gets the last word:

He ceased. Great Punchius rubbed his eagle
    beak,
And said, "I think we'll take the rest next
    week!"

He does, and there is more "moaning of the bards" when Tennyson had "put out to sea."

The bard's battle ended on 1 January 1896 when London papers announced that the queen had appointed Alfred Austin to be the poet laureate to Her Majesty. With no other major living poet acceptable to Victorian orthodoxy, Austin, the little man who had called Clough, William Morris, Swinburne, and Browning all inferior poets, gleefully accepted the laurels. "Alfred the Little" *Punch* called him in the 11 January issue (figure 64). With the bitter Edwin Arnold and the moody Lewis Morris in the shadowed background, Austin is standing on his publications (the latest of which had been *England's Darling*), which are insufficient to extend his reach to grasp the lyre hanging atop the Tennyson memorial. The accompanying verse narrates the occasion:

Figure 64. "Alfred the Little," Punch, *11 January 1896.*

NEW YEAR'S DAY

(*On Parnassus*)—

OR, THE APOTHEOSIS OF ALFRED THE LITTLE.

Alfred the Little tunes up on his new Official Harp to an old air of Alfred the Great's:—

YOU must take and call me Laureate, Poet
    Laureate, brethren dear,
For to-morrow I'll be the happiest bard of all
    this glad New Year;
My glad Muse chimes, not "vapid rhymes," but
    the maddest, merriest lay,
    For I am QUEEN's Poet to-day, brethren, I
    am Court Minstrel to-day!

There's many a gushing muse, men say, but
    none can gush like mine;
There's ARNOLD and there's MORRIS, both can
    lip the laureate line:
But none so well as little ALFRED in all the land,
    they say,
So I'm to be Poet Laureate, brethren, all upon
    New Year's Day!

I'll now sleep sound o' nights, from dreadful
    dreams no more I'll wake,
That ALGERNON or WILLIAM they will Poet
    Laureate make.
But I must gather flowery tropes and flatteries
    fine and gay,
For I'm ALFRED THE GREAT's successor,
    brethren, dating from New Year's Day!

As I came down the street called Fleet, whom
    think ye I should see,
But EDWIN, bland and Japanesque, bard of the
    Daily T.
He thought his chance was good, brethren,
    lord of the Orient lay,
But I've whipped him on New Year's Day,
    brethren, done him on New Year's Day.

He looked pale as a ghost, brethren, exceeding
    weird and white,
For the singer of "The Season" now had
    dimmed his Asian Light.
They say I'm a Party pick, brethren, but I care
    not what they say,
For I'm crowned upon New Year's Day,
    brethren, laurelled on New Year's Day!

They say that limpid LEWIS is as mad as mad
    can be;
They say young ERIC is making moan—what is
    that to me?
There's many a better bard than I, or so sour
    critics say,

But little ALFRED has taken the cake, all upon
    New Year's Day.

Little ALFRED has licked them all, as shall right
    soon be seen,
The loyallest lyrist of all the lot to his Country
    and his Queen.
    I've out-sonnetted WILLY WATSON in my
    Tory-patriot way,
So I've passed dear WILL up the "Sacred Hill,"
    all upon New Year's Day!

For WILLY, with wild and whirling words, had
    pitched into the Powers,
And invoked the name of the old recluse who at
    Harwarden groans and glowers;
For he's got a bee in his bonnet about the woes
    of Ar-me-ni-a:
So I look down on *him* from Parnassian peaks,
    all upon New Year's Day!

Yes, I am "Fortunatus," brethren, and
    "England's Darling"! Hum!
This harp *is* big, and wide in stretch, and needs
    long arms to thrum.
But if I stand a-tiptoe I shall manage it, I dare
    say,
And I'm Poet Laureate, anyhow, all upon New
    Year's Day!

I wonder now if ALFRED THE GREAT—and
    gruff—with joy would thrill
If he saw *me* twanging the Laureate lyre on the
    Parnassian Hill?
He once was a leetle rude to me when on him I
    had said my say,
Like LYTTON to him; but *I'm* Laureate now, all
    upon New Year's Day!

So you must take and call me Laureate, Poet
    Laureate, brethren dear,
And I'm sure that EDWIN, and LEWIS, and
    WILLIAM will wish *me* a Happy New Year.
"My Satire and its Censors" have *not* stood in
    my upward way;
"Ambition ended" I'm Laureate—at last—upon
    New Year's Day!!!

                      (11 January 1896)

Austin had been earlier caricatured by *Punch* in an 1883 "Fancy Portrait" (figure 65), and *Vanity Fair*'s "Spy" (Leslie Ward) drew him in 1896 as a little man with more taste in dress than in poetry (figure 66). "His dress was that of a country squire and not that of a long-haired poet. He stood but a few feet high," said Ward, who also noted that it took "but a tiny scrap of paper" to take notes on the artist's interview with the poet![4]

Figure 65. Punch's *"Fancy Portrait" of Austin, 3 March 1883.*

Figure 66. "Spy's" Vanity Fair *portrait of Austin, 20 February 1896.*

Austin was vulnerable to satire because of his two most prominent features—lack of height and lack of talent. *Punch* took full advantage of both. "The Poet Laureate on Turkey" (figure 67) appeared shortly after his becoming laureate when he decided that "the virtue of the office" made it incumbent upon him to comment on an 1896 Turkish massacre in Armenia. In a series of *Punch* Christmas greetings in 1900, the empty-handed poet stands perplexed, saying, "Has anybody seen a lyre? I can't find mine anywhere!" (figure 68). As the reign of "Alfred the Little" plodded on after his reappointment in 1901 (see figure 49), his laureate contributions were fewer and fewer. *Punch's* mock "Coronation Ode," playfully attributed to Austin, was about as good (or bad) as what Austin himself might have written (see figure 50 for accompanying caricature):

> WELCOME, thrice happy morning! None too
>   soon
>   Certain preliminary days are past;

> The veritable Twenty-sixth of June
>   Is here at last!

> O lift your voices in united strain
>   To welcome Him—and eke to welcome Her
> Who take their place within the ancient fane
>   Of Westminster.

> First listen to the immemorial vows
>   Phrased with befitting dignity of speech;
> Next, place Two Crowns upon Two Royal
>   Brows,
>   (One upon each).

> And then keep silence, while in roundelays
>   Which, I opine, "may soothe some sufferer's
>   lot"
> When "new and noisier notes" (namely R.K.'s)
>   Are clean forgot

"Oh make the Bard, if possible, a Peer—
A knight, at least."

(25 June 1902)

Punch's attitude toward Austin is cleverly reflected in an illustrated "Sketchy Interview" in the issue of 18 June 1902 (figure 69):

MR. PUNCH'S SKETCHY INTERVIEWS.
I.—THE POET LAUREATE.

I FOUND Mr. AUSTIN at work in his study at Swinford Old Manor—a charming snug apartment with *Walker's*

Figure 67. Austin Turkeyback, Punch, *10 October 1896.*

I bid the Lion of the Land arise,
    Grasping that Flag of Freedom in his paw,
Which in such various localities
    The *Ophir* saw.

Dread Destiny withal I charge to fill
    With devastating draught her cruel cup,
Which having drunk, our envious rivals will
    Simply curl up.

I bid the Lion-cubs to gather fast,
    Flying, as swallows fly, across the waves
Adding that Britons never will be classed
    Withal as slaves.

I sing of Realms imperishably set
    Above the sands of time, of Empires fixed
Upon "the wave-wide track;" in fact, I get
    A trifle mixed.

And, as I warble to each hemisphere,
    Comes the responsive cry from West and
        East:—

Figure 68. Austin's Christmas greeting in Punch, *25 December 1908.*

"ENGLANDS DARLING WAS WRITTEN IN THAT ARM-CHAIR."

"BY THE WAY WHEN I WROTE ENGLAND'S DARLING I WORE WOAD."

"THE WASTE-PAPER BASKET CAME FROM FARINGFORD, TENNYSON'S PLACE."

"NOW, HE SAID, LET ME SHOW YOU THE POULTRY."

"SOMETIMES I JOIN THEM IN THEIR GAMBOLS, ON A BANTAM."

"ALLOW ME TO OFFER YOU A STIRRUP CUP OF MALMSEY."

Figure 69. Punch's *"Sketchy Interview,"* 18 June 1902.

Rhyming Dictionary on the shelves. He extended a welcoming hand.

"Yes," he said, "I do most of my work here. *England's Darling* was written in that arm-chair: the holes in the leather were made while I was thinking of the next line. Ah, the next line—that is at once the poet's triumph and his tragedy! I would not have it re-upholstered for worlds, although several Ashford firms have tendered very reasonably. By the way, when I wrote *England's Darling* I wore woad, and the cook had orders to be continually burning cakes—it seemed to give the atmosphere.

"*The Garden that I Love* was composed in the window seat commanding a view of the geraniums. Ah! sweet Nature—what an influence! what an inspiration! She is the best padding.

"I wrote *The Conversion of Winckelmann* at Herne Bay—not indeed that winkles are too plentiful there, but I found that one could worry along on shrimps. After all, what is a poet if not adaptive?"

"Your study is charming," I said.

"Yes," he said, "I have many treasures. The waste-paper basket came from Farringford, TENNYSON's place. That Dutch clock was Doctor JIM's. The paper-weight was ALFRED THE GREAT's. The goose-quill I have been using was the Laureate PYE's."

"Let me repeat you something," he said; and so saying, the poet, lifting his hand to enforce a silence that I should never have thought of breaking, delivered with admirable emphasis his charming poem beginning "The lark went up"—a little masterpiece fraught with open-air gladness and redolent of the dewy Spring.

"Now," he said, "let me show you the grounds," and he led the way to the chicken run. "I give them all names," he said; "that is MUDFORD, that is CURTIS; over there you see GORDON SPRIGG; in the corner is LIONEL PHILLIPS, and so on. Sometimes I address them in impromptu verse. I am often very happy in impromptu verse in the chicken run."

"And now," said Mr. AUSTIN, as we returned to the house, "if you must go" (although I had still plenty of time before me and had made no movement), "allow me to offer you a stirrup-cup of Malmsey."

He produced a beaker and filled it to the brim.

"Notice," he said, in that incorrigibly poetic way of his, "how the beaded bubbles wink."

Thus fortified, I tore myself away, feeling that I, too, had dwelt in Arcadia.

Finally, two years before his death in 1913 (marking the conclusion of Austin's reign as laureate and the beginning of Robert Bridges's), the American *Life* offered its own "Impudent Interview" with Austin in a bit of doggerel by Arthur Guiterman:

Alfred Austin

Ah, yes, no doubt it's mighty fine
    To be a Poet Laureate,
And pipe each year a pipe of wine,
    With sundry guineas aureate;

But when the plodding universe
    Observes again those fatal days,
Who else must hymn in puny verse
    Britannia's royal natal days?

Who else must hammer rhymes for "George,"
    "Prince Albert," and "Victoria"?
For which I'm tempted oft to forge
    A crime like "infusoria."

'Tis I must show my gratitude
    To condescending Royalty,
With patriotic platitude
    And incandescent loyalty;

Or even pass, with kindly smirk,
  A bit of jobbing knavery,
And praise a raider's dirty work
  As Brilliant British Bravery.

Assail me not with verbal bricks
  And shoulders hyperborean!
I've got to keep my politics
  Consistently—Whig-Toryan.

Like Horace, I've a lyric vein,
  And really should be pitied, for
The fact that I must pipe a strain
  My reeds were never fitted for.

My tapestries have softer tints,
  Wordsworthian and Herricky.
(The *Independent* often prints
  My verses in Ameriky.)

I've learned Apollo's higher laws,
  I've drained the Muses' tippling-can,
But still they mock at me, because
  I cannot shout as Kipling can;

While friendly literary sharks
  In giving me their benison,
Will add irrelevant remarks
  In praise of—Alfred Tennyson!
                          Arthur Guiterman.
                          (9 February 1911)

With this brief offering from "the other side of the Atlantic," we return to Alfred I to sample American responses to Tennyson.

American caricatures of the laureate were far less plentiful than British, although reproductions of paintings, drawings, and photographs were used freely as illustrations for serious reviews and verse tributes that appeared in such periodicals as *Mac-Millan's* and the *Review of Reviews.* What appealed to the humorists was the large body of poetry that their readers could be counted on to recognize. Direct parodies of many poems—"The Charge of the Light Brigade," "Enoch Arden," and portions of "The Idylls of the King"—however, can be found in humor magazines as diverse as the Chicago *Figaro* and Frank Leslie's *Budget of Fun.* Tennyson's poetry was the vehicle for dealing with the fisheries question, taxation, and various presidential races; he was further made to comment on smashed baggage, the Fourth of July, and women's rights. Passing reference was made to his works even in parodies of other authors. In short, his name evoked for the American reader a set of preconceptions not only about what poetry is but about what it should be,

and while isolated examples in the parodic response are critical of his meter or rhyme, for the most part the parodists flattered by imitation.

Tennyson's widespread appeal, from the working-class readers of the Leslie publication to the more sophisticated but democratic-minded readers of *Life,* was in part responsible for the American surprise—and disappointment—at his acceptance of the baronetage. The Americans were amazed that the poet who expressed for all men what one writer calls "The 'honest doubt' concerning religious beliefs; the generous attitude toward the cause of women; the acceptance of science; the liberal politics; the pleas, sometimes a little prudish, for that higher manhood which would hold under the 'ape' and 'tiger' in man"[5] could array himself, as the Boston *Globe* put it, in a "piece of fustian"—a title representing an exclusivist and outmoded form of government (18 December 1883, p. 2). While the *Globe* further complained that unlike the "sweet pure poet," the "old barons were brutes, blood-thirsty savages" (23 December 1883, p. 16), *Life* went to the other extreme; it trivialized the title, dubbing Tennyson "Chief Lord of Her Majesty's Rhymster, and Knight of the Triolet," and published a sketch of the new baron as he looked arrayed in Lord Coleridge's robes, which are much too large (figure 70).[6]

As the American response makes clear, poetry and government don't—or shouldn't—mix, especially when the poet has so democratic an appeal and the government in question is a monarchy. A parody of "Lady Clara Vere de Vere," reprinted in *Judge* from the Norristown *Herald,* states this point of view very well:

Tennyson Takes his Seat

Baron Alfred, Prince of Bards,
  You seek to strengthen your renown
By sitting in the House of Lords,
  And wearing an embroidered gown.
You now refuse to court the muse,
  And with high dignity disport;
You heave a sigh and play the deuce
  While aiming to amuse the court.

Lord of Lyric, King of Verse,
  We know you're proud of your new name;
Your pride could never be much worse
  Than if you had the bulge on fame.
Why do you frown upon the gown
  Of poesy, with all its charms?

A simple poet's laurel crown
  Is worth unnumbered coats-of-arms.

O, monarch of the Muse, you're strong,
  Yet have a weakness for the towers
And titles that to "nobs" belong;
  They're more to you than sylvan bowers.
With brilliant fame and piles of "rocks,"
  And promise of poetic bliss,
With old age silvering your locks,
  'Tis strange you play a prank like this.

Alfred, Alfred, Laureate,
  If time be heavy on your hands,
Are there no singers at your gate,
  Nor inharmonious brass bands?
Ah, teach the amateur to toot,
  Or show some rhymster [*sic*] how to grind!
Go teach the young idea of shoot,
  And keep your title in your mind!
                    (5 April 1884, p. 13)

Puck's reaction to the honor is anything but complimentary. In a comic interview published 19 December 1883 the new lord is portrayed as a money-hungry versifier for whom inspiration is an uncertain thing. He offers samples of his work, all

Figure 70. "Baron Tennyson's Robes Stolen," Life, 20 March 1884.

parodies of the originals. For *In Memoriam*'s "'Tis better to have loved and lost / Than never to have loved at all," he gives,

I hold it best, whate'er befall—
  I feel it when I sorrow most—
  'Tis better to have quail on toast
Than not to have a quail at all.

As he claims, "'I sell such a thing as that for three 'arf-crowns, I'm always sure of five bob; but I manage generally to get the extra two and six.'" "Mariana" is likewise altered:

My heart is wasted with my woe,
  Sary Anna;
I'm sitting at a minstrel-show,
  Sary Anna;
The night is dark, the night is cold,
Because the minstrel-jokes are old,
  Sary Anna.

Puck's reporter discovers that the poet has made a deal with the Prince of Wales and the Duke of Edinburgh to gain a peerage. Tired of being paid in Queen Victoria's "Hindia" shawls rather than in cash, he threatens to stop writing: "'"Look 'ere, young fellers," I said: "I ain't a-going to write any more until I get the spondulix for the stuff I let your mother have according to contract."'" Several days later he is notified by mail of his peerage, which he sees as a way of making a living: "'I don't know how I'm going to keep up the dignity, but I feel a bit encouraged, and I may get extra work from the other chaps in the House of Lords. Besides, I'm 'ard at work on Epp's Cocoa and Pears's Soap poetical ads.'"[7]

According to *Life* one of the least attractive aspects of Tennyson's "job" was the nature of the verse he was required to write. One poem that appeared[8] suggests that Tennyson takes a childish delight in his new status:

I tell you, Mrs. Tennyson—Your Ladyship, I
    mean—
There are certain things that can't be done, yes,
    even for the Queen!
I've written up her family, dear knows, from A
    to Z,
Or to B, to be exact, but she is growing much
    too free!

I'm sure I've earned my salary, and pretty hard
    sometimes.

Just think of all the names I've had to fit into
    my rhymes!
And I've never made objections, when she kept
    within the bond,
But the last two things she's asked of me are
    very far beyond!

She made believe she thought I could not find a
    rhyme for Brown—
I have more than half-a-dozen, but I'd scorn to
    write them down!
She could really go no farther, I thought, than
    she went then,
But it seems I was mistaken—she's been after
    me again!

I declare, I blush to mention what she's tried to
    set me at—
She wants a sonnet-epitaph for her Angora cat!
She gave me the particulars, its name, and age,
    and ways,
And she said I couldn't possibly say too much
    in its praise.

I half took off my coronet to throw it on the
    floor,
But I thought, suppose she shouldn't let me
    have it any more?
So I curbed my fiery temper—it's hereditary
    too—
And I calmly said, "Your Highness, that's a
    thing I *cannot* do."

"I will rhyme for all your children, be it
    marriage, be it death,
And I'll rhyme for you, my Empress, with my
    last remaining breath.
And I'll even rhyme your grandchildren,
    though I bargained not for that,
But how dare you ask a Laureate to write about
    a cat?"

She quailed; she begged my pardon; she
    withdrew her bold request;
But the scene was too exciting. I must have a
    little rest.
I wish you'd take my coronet—you can hold it
    in your lap—
And if any of them call, just say I've gone to
    take a nap.

                  (7 February 1884, p. 82)

Likewise, "Seraph" in *Spirit of the Times* suggests that Tennyson has found a way of coping with his onerous duty of writing "apropos verses":

Babble Ballads
Drinks All Round
After Tennyson

First pledge our noble selves, and then
    A health to every other guest!
Come, landlord, set 'em up again!
    He writeth best who drinketh best!
I am the Poet Laureate,
    And so my duty is to grind
Apropos verses, which I hate!
    By facts I'm cabined, cribbed, confined!
Drinks all round! All teetotallers confound!
    I've got to write another ode, my friends,
And my poor head is whirling round and
    round!

Now, there's a rascal named McLean—
    A cranky, crazy sort of sot—
Has fired a pistol at the Queen,
    Who narrowly escaped his shot!
Well, I'm to put that into song—
    Express in verse all England's thoughts!
Fancy me, boys—Here's luck! S'long—
    Turning out rhymed police reports!
Drinks all round! All teetol [*sic*] cranks
    confound!
    I've got to write another ode, my friends,
And my poor head is swimming round and
    round!

What can I say of such a case?
    I'll blow the old, familiar gaff—
Call England "loyal," traitors "base,"
    Alix in Canadian wheat (no chaff!)
With India and Australia too,
    And wind up with a benison!
I tell you, any jot will do
    When signed by Alfred Tennyson!
So, drinks all round! Rhymes to order (hic);
    confound!
    I've got to write another ode, my friends,
And my poor head is buzzing round and
    round!

                (1 April 1882, p. 236)

One part of the laureate's job was, of course, to write official commemorations of births and deaths. When John Brown, the queen's personal servant, died, Tennyson supplied (as one biographer notes) "a singularly gawky inscription" for the memorial statue at Balmoral: "Friend more than servant, loyal, truthful, brave: / Self less than duty even to the grave."[9]

While imaginative reconstructions of the laureate's relationship with the queen clearly amused an American public ever ready to enjoy a joke at royalty's expense, Tennyson's meter was also used for quips that were purely American. *Life*, a staunch New Yorker, claimed that Gotham girls were preferable to all others and so gibed at Boston bluestockings and Chicagoans alike: "If [Tennyson] mentions Chicago girls he will have to use very long lines so as to admit their feet" is typical (16 September 1886, p. 160). Philadelphia belles came in for their share as well. In "The Day-Dream; or, A Hitch in the Programme, Written expressly for LIFE by Lord A-f-d- T-nny-n and others," Prince Charming is unable to awaken the Sleeping Beauty:

> A touch! a kiss! the charm was snapt;
> There rose a noise of striking clocks
> And feet that ran and doors that clapt,
> And barking dogs, and crowing cocks;
>
> And gathered fast a noisy throng
> Of courtier, peasant, lord and churl,
> But still the Sleeping Beauty slept!
> She was a *Philadelphia girl*.
> (4 November 1886, p. 271)

More extended comments on American manners appeared as parodies of the very popular "Charge of the Light Brigade," which by 1897—forty-three years after the original incident—was listed by *Life's* readers as one of their ten favorite poems.[10] Twice transmogrified in *Life* to "The Charge of the Tight Brigade," Tennyson's stirring eulogy to the cavalry men who were killed in Balaclava becomes a record of a rowdy party on the one hand and an attack on fashion on the other. The first poem is by versifier Timothy Hagen:

> Half a night, half a night,
> Half a night drinking,
> All through the supper-room
> Stode the Four Hundred.
> "Forward the Tight Brigade!
> Charge on the wine!" they said.
> Into the supper-room
> Strode the Four Hundred.
> . . . .
> Bottles to right of them,
> Bottles to left of them,
> Bottles in front of them
> Popp'd, popp'd and thundered.
> Stormed at with cork and glass,
> Boldly they strove to pass
> Into the supper-room:

> Into the room *en masse*
> Strode the Four Hundred.
>
> Smashed all their drinking ware,
> Smashed over solid fare,
> Grabbing the waiters there,
> Charging the table, while
> All the world wondered.
> Plunged in the sparkling froth
> Fought they, exceeding wroth;
> Dudes and the deadheads
> Reeled from the table-cloth
> Spattered and sundered.
> Then they strode back, but not,
> Not the Four Hundred.
> . . . .
> When can *their* glory fade?
> Oh, the wild charge they made!
> Society wondered.
> Honor the charge they made,
> Honor the Tight Brigade—
> What a Four Hundred!
> (23 May 1889, p. 297)

The other is a spoof of the hobble skirt, a fashion that made its wearers resemble an umbrella in silhouette:

> Half a leg, half a leg,
> Half a leg onward,
> All in pursuit of style
> "Hobb'd" the Four Hundred.
> "Forward the Tight Brigade!
> Charge—it's the style," they said;
> Oh, what a price they paid—
> Hobbled Four Hundred.
>
> "Forward, the Tight Brigade!"
> Was there a man dismayed
> At wifey so arrayed!
> Some one had blunder'd:
> Theirs not to make reply,
> Theirs not to reason why,
> Theirs but to see and buy—
> Funny Four Hundred.
>
> Hobbles to right of them,
> Hobbles to left of them,
> Hobbles all sides of them—
> What if they'd sunder'd?
> Maude, Bessie, Kit and Nell,
> Wrapped like an umberell,
> Should one have tripped and fell
> She would have looked like—
> Well, less than Four Hundred.

Flashed all their curves so rare;
Flashed—yes, and *bulged*, so there!
All but the skinny ones,
While the world wondered.
Some couldn't stand the strain;
Some, yes, some *shrunk* from rain;
So now they're on the wane;
Gone is the hobble day—
Hoop-skirts are next, they say,
Fickle Four Hundred.

When can their glory fade?
Oh, what a stir they made;
All the world wonder'd
What more could be displayed;
Dear, naughty, Tight Brigade—
Dear old Four Hundred.

> (*Life*, 2 March 1911, p. 442)

Two other parodies deserve mention. "The Going of Arthur" is a series of outrageous puns, of which this is a sample:

Came from the sunset bounds of Lava-bed,
And all the Creeks came creaking down to him,
And the Crows shrilled about him with the
    Kaws,
And the Pawnees brought in their uncle's
    pledges,
Whereat he laughen, saying, "Yes, I know,"
As one who had been there himself, long time
    ago . . .
Came the Navajoes, calling him by name,
And saying that a genuine Chippewas
Of the old block, and that he Ottawa
Their wishes well.

> (*Life*, 13 September 1883, p. 125)

The more sophisticated and topical "'Dream of Fair Women': For Which the Published Reports of the National Council of Women Were Probably Responsible" is notable for its humorous expression of the current sentiment against women's liberation. The author, Harold R. Vynne, experiences an "astounding" dream in which men are "relegated . . . to second place":

Our President was a most comely wench—
    Her Cabinet composed of maidens fair;
Sweet lady Judges sat upon the bench;
    Lawyers in skirts talked juries to despair.
The halls of Congress rang with dulcet notes
    Of members' voices—school girls in their
        teens—
The Army mounted guard in petticoats,

The Navy swarmed with feminine Marines.
Grandames austere, be-spectacled and sleek,
    As Merchants posed in offices all day,
Whose male stenographers (at ten a week,)
    Be-banged and rouged, cast sheepish eyes
        their way.

Professional usurpation was the least of the dreamer's woes, however:

Bald-headed gentlemen the ballet graced,
    And executed kicks and pirouettes,
While comely girls, in front rows snugly
        placed,
    Gazed at their caperings through big
        lorgnettes.
Proud, dashing dames drove tandem to the
        track
    To view the races—that most royal sport!—
And swore devoutly when the nags they'd back
    Failed to win quite as often as they ought.
While younger beauties—saucy little sparks—
    From their club-windows ogled passers-by,
Chewing their canes and passing pert remarks
    Upon such chaps as chanced to meet their
        eye.

He discovers, however, that there is a reason for his nightmare:

Just then I woke. By dint of many rubs
    My eyes were opened, and I saw it all:
'Twas at the meeting of the Women's Clubs—
    I'd gone to sleep in Central Music Hall.

> (Chicago *Figaro*, 14 May 1892, p. 187)

Whether writers chose to mimic "The Coming of Arthur," part of "Idylls of the King," or "The Dream of Fair Women," itself built around Chaucer's "Legend of Good Women," the topics were American ones. Similarly, political questions were likely to be interpreted in Tennysonian rhymes and rhythms. The controversy over the new fishery law enacted by the United Kingdom on behalf of Canada in November 1884 prompted just such a response. According to the revision, Canada would not just fine but confiscate any ship that came within one marine league of its coast "for any purpose not permitted by treaty or convention or by any law of the United Kingdom or of Canada for the time in force."[11] The change meant that deep-sea fishermen could not put into a Canadian port, either for bait or for repairs. While the American press was generally outraged over what it perceived to be an unfair economic sanction, *Tid-Bits* viewed the matter humorously, publishing "Three Great English Poems." One, by Swinburne, is a burlesque of the poet's alliterative tendencies:

> THRILLED by the throb of the thought of the thinkers,
>   Pulsing with power and pallid with pain,
> Drunk with the pain draught of the demon of drinkers,
>   I deluge the day with a dirge of disdain!
>
> Fish, fowl, flesh, folly, flamboyant and flaunting,
>   Shall I weight all my woe on the wing of a wish
> And hunt where the humanized horrors are haunting,
>   And focus my fate on the fin of a fish?

Another, attributed to Browning, is a monologue characterized by brevity and obscurantism:

> SAN BRANGANZA singing,
> (If so, whence or why not?)
>   Strove to make amends.
> Saw the light upspringing,
> Said that he would try not—
>   Will be friends.
>
> Antinonian Nero,
> (Serpent tongues had hissed her)
>   Didn't it? Course it did.
> Truculent old hero—
> How superb he kissed her—
>   What is lost is hid.
>
> Hearest thou? then trust not;
> (Winds are featly blowing)
>   Mackerel—that's the stuff!
> If our bastions burst not—
> See the glow-worm glowing;
>   Silence! That's enough!

Finally, the laureate himself suggests that the way to end the dispute is to go fishing:

> COMRADES, leave me here a little, victim of a wayward wish,
> To withdraw myself from action and to meditate on fish.
>
> O, the fish can clothe a nation with a glory not its own,
> And the wiggle of a codfish shape the counsels of the throne.

Bait, you whisper—ah, I know it—Europe grapples with its fate,
And Columbia grovels prostrate on the stumbling-block of bait.

Men are rascals, faith has perished, truth a farce, and peace a lie!
Dig your bait, and throw your fish-hook, out your pole, and let her fly!
                                        (12 May 1887, p. 12)

The many parodies and comments published by the popular press demonstrate that Americans were warmly interested not only in what Tennyson wrote but in what he did. That they sometimes pointedly criticized his work and expressed concern that his powers were waning is further testimony to reader interest. One early parodist in *Nick-Nax for all Creation* complains that Tennyson's "The War," first printed in the London *Times*, is valueless. His verse seems to include "Maud" in the same general condemnation:

> There's a little trash just from your quill—
> A halting, wild, spasmodic display,
> Ground, no doubt, from a rhyme-making mill;
> Alfred, why do you write in this way!
>   Don't! don't! Tennyson, don't!
>   You'll really oblige us, sir, if you won't!
>   Tennyson, Tennyson, Tennyson, don't!
>
> Be not deaf to the voice that warns:
> Your's are but *Maud*–lin lines indeed;
> Rather figs of thistles and grapes of thorns,
> Than laurel spring from roadside weed.
>   Don't! don't! Tennyson, don't!
>   You'll really oblige us, sir, if you won't!
>   Tennyson, Tennyson, Tennyson, don't!
>   (July 1859, p. 81)

The parodist shows his disapproval of the "Spasmodic School," a name given by the critic William Aytoun to those who wrote in the style of Philip Bailey, author of a lengthy version of the Faust legend. He further warns that Tennyson, a lyric poet, will lose his laurel crown if he persists in producing such "weeds."

The caricaturist who drew a group of "Remarkable Resemblances" for Collier's *Once a Week* in 1893 might agree; he pairs the laureate with Joel Benton, a well-published American poet who was popular for his sentimental and humorous versifying (figure 71). Even in the pages of a single periodical the response was mixed. Robert Bridges, *Life*'s book

Figure 71. "A Group of Remarkable Resemblances,"
Once a Week, *24 June 1893.* (Courtesy of the Library of Congress.)

reviewer, firmly defends the later works not only for their "clear vision" and "beautiful fancy" but for "that unmatched melody and imagery which made Tennyson great in youth" and for "the perfect simplicity of phrase which gives to Saxon monosyllables the melody of Latin tongues."[12] On the other hand, his fellow writer George W. Metcalfe humorously suggests that since Tennyson is responsible for infecting a generation of otherwise harmless individuals with the "divine afflatus," he offer himself as a sacrifice:

His is an extreme case of Prosophobia, and in the hands of a literary Pasteur we doubt not he could furnish the wherewithal to inoculate the many sufferers from the attacks of the muses and avert the calamitous condition of affairs, which, as one of the poetic guild remarked in a recent poem, "is staring us in the face like a ship tossed upon the calm bosom of the boundless west." (*Life,* 23 September 1886, p. 176)

"Locksley Hall Sixty Years After" was parodied innumerable times to demonstrate not ony that Tennyson's title had changed his view of progress but that he was in his dotage and thereby saw the future foreshortened by age. Metcalfe is again critical; purporting to be the emissary for a weary postman on St. Valentine's Day, he forwards to Tennyson a card decorated with "a little green laureate holding a blue pen marked 'Pessimism' in his hand, combating with a purple giant labeled 'Progress.'" The accompanying verse is as follows:

Upward, downward, downward, upward,
    beating in and 'bout the stump;
See the poet, with his pencil, giving Progress
    many a thump.

It is natural that the second blast from out the
    poet's pen,
Should be rankly pessimistic while 'twas
    optimistic when

He was young, for then he had some thing to
    look to up on high,
Which was far above his station, far as earth is
    from the sky.

He could toady and be happy, looking up to
    the lords and earls,
He could write the poems that would suit the
    critics and the girls.

Now the poet has grown older, and he wears a
    noble's clothes,
And as suited to his station, up Lord Alfred
    turns his nose.

                 (17 February 1887, p. 90)

Metcalfe's assessment was amplified in the Boston *Gazette*, where a similar offering appeared and was reprinted in *Life*'s "Aut Scissors Aut Nullus" column:

Backward Tennyson

In his age did daintiest Alfred turn once more
    to Locksley Hall;
In his age the Lordly Laureate piped in accents
    deuced small;
Sang the world was rent asunder into very little
    bits,
And the lion toppled over into very desp'rate
    fits.
O my Alfred! O my poet! with your senile
    groans and sighs,
Once more comes your second childhood, and
    you revel in mud pies.
             (*Life*, 13 January 1887, p. 27)

Metcalfe's review of *The Foresters*, first performed at Daly's Theatre on 17 March 1892, is even more devastating in its suggestion that the play is a pastiche of Shakespeare's words and Sullivan's music, successful only because of Daly's brilliant stage management; nonetheless, John Eidson's review of the play's critical reception suggests that such a response was not uncommon.[13] What makes Metcalfe's review out of the ordinary is that it is written as a scenario in which Tennyson, the ghost of

Shakespeare, and Shakespeare's Muse participate. Tennyson is moved to confess that because of his age, his "brain in labour brings forth nought but words," an assessment with which the shade agrees. Shakespeare's help saves the play from its otherwise deservedly brief run in front of "the sickly crowd / That worships names because the names are known":

The music of Sir Arthur is the essential thing
That may thy half-dead child to life revive.
And further yet, call to thy pressing need
Augustin's aid, who good and comely actors
    hath
And taste withal, to give the poorest play
Most excellent presentment in the public eye.
            (7 April 1892, pp. 218–19)

As Eidson points out, the play was a popular success, partly because of the lavish scenery and partly because of the support of such performers as John Drew and Ada Rehan.

Despite the mixed reviews, *Life* is remembered for its sympathetic evaluation of Tennyson, as Bridges's comments suggest:[14]

What seems like pessimism . . . is really a note of warning against a Realism which has taken the glory from fiction and poetry, and robbed life of its charm. It remains for young men to take up the cry of the aged idealist, and fight the battle which he is too old to lead.
            (6 January 1887, p. 435)

Bridges's was not the only voice crying in a wilderness of popular criticism; C. M. Snyder, writing for *Tid-Bits*, allows Tennyson to castigate his critics for their slangy diction:

The Laureate on the Sands of Cromers

The barren Baron stood on the sands
And inward grief his soul commands.
"Alas!" cried he, "for poetry,
'Tis fallen into alien hands."

How do the members of that tribe
We designate "newspaper scribe"
Measure the times with jingling rhymes
And shock with sacrilegious gibe!

A man is "busted" in his loss,
And "boodle" call they golden dross,
And politics are "shady tricks;"
A leader they baptize as "boss."

Their speakers only "work their jibs,"

Their repartees are labelled "squibs;"
And worst of all, they sometimes call
An Englishman "his blooming nibs."

And love they designate as "mash,"
The hungry wrestle with their "hash,"
A man's a "chap" "euchered"—mishap,
And ruin is "eternal smash."

Pursuit of wealth they call a "game,"
Possession reads, "He's staked his claim;"
And of success in happiness
They say, "We got there all the same."

But when these wretches designate
Old England's foremost Laureate
As "worn to shreds," and "ravelled threads,"
No wonder they exasperate.

(11 September 1886, p. 3)

Nineteenth-century readers of American popular periodicals thus found Tennyson parodied in both trivial and profound ways. Much of his popularity was, of course, a function of his quotability; Charles Coupe, whose dialogue among a "matter-

Figure 73. Tennyson in Christmas Number of Truth, *25 December 1880.*

Figure 72. "Gallery of Beauties," Life, 16 May 1889.

Figure 74. Tennyson leads the Westminster Boys' Choir for the Queen's Jubilee Procession in Life, 23 June 1887.

Figure 75. Tennyson with the queen in Life, 23 June 1887.

Figure 76. "Musicians" Tennyson and Gladstone as "Pessimist and Optimist" in Life, *27 January 1887.*

The British Muse—see 'um ?

Figure 77. A Punch *pun on Tennyson, 7 May 1887.*

of-fact" lawyer, a literary woman, and a metaphysical professor was principally composed of Tennyson's references to the sea, amply illustrates this point.[15] Quite simply, his poetry was accessible to readers from all walks of life. As one critic points out, "You can hardly overemphasize the importance of ease of understanding of Tennyson in fixing him in the minds of the public."[16] The image that seems best to represent the general kindliness with which the laureate was viewed in America was published as part of *Life*'s "Gallery of Beauties" series in 1889 (figure 72). Shedding such earthly encumbrances as umbrella and briefcase, the aging Laureate ascends gracefully into the heavens, the bar he is crossing neither British nor American, but universal.

1. Previous collections of Tennyson parodies are in Hamilton, *Parodies*, I: passim; Jelle Postma, *Tennyson as Seen by His Parodists* (1926; reprint ed., New York: Haskell, 1966); Walter Jerrold and R. M. Leonard, eds., *A Century of Parody and Imitation* (London: Oxford University Press, 1913); and George O. Marshall, Jr., *Tennyson in Parody and Jest: An Essay and a Selection* (Lincoln, England: Tennyson Research Centre, 1975).

2. Marshall, *Tennyson in Parody*, p. 11.

3. Marshall, for example, includes a parody, "Wanderers," from an 1867 issue of *Once a Week* in *Tennyson in Parody*.

4. Leslie Ward, *Forty Years of "Spy"* (London: Chatto and Windus, 1915), p. 291.

5. Cornelius Weygandt, *The Time of Tennyson: English Victorian Poetry as it Affected America* (1926; reprint ed., London: Hogarth, 1973), p. 101.

6. Other than the suggestion that Tennyson does not measure up to his "peers," the source of the cartoon is obscure. The *New York Times* (30 March 1884), reprinting a report from the London *Times* (12 March 1884) on the robing ceremony, does not list Lord Coleridge as being present.

7. Parodic examples of such "poetical ads" may be found in *Life*'s "Poetry Made Practical":

> Tell me not in mournful numbers
> Life is but an empty dream;
> Nightly, e'er you seek your slumbers,
> Rub your face with Camphor Cream.

Lady Clara Vere de Vere,
 Of me you shall not win renown
Unless you wear Supernal Shoes,
 The finest made in all the town . . .

You must wake and call me early,
 Call me early, mother dear,
To-morrow'll be the happiest time
 Of all the glad New Year—

Of all the glad New Year, mother,
 The maddest, merriest day,
I'll get a Seraphina
 Pianola for to play.

(7 April 1910)

8. See Postma, *Tennyson as Seen by His Parodists*, for other attributions.

9. Longford, *Queen Victoria*, p. 452.

10. Flautz, *Gentle Satirist*, p. 123.

11. "Canada's New Fishery Law," *New York Times*, 6 January 1887, p. 4, cols. 6–7.

12. "Tennyson's Protest Against the Realists," *Life*, 6 January 1887, p. 435; and "The Last Poems of Tennyson," *Life*, 17 November 1892, p. 282.

13. John Olin Eidson, "Tennyson's *The Foresters* on the American Stage," *Philological Quarterly* 43 (1964): 549–57.

14. Flautz *Gentle Satirist*, p. 122, however, notes that *Life* "automatically" ranks poets of the "genteel tradition" over Tennyson, an assessment not borne out by Bridges's comments.

15. Charles Coupe, "Tennysonian Sea-Echoes," *American Catholic Quarterly Review* 28 (1903): 455–63.

16. Weygandt, *Time of Tennyson*, p. 110.

M IS MacDuff, who's prevailed upon Milton,
Montaigne and Miss Manon
To each try a kilt on.

N IS Napoleon shrouded in gloom,
With Nero, Narcissus and Nordau, to whom
He's explaining the manual of arms with a broom.

5
Robert Browning Meets the Press

HAD ROBERT BROWNING'S MUSE OF PAINTING been slightly more active than was his Muse of Poetry, it is quite possible that Browning might have been a contributor to the drawings in this book, rather than one of the subjects of the drawings. Browning's father had a knack for making caricature sketches which, according to Rossetti, showed "a real genius for drawing."[1] Among these were several done to illustrate his son's poems, such as that of the dying bishop in "The Bishop Orders His Tomb at Saint Praxed's Church" (figure 78). Partly, no doubt, from his father's influence, the poet himself developed an early interest in art, an interest that remained with him as evidenced by the subjects of several of his best-known poems. One might suspect a touch of autobiography, for example, in the lines from "Fra Lippo Lippi" where Lippi describes his childhood doodling in the monastery:

> I drew faces on my copy-books,
> Scrawled them within the antiphonary's marge,
> Joined legs and arms to the long music-notes,
> Found eyes and nose and chin for A's and B's,
> And made a string of pictures of the world
> Betwixt the ins and outs of verb and noun,
> On the wall, the bench, the door.

Browning himself, according to W. Hall Griffin, was a schoolboy doodler, fond of making pen-and-ink caricatures, which he did with a cleverness that reflected the talent of his father.[2] That the poet must have encouraged the same trait in his own artistic son Barrett ("Pen") is evident not only in Pen's later paintings but also in a childhood cartoon of "Papa" (figure 79) depicting Pen's impression of his father as a knight on horseback. While Pen's drawing deserves mention for its personal touch and charm, it may also qualify as the earliest known caricature of the poet. It was not until the 1870s that Browning began to appear in cartoon and caricature in the British comic periodicals and quite a bit later that he made his way in their American counterparts.

In this chapter we offer a selection of caricatures, cartoons, and illustrative sketches either of or pertaining to Browning, most of which first appeared in British and American periodicals from the 1870s to World War I. A few have been selected, however, from a later period, such as the relatively unknown 1936 *Manchester Guardian* drawing by Max Beerbohm, because they offer interesting comparisons to the earlier examples.

Probably the earliest published caricature of Browning was the one by Frederick Waddy in the 17 February 1872 issue of *Once a Week* (figure 80). Captioned simply "Browning," the cartoon was one in a series of several dozen literary figures contributed by Waddy during that year.[3] Beneath the drawing of the poet, depicted as the "Pied Piper,"

Figure 78. Drawing by Browning's father to represent the dying bishop in "The Bishop Orders His Tomb at Saint Praxed's Church." This is number seven of thirteen sketches laid into copies of pamphlets III (Dramatic Lyrics, 1842) and VII (Dramatic Romances and Lyrics, 1845) of the "Bells and Pomegranates" series. These are a part of the Armstrong Browning Library collection.

are lines 71–75 of Browning's poem "The Pied Piper of Hamelin":

> "Please, your honours," said he, "I'm able,
> By means of a secret charm, to draw
>   All creatures living beneath the sun
>   that creep or swim or fly or run
> After me so as you never saw!"

While the Waddy cartoons themselves were sometimes unflattering, the biographical and critical comments accompanying them were generally appreciative. Such was the case with Browning. Since Waddy's interesting commentary, originally written to gloss the cartoon, is no longer readily available, it seems appropriate to offer several paragraphs:

Strong, rugged, independent;—no fashioner of pretty songs modelled upon patterns designed by greater men, no warbler of sweet and soft love ditties, no dealer in unreal and exaggerated passion, no puling complainer of mock sorrow, no dreamy poet of conventional life, is Robert Browning. When, so many years ago, he set himself to make poetry the work of his life, he undertook the task in his own sturdy and independent way. Verse should be his slave, and should express his thoughts as he designed. Now, most poets are the slaves of verse, and can only get their thoughts expressed by a sort of coaxing, and in a round-about fashion. Then, the life they describe is conventional: Browning's should be real. The motives and springs of action which they describe are simple: those of life are really complex, manifold, various, and overlapping each other. In Browning, we find the psychologist trying to show us, in his analysis, some of the many influences under which the soul acts. With most poets the soul is, as it were, a river. Browning recognizes the fact that it is a mighty ocean. Currents flow backwards and forwards: there are depths and shallows: there are storms on the surface and stillness below, or there are whirlpools below and calm on the surface. The sun shines on it, and the clouds rain upon it: perpetual change is going on, but it remains the same. It has infinite possibilities: it contains infinite treasure. It is ever in unrest, ever flowing and ebbing: ever disturbed, uncertain, and wayward. To describe, to dissect, to observe these currents and moods is the hardest task that a poet ever set himself; and it is Browning's self-imposed task. If he has failed, he has failed splendidly. It is a defeat which is a great victory.

After describing Browning's "dramatic power," which "presses verbs and adjectives to do service which have never before worked for mortal bard," Waddy continues:

He is like a driver who drives furiously over rough ground: driving not for pleasure, but because work has to be done. If you want to float lazily on a summer sea, there is Tennyson; if you would glide down the stream without an effort, there is Byron; if you would drive along a smooth road and admire the hedges on either hand, there is Pope. But if you are not afraid of hard work, rough work, tough work, go with Browning, and follow him while he clears the jungle of thoughts, aims, motives, and passions, and shows you a human heart as poet never showed before.

Waddy finds Browning's theatrical efforts, despite their "vigour, cleanness of plot, and strong accentuation of character, and rapid action," unsuited for acting because of the poet's "chief failing," a "deficiency of tenderness":

Figure 79. Barrett ("Pen") Browning's cartoon sketch of his father, dated 23 January 1853. The original, in the British Museum, has been reproduced in Maisie Ward's The Tragicomedy of Pen Browning *(London: Sheed and Ward, Inc. and New York: The Browning Institute, 1972), p. 74. It is also in* Robert Browning's Portraits, Photographs and Other Likenesses *by Grace Elizabeth Wilson (Waco, Texas: Baylor University, 1943), p. 80.*

Sympathy he must have, because he sees so deeply; but it is the sympathy of a sort all his own. It does not lead him to be tender. It is the sympathy which comes from knowledge, and not that which springs from the feeling of *possible* partnership in misfortune or remorse. It is the pity of a strong man for the weak, mingled with a little contempt. But this is fatal to dramatic success. On the stage, above all, we must be human.

Waddy recognizes Browning's then limited popularity and attributes it to the unusual intellectual effort needed to "follow him through all the mazy windings and involutions of his thought," and he relates the story of Douglas Jerrold who, "recovering from an illness, took up 'Sordello' and began to read it. Presently he burst out into tears and threw the book away. 'Good God!' he cried, 'I have lost my intellect!'" But for the few who are prepared to accept the challenge of Browning's frequent difficulty and obscurity, Waddy says that "with the reading of Browning grows one's love for him. *L'appétit vient en mangeant.* And when the taste is once formed, there can be for his admirer but one living poet."

Although Waddy finds much to admire in many such shorter pieces as "Count Gismond" and "Soliloquy of the Spanish Cloister," he chooses Browning's humor in "The Pied Piper" as the theme of his cartoon. He draws the bard, pipe in hand, according to Browning's descriptive lines,

> His queer long coat from heel to head
> Was half of yellow and half of red;
> And he himself was tall and thin,
> With sharp blue eyes, each like a pin.

figures in *Vanity Fair* is an especially fine lithograph of Robert Browning (figures 81 and 82). Appearing in the 20 November 1875 issue, the drawing was done by Carlo Pellegrini (1839–89) who signed his usual sobriquet, "Ape." Although Leslie Ward's "Spy" signature is, perhaps, most familiar today, Pellegrini was clearly the early presiding genius of the magazine's popular art, and he was its chief contributor during the years from 1869 to 1888. Pellegrini's pseudonym was quite in keeping with his tendency, at least in his earlier cartoons, to treat his subjects (or "victims") with cruel satire, giving most of them apelike faces and often grim and gro-

igure 80. Browning as Pied Piper in Once a Week *(17 ebruary 1872) cartoon by Frederick Waddy. See also ver and note in* The Browning Newsletter, *no. 3 Fall, 1969).*

Waddy's conclusion leaves no doubt about the artist's admiration for the poet:

We have, besides the usual throng of verse writers common to every age, one or two leading poets besides Browning. But there is not one who has a better chance of that best kind of posthumous fame: not one who will! so certainly be remembered as the highest product of his time. (17 February 1872, pp. 164–67)

Among the more than eighty cartoons of literary

Figure 81. Unfinished preparatory sketch by Carlo Pellegrini. See The Browning Newsletter, *no. 1 (October, 1968), 26.*

Figure 82. Finished chromolithograph by Carlo Pellegrini ("Ape") in the 20 November 1875 issue of Vanity Fair. *The actual print is 12" × 7". See note on this print in* Studies in Browning and His Circle, *5, no. 2 (Fall, 1977), 49, 71–74.*

tesque postures. This unique caricature style, established in France as a *portrait chargé* tradition, was imitated by Pellegrini who introduced it in England in his cartoons of Disraeli and Gladstone, the first to be published in *Vanity Fair*.[4] While the likenesses are good, the caricatures are far from flattering. Given this background, we think it significant that the Browning drawing is *not* in Pellegrini's usual

portrait chargé style. Depicting Browning at age sixty-three, the caricature shows a slightly dwarfed and portly physique (in rather marked contrast, incidentally, to the tall and slim "Pied Piper" Waddy drawing!). But the *Vanity Fair* cartoon's profile is a reasonably good likeness of Browning, and the drawing is not at all in Pellegrini's usual style of deliberate distortion and exaggeration of features. The reason for the artist's uncharacteristic kindliness was, we suspect, his admiration for Browning as a man and poet. It is quite possible that Pellegrini, an Italian, looked with favor upon the English poet whose love of Italy was evident in his life and work.

Vanity Fair editor, Thomas Gibson Bowles, was not known for his unqualified praise of his subjects, and in his commentary on Anthony Trollope, for example, he said that Trollope's books would be much more likely to survive if he were to limit himself to writing only one a year![5] Not so in his commentary on Robert Browning. Bowles, like Pellegrini, apparently admired Browning. Since his commentary accompanying Pellegrini's cartoon may offer a fair summary of Victorian England's most popular society magazine's evaluation of the poet, we offer it in its entirety:

Three and sixty years ago Mr. Browning was born to poetry, and very soon discovered it by composing verses, some of which are still extant. He conceived a passionate admiration for Byron and Shelley, whose influence, though since outgrown, was strongly marked in his first efforts; he passed most of his youth in Italy, and at twenty-three he had already published "Paracelsus." In this, as in "Pauline" and "Sordello," he described the effort to transcend those limitations of fact towards which he subsequently adopted a more questioning attitude, and which of late he has almost accepted. Yet he does not accept them without a struggle, for he is combative by nature, is always resisting or defending what seems to him untrue, and will resist even the truth itself if it seems to him presumptuous. Essentially vigorous and with redundant imagination, he is ideal in his mode of conception yet an unflinching realist in his method of work. There is nothing loose or shadowy in his productions, no swooning or melting away in emotion, but a steady building up of thought and feeling through the fact and incident of common life. He never omits a detail, but he omits all the words he can spare, and he has an especial objection to articles, which he picks out as one would pick out the basting stitches from a finished garment. He has expressed an infinite variety of human feeling and experience, and though he has been accused of being unmelodious, he sinks into the mind with a

Figure 83. Linley Sambourne's "Fancy Portrait" of Browning in Punch, *22 July 1882.*

ries years and experience with the air of youth. And hence also it is that after having written all his life, he is still fresh and young enough to give us now in the "Inn Album" one of the most powerful and moving expressions extant of human passion. (20 November 1875)

This evaluation in caricature and commentary, coming as it did at the height of Browning's most productive period, offers a perspective from the past that is remarkably in line with the poet's most appreciative readers a century later.

Another prominent and, perhaps, the most famous of all British comical periodicals was *Punch,* a weekly journal of satire and parody which, according to Browning, always "treated him gently." Next to Tennyson, Browning was one of the most frequent subjects of caricature and poetry in *Punch,* at least as far as the better-known Victorian poets were concerned. On 22 July 1882 he appeared in *Punch* as one in a series of cartoons called "*Punch's* Fancy Portraits," a cleverly drawn gallery of prominent personalities including several well-known writers. The drawing (figure 83), signed by the talented *Punch* artist Linley Sambourne, is captioned "Robert Browning, D.C.L., The Ring and Book-Maker from Red Cotton Night-Cap Country." As background to Sambourne's clever sketch of the poet in his nightcap, we offer the following comments from W. Hall Griffin's *The Life of Robert Browning:*

On the completion of his seventieth year another distinction awaited him, the University of Oxford conferring upon him the honorary degree of D.C.L. In the course of the ceremony an undergraduate jester let down from the gallery a red cotton nightcap, and dangled it above the new doctor's head. He was like to pay severely for his prank, but Browning interceded with the Vice-Chancellor, and the culprit was forgiven. An observer who watched the procession to the Sheldonian remarked how lightly Browning carried his seventy years, how briskly he stepped along, in his new red gown, with head thrown back and eyes on the buildings, roofs, and sky.[6]

Accompanying the drawing is a brief parody of Browning's "At the 'Mermaid,'" which alludes to the founding of the Browning Society by Furnivall a year earlier and pictures the poet as having survived the stone-casting of his critics.

ROBERT BROWNING,
D.C.L.

(A Long Way after "At the Mermaid")

searching power all the more deeply because his tone in its maturity is habitually gruff from the jarring of the voices within him. He is as complex as life, as various as men and women, and, take him for all in all, the best of our professors of modern poetry. Quickly and passionately sensitive, the meaning of his own feelings does not always reach him at once, and he appears vindictive because he does not become conscious of resentment till the first impression of wrong has faded away; whence also it follows that as he hates well, so too does he love much and long. Although he has in him several men, and at least one woman, he has a profound contempt for most of his fellows in the world, and seeing them to be so little, does not carefully conceal that he knows himself to be proportionately great. Hence it is that in spite of a certain power of sympathy he is hard of approach, and stands forth like a monologue which is never to be interrupted. With all this he has an unquenchable vitality which car-

"This figure that thou seest well,
  Is ROBERT BROWNING, D.C.L."
                              B. Jonson (adapted)

I'm a D.C.L., my hearties,
  What some others fain would be:
There's war 'twixt poetic parties,
  And some folks cast stones at me.
I have sown some song-sedition,
  Easy is it to provoke
Cackle on a bard's ambition
  But I win—and there's the joke!

Though the world may cry out, frowning,
  "Hard is he to understand!"
See societies called "Browning"
  Flourish largely in the land.
I'm too crabb'd, confus'd, and mystic
  So brays out each kindly ass,
Sounds his trumpet eulogistic,
  Ορειχαλκος—made of brass.

Let the world wag on, these letters
  Show one poet's got his due;
I've received them like my betters,
  Smaller men have gained them too.
But, in spite of all the stir made,
  Put the robes upon the shelf:
I've my corner at "The Mermaid"
  With "rare Ben" and Shakespeare's self.
                              (22 July 1882)

Figure 84. Browning, Tennyson, and Swinburne
Punch, *27 December 1884.*

Along with Tennyson and Browning, another frequently satirized poet in *Punch* was Swinburne. In the 27 December 1884 Christmas issue, the three appear together as "Christmas Waits" (figure 84). The trio sings,

  Oh, bless you, gentlemen, whose looks
    Are very far from frowning,
  Pay cash, and buy the latest books
    Of Tennyson, Swinburne, Browning!

The implication that successful poets write primarily for "cash" was a frequent theme in *Punch*'s parodies, caricatures, and satirical commentaries, and it was often even more blatantly stated than in the cartoon's caption. Informed *Punch* readers would have been amused by the cartoon itself, especially if they were familiar with the trio's "latest books." Front and center stands Tennyson in his laureate's robe, reading from his 1884 Macmillan edition of *Becket*. Behind him and to his right is Browning, in work clothes, his head thrown back in rigorous and philosophical song from his own recently published *Ferishtah's Fancies*. To Tennyson's

left is Swinburne (who himself had parodied both Tennyson and Browning in *Heptalogia* a few years earlier), in top hat and dress coat, standing mute with chin on clasped hands in the winter scene. Perhaps the cartoonist Linley Sambourne is suggesting that the manuscript sticking out of the pensive poet's coat pocket contains thematically inappropriate material for Christmas singing. Swinburne's most recent publication had been *A Midsummer Holiday*!

Frequently, Browning appeared in less conspicuous ways in the pages of *Punch*. Two amusing examples are small cartoons of about 1½″ × 2″ presented here, considerably enlarged from the originals. The first (figure 85), "Browning Frowning," makes comic comment on rival poets. The second (figure 86) is from a grouping of six others as part of the magazine's series spoofing "Grosvenor Gallery Gems." On the same page is a similar-sized cartoon of Gladstone (figure 87), and the caption beneath the Browning cartoon says,

Robert Browning, dressed up as a "well red person," and very angry. He is evidently saying, "Now then, what are you laughing at? You don't see anything absurd in me,

104

Figure 85. Inspiration. Browning Frowning—on Alfred Austin. From Punch, *15 July 1882.*

do you? No, I'm not an advertisement for cheap mother-of-pearl studs. Yes, my shirt-front is a well-studded effect. If you want to laugh, just look at Gladstone over there!"

The pun on the poet as a "well *red* person" refers to the original 1882 portrait by Barrett Browning (figure 88) in which Pen paints his father in the scarlet academic robes presented to him in 1867 when he was made an Honorary Fellow of Balliol College. The *Punch* cartoon appeared in the 9 May 1885 issue. A month later Barrett's portrait was presented to Balliol College, followed by numerous words of praise, including those of W. M. Rossetti, who considered it "the best of all" among the son's many paintings of his father.

Any representative selection of cartoons and caricatures of Browning must include examples from the pen of "The Incomparable Max," and two of Max Beerbohm's best-known contributions are "Browning, taking tea with the Browning Society" (figure 89) and "Mr. Browning brings a Lady of Rank and Fashion to Mr. Rossetti" (figure 90). The "Browning Society" cartoon, probably the most famous caricature ever done of Robert Browning, is the subject of an interesting, well-documented, and well-illustrated article by Michael Hancher in *The Browning Newsletter*, no. 9 (Fall 1972): 23–33. Hancher discusses and illustrates three versions of the Beerbohm caricature: the preliminary pencil sketch owned by the Armstrong Browning Library, the original color drawing in Oxford's Ashmolean Museum, and the black-and-white reproductions from the color plate that was adapted from the original drawing and published in 1904. He also speculates on the identities of several person in the drawing (F. J. Furnivall and Emily Hickey, cofounders of the society, and Arthur Symons) and concludes that most of the figures are probably caricatures of types rather than of persons: "It served Beerbohm's satiric purpose to picture the whole Society as a coterie of spineless aesthetes, a sharp contrast to their notoriously healthy hero."[7] J. G. Riewald also gives brief comment on the drawing of

Figure 86. Browning in Punch, *9 May 1885. The cartoon is after Barrett Browning's portrait (see figure 88). The original cartoon is only 1½" × 2".*

the ceremonially polite poet, seated on a pink-upholstered chair, surrounded by fifteen unsmiling figures with an amusing variety of emotional expressions.[8] While on the topic of the Browning Society, we might note the following that appeared in the 24 October 1891 issue of *Punch:*

BROWNING SOCIETY VERSES

(Dr. Furnivall announces that the Browning Society is about to be dissolved.)

> Hark! 'tis the knell of the Browning Society,
>   Wind-bags are bursting all round us to-day;
> Furnivall fails, and for want of his diet he
>   Pines like a love-stricken maiden away.

> Long has he fed upon cackle and platitude,
>   Furnivall sauce to a dish full of dearth,
> Still, in the favourite Furnivall attitude,
>   Grubbing about like a mole in the earth.

> Now must he vanish, the mole-hills are flat
>   again,
>   (Follies grow fewer it seems by degrees);
> Lovers of Browning may laugh and grow fat
>   again,
>   Rid of the jargon of Furnivallese.

Four years later *Punch's* anonymous poet-parodist imagined the "Shade of the Author of 'Sordello'" singing in approval of the inauguration of the Robert Browning Social Settlement, an educational and cultural center established to deal with mounting social problems in the overpopulated and poverty-stricken Walworth Road district in London: "The hall where the meeting was held, known of old as Lock's Fields Meeting House (built in 1790),

Figure 87. William E. Gladstone in Punch, *9 May 1885.*

Figure 88. Oil painting by Barrett Browning, 1882. The Punch *cartoon (figure 86) is from this painting.*

was once a Congregational chapel in what was long a well-to-do neighbourhood, and was attended by Robert Browning's family, the poet himself having been baptised there." In a twelve-stanza parody, "Browning at Browning Hall; Or, Love Amongst the (Human) Ruins," the *Punch* poet uses the stanza form from "Love Among the Ruins" to present Browning's smiling favor toward the project.

Figure 89. Robert Browning, taking tea with the Browning Society. This frequently reproduced cartoon by Max Beerbohm is in the Ashmolean Museum, Oxford. Interesting discussions of the cartoon include Michael Hancher's "The Beerbohm Caricature of Browning and the Browning Society," The Browning Newsletter, *no. 9 (Fall, 1972):23–33; J. G. Riewald's selection and commentary in* Beerbohm's Literary Caricatures from Homer to Huxley *(New York: Archon Books, 1977), pp. 52–53; and Lola Szladits's foreword in John D. Gordan's* Joint Lives: Elizabeth Barrett and Robert Browning *(New York: New York Public Library, 1975).*

Figure 90. Mr. Robert Browning Brings a Lady of Rank and Fashion to Mr. Rossetti. Another amusing and frequently reproduced caricature by Max Beerbohm.

Well! It does me truer honour, I protest
   Than the quest
Of my minor mystic meanings, cryptic, crude,
   By the brood
Of "disciples" who at meetings
   Browning-Clubbish
   Talk such rubbish!

And the parody concludes

Well, a Walworth chap may not quite grasp
   Sordello,
  Poor, good fellow!
But the author of *Sordello* hath the whim
   To grasp *him;*
And for Hall and Settlement to bear *his* name,
   He holds fame!

With this Robert Browning Social Settlement
   I'm content.
Over poverty, pain, folly, noise and sin,
   May they win.

As I sang, despite wit, wealth, fame, and the
   rest,
  "Love is best!"

(21 December 1895, p. 298)

Beerbohm's cartoon of the polite but uncomfortable poet in the midst of Browning Society members seems, therefore, to provide a visual parody quite in line with the verbal ones appearing in *Punch.*

Since Beerbohm never saw Browning, it is possible that his caricature may have come from a photograph such as the one by Fradelle and Young in 1882.[9] This photograph may also have been his model for "Mr. Browning Brings a Lady of Rank and Fashion to Mr. Rossetti" (figure 90), probably the second-best-known Beerbohm drawing of Browning. Two other Beerbohm drawings, probably less known, deserve brief mention. Beerbohm owned a 1907 copy of Browning's *Poems* in which he strangely altered the portrait and "improved" the title page by the addition of a Victorian woodcut in comic allusion to Browning's elopement with

Figure 91. A Catalogue of the Caricatures of Max Beerbohm, compiled by Rupert Hart-Davis (Cambridge, Mass.: Harvard University Press, 1972), reproduced the drawing with the following note: "Browning *(Robert)* Poems, *the portrait strangely altered by Max Beerbohm, and the title-page 'improved' by him by the addition of a Victorian woodcut in comic allusion to the Browning elopement. Beerbohm's signature on reverse of portrait, original cloth. 8vo 1907.*" Actually, the drawing first appeared in Punch *on 14 August 1841, four years before the Brownings' courtship. Therefore, Beerbohm used it to represent the Brownings, even though this could hardly have been the intention of the* Punch *artist.*

Elizabeth Barrett (figure 91).[10] And, in the 13 March 1936 issue of *The Manchester Guardian*, Max "strikes again" with a composite sketch of several eminent Victorians (figures 92 and 93). Headlined "The Return of 'Max': He Shears the Victorians," and captioned by Beerbohm, "If they were flourishing in this our day," the sketch includes sixteen influential Victorian statesmen, scientists, artists, and writers, including Browning (see identifications on figures 92 and 93). Beneath the *Guardian* drawing is the following commentary:

He has chosen for his subject the Victorians who are now so fashionable on the stage and in books, and shows us how they would fare if they had lived to-day and followed our barber customs. Their long hair, beards, whiskers, chin-tufts and heavy, curly moustaches would, of course, go. They would have Chaplin (or Hitler) moustaches; they would abandon pince-nez and monocle for horn-rimmed spectacles; they would brush their forelocks back instead of forward. One had not thought of all these things, but "Max" has done so. Shorn of all their hirsute decorations, they do not look such very grand figures now. Nor would our little heroes of to-day look so ordinary beside them! Anyway, there are the Victorians "if they were flourishing in this our day." How many of them could our friends—even the cleverest of them—identify? (13 March 1936)

While it is hardly in the Beerbohm tradition of caricature and is probably better classed as illustration than cartoon, Walter Crane's homage to William Morris (figures 94a and 94b) provides yet another example of how Browning has been drawn in the light of his relationship to his contemporaries. The Crane drawing shows Browning, along with Tennyson, Arnold, and Swinburne, surrounding the central figure of William Morris, the socialistic artist-poet so admired by Crane. Morris sits in the foreground, picking flowers and holding *The Earthly Paradise*. Swinburne holds *Atalanta in Calydon*, and Browning *The Ring and the Book*. Behind is the Muse of Poetry, backed by the sculptured images of Chaucer, Shakespeare, and Milton. In his autobiography, *An Artist's Reminiscences*, Crane comments on his drawing:

Among the smaller occasional designs I did while in Rome during the winter of 1883–84 was a frontispiece for Messrs. Kegan Paul, Trench, & Co.'s selection from "Living English Poets," which may claim a certain interest from the fact that of the groups of poets I represented on the slopes of an English Parnassus, including Tennyson, Browning, Matthew Arnold, William Morris, and Swinburne, the last named only now survives.[11]

During the 1880s and 1890s, British and American comic periodicals were filled with verbal and visual commentaries on Browning, most of them relating to the alternating rising and declining of his popularity among "fashionable" Browning clubs and cults. In this section we offer a potpourri of examples, most of which are commentaries *on* Browning rather than caricatures *of* him. An 1887 issue of the American *Puck* printed an amusing little

Figure 92. "The Return of 'Max': He Shears the Victorians," by Max Beerbohm, in The Manchester Guardian, *Friday, 13 March 1936. Max depicts the sixteen eminent Victorians as "if they were flourishing in this our day." Back Row: Sir William Vernon Harcourt, Lord Leighton, Sir Henry Irving, Darwin, Whistler, Lord Randolph Churchill, Oscar Wilde. Middle Row: Browning, Herbert Spencer, D. G. Rossetti, Swinburne. Front Row: Gladstone, Ruskin, Disraeli, Carlyle, Tennyson.*

series of cartoon vignettes (figure 95) depicting Boston Browningites in five social situations. While the illustration itself is really more a marginal design and somewhat difficult to decipher, the accompanying commentary by Zenas Dane clarifies the matter:

Figure 93. Detail of Browning from Beerbohm's Manchester Guardian *cartoon (see figure 92).*

Browning in Boston
In Business Circles

"Ha, Brown, good marning!"

"Good morning, good morning, Whyte! How's business, anyhow?"

"Fair. Coal's going up. Everything pretty lively down your way?"

"Yes, cold weather's helping trade. Had a good run in all our departments yesterday. Stocks pretty steady?"

"Yes, rather. Didn't see you at the Browning Club last night."

"No, *had* to stay away. Mighty sorry. Had a good time, didn't you?"

110

Figures 94a and 94b. Working sketch and finished drawing of Walter Crane's homage to Morris. Morris sits in the foreground, picking flowers, below the muse of poetry. Looking on (left to right) are Swinburne, Browning, Arnold, and Tennyson. This is described as the frontispiece to English Living Poets *by Crane in his autobiography,* An Artist's Reminiscences *(New York: Macmillan Co., 1907), p. 250.*

"Fine. Several new and capital interpretations were given
   sonnets. Ought to have been there!"
"I shan't miss again this winter."

At Houri Silk Counter

"Why, Sadie, is this *you!*"
"Yes, *indeed;* where did *you* come from?"
"I just now ran in; *so* glad to see you."
"How *well* you're looking!"

"Oh, thanks, I saw you at our Browning Club last
   night."
"And I saw *you.* Wasn't it just too splendid for *anything!*"
"I never knew before how perfectly beautiful dear old
   Browning was."
"I think he's just *sweet.*"
"So do I. I'll see you at the Club next week?"
"Yes, indeed; I wouldn't miss it for *anything!*"
"Nor I."

Figure 95. From Puck, *26 January 1887, p. 361.*

On Hampden Street

"The top av the mornin' to yeez, Mistur O'Rafferty!"

"The same to yerself, Mistress Gilligan."

"Bedad, an' it's a snifter we're havin' in the way of bad weather, ma'am."

"It is that same, Mrs. Gilligan. But sure an' I don't moind it, ma'am, so long as I've a bit o' beer in the house, an' me copy av Mr. Browning's writin's."

"Browning, is it, ma'am? An' it's a divilish foine writer he was, ma'am. Me ould man an' me are r'adin him the blissid toime!"

"Ye'll be at the Browning Club to-night, Mrs. Gilligan?"

"I will that, ma'am."

At Young's Hotel Restaurant

"Ah, deah boy, but it's pleasant to bweak bwead with you again."

"Thanks, old chappie; thanks awfully; you're looking monstrous well, deah boy."

"Ah, thanks, awfully, old fel, I believe I *am* well. Whacher doing to kill time, me boy?"

"Why, doncher know, weading Bwowning, to be sure, old chappie."

"Ah, shake, deah boy. I'm weading Bwowning myself. Belong to six Bwowning clubs, doncher know."

"So do I. Chawming fellow Bwowning must have been, chawming."

"Oh magnif! you must join my Bwowning club."

"I will, deah boy, if you'll join mine."

Extracts from Boston Papers

The West and South End Browning Clubs meet on Tuesday nights.

The clubs in the North and East End hold meetings on Wednesday, Friday and Saturday evenings.

A Browning Club was organized yesterday on Deer Island by a number of philanthropic ladies from the West End.

Twenty-nine new Browning Clubs were organized on the Back Bay last week.

Figure 96. Cover of Life, *2 May 1889. "A Distinct Decline."*

Mrs. B: "The Browning Cult has rather subsided in your city, has it not?"

Mrs. L (from Chicago): "Yes, indeed! Now that we have got on to his curves it is scarcely an exaggeration to say that Browning is already in the soup."

Mr. Arthur Pickering gave some delightful interpretations of Browning, before Cambridge's sixteen Browning Clubs on Friday.

Two of the drivers on the Metropolitan car-line came to blows yesterday, over a disputed interpretation of Browning. They spent the night in the cooler, but their fines were paid this morning by members of the Soulful Insight Browning Club, from South Boston.

The newsboys of the city are organizing into Browning Clubs, and they are to be joined by the Cash Girl's Clubs.

Zenas Dane.
(26 January 1887, p. 361)

Another American journal of satire, somewhat akin to the British *Punch*, was the early *Life*, a magazine started by a group of Harvard men in 1883. While the periodical's name suggests its connection with the later and now better-known pictorial magazine, the early *Life* was a distinctly different product, offering satirical observation on matters literary, political, and social. The cover of the 2 May 1889 issue featured two fashionable ladies in conversation (figure 96). Under the caption, "A Distinct Decline," is their brief dialogue:

Mrs. B: The Browning Cult has rather subsided in your city, has it not?
Mrs. L (from Chicago): Yes, indeed! Now that we have got on to his curves, it is scarcely an exaggeration to say that Browning is already in the soup.

Another *Life* cartoon, captioned "Next! Latest From Our Boston Correspondent" (figure 97), suggests that Browning's reputation, along with Tolstoy's, was being swept away (note the broom on the steps) by the rising Ibsen cult. In this 1890 cartoon by Attwood, Ibsen sits swamilike on his pedestal, while "Apparitions" of dethroned literary heroes (including the prominent but discarded bust of Browning) fly away with the smoke of sacrifice to the new guru.

In England during the 1890s *Punch* continued to comment on Browning's popularity in fashionable literary circles. An 1891 Du Maurier cartoon captioned "True Literary Exclusiveness" (figure 98) shows a well-attired couple in politely bored conversation at a party:

"Don't you admire Robert Browning as a poet, Mr. Fitzsnook?"
"I used to once; but *Everybody* admires him

Figure 97. *"Next! Latest from our Boston Correspondent," Life 15 (22 May 1890).*

now, don'tcherknow—so —'ve had to give him up!"

(10 October 1891)

An 1897 cartoon, captioned "Confidences," shows a youthful "Miss Girton" asking a "Muscular Undergraduate," "And do you like Browning?" Her athletic escort replies, "Well, to tell the truth, I'd as soon read a time-table!" Another, captioned "An Honest Penny" (figure 99), shows two monocled males in conversation:

"What have you been doing all day?"
"Writing an article for the *Gadfly*."
"Who about?"
"Robert Browning."

113

Figure 98. From Punch, *10 October 1891, by Du Maurier.*

"Suppose you've read a lot of him?"
"Not I! But I met him once at an afternoon
  Tea."

(11 April 1896, p. 169)

The theme, frequent in *Punch* during the 1890s, that Browning's reputation rested less upon an appreciative understanding of his poetry than upon knowing just enough to "drop" his name at fashionable gatherings, was often echoed in the American *Life* as well. The 3 October 1895 issue contains a drawing of a nymphlike student floating on a tree branch (figure 100). Captioned "The Wonders of America : A Scene on Boston Common," the drawing shows the girl reading from a Browning book that is propped up by the wings of a comically exotic bird with a silly grin on its beak and a gleam in its eye! This idea that Browning's poetry, however uncomprehended, should be read by young would-be "Browningites" is treated comically in *Hood's Comic Album* by Charles J. Dunphie in a parody to accompany a drawing, "Browningites at Sea" (figure 101):

Undeterred by fear of drowning,
Though the skies were fiercely frowning,
Students four of Mr. Browning,
  Let what might befall,
Vowed that they were each man willing
To subscribe a splendid shilling
For a voyage brief and chilling,
  In a Ramsgate yawl.

By a chance quite accidental,
Three were Mashers sentimental,
One a Welsher; and intent all
  On a spree were they.
Love of Mr. Browning banded
Them together, though the candid
Hint that he not understanded
  Was by them alway.

Quoth the youngest of the party,
Hailing from the town Cromarty,
"If you'd still feel hale and hearty,

Figure 99. Another cartoon by Du Maurier in Punch, *11 April 1896.*

114

Figure 100. "The Wonders of America: A Scene on Boston Common," Life, 3 October 1895.

And from sickness keep,
Mr. Browning's book *Sordello*,
Will I read while tempests bellow";
And he did—the charming fellow.
  They fell fast asleep!

Thus while angry skies were frowning,
And the yawl was up-and-downing,
Students four of Mr. Browning
  Had a high old time.
Each was an unconscious ranger,
Quite insensible to danger,

And to sickness, which is stranger
  Through their poet's rhyme.

MORAL

When afloat you're going,
And the breeze is freshly blowing,
Trust to Browning, there's no knowing
  What a comfort he will be.
The Nepenthe of his verses
In Lethean waves immerses
Him who hears them, or rehearses.
  Like these Browningites at sea.

As we have tried to illustrate thus far, cartoons, caricatures, and comic commentaries on Robert Browning take many forms. Although the cartoons and caricatures of Browning seldom flatter, rarely do they belittle, even when they suggest that his poems are difficult or obscure. The comic press, like the more serious critical press, seemed less certain of Browning's achievement than it did of that of Tennyson or of Arnold, Browning's most important contemporaries. On the other hand, Browning was never treated as a comic personality, as was Oscar Wilde and, sometimes, Swinburne. While Browning rarely appears in caricature in most twentieth century popular comic periodicals, characters from his poems sometimes do, as, for example, in S. W. Stanley's 1912 *Punch* cartoon of the "New Version" of Pippa passing as "The Terror of Bond Street" (figure 102).

Closely related to the caricatures and cartoons are the parodies and comic commentaries that frequently accompanied them. We have included several of these where it seemed appropriate but have resisted the temptation to add numerous other good ones[12] because our intention has been to focus primarily upon visual, rather than verbal, examples. We conclude, however, with a poem that is neither parody nor comic commentary. It appeared in *Punch* several days after Browning's death.

Robert Browning
Born, May 7, 1812   Died, December 12, 1889

In mid-winter, in the silent songless snow-time,
  Your last song, all gallant glee,
Flashed upon us—and while we yet gladly
    listened,
Low you lay in sunny Venice that you loved
    so,
    Singer free!

115

Figure 101. From Hood's Comic Album.

England loved you, though your song was oft
    mistaken,
    For your Muse, scarce trim, was true.
Nothing hopeless, nothing maudlin or
    unmanly,
Nought of sick erotic hot hysteric drivel
      Came from you.

One who never wooed the night, but loved the
    daytime,
    Never doubted dawn would break,
Never dramed delirious dim narcotic visions,
Never culled pale flowers of sin in Stygian
    meadows,
      Sleep—to wake!

You at noonday, in the struggle of men's
    toil-time,
    Gave us song to strengthen, cheer:
Now you sleep, but not your fame; the world
    you wakened
Will not let your memory die, but hold it ever
      Sweet and dear!

              (21 December 1889)

The "last song" referred to in the first stanza is
Browning's "Epilogue." While *Punch*'s poet offers a

Figure 102. Punch, *13 November 1912.*

fairly skillful imitation of Browning's final poem, it is obvious that parody has given way to praise.

Commenting on the Litzinger and Smalley edition, *Robert Browning: The Critical Heritage* (1970), P. J. Keating observes that "the history of [Browning's] reputation in the Victorian period . . . makes, as one would expect, depressing reading: so much incomprehension, so many feeble witticisms about his obscurity, so little real communication between author and reader."[13] One might expect this statement to apply even more to the intentionally satiric criticism from the comic press. To a great exent, it does. On the other hand, Keating notes that while "throughout his life Browning was haunted by what he considered to be the wilful misunderstanding of critics and reviewers," he also gratefully enjoyed the loyal support of a handful of perceptive admirers, many of whom were his fellow writers. Many of these, also, must be numbered among the artists and writers who caricatured and parodied the poet in the popular press, providing us with those "other likenesses" that both amuse us and awaken us to an added dimension in the history of Browning criticism.

NOTES

1. W. Hall Griffin, *The Life of Robert Browning* (London: Methuen and Co., 1938), p. 12.

2. Ibid.

3. The following year, Waddy collected the cartoon series in *Cartoon Portraits and Biographical Sketches of Men of the Day* (London, 1873).

4. Eileen Harris has written a well-documented introduction to *Vanity Fair* magazine and its caricatures in the National Portrait Gallery's exhibition booklet, *Vanity Fair: An Exhibition of Original Cartoons*, published by and available from the National Portrait Gallery, London WC2H OHE. See also Savory, *Vanity Fair Lithographs*, and *The Vanity Fair Gallery: A Collector's Guide to the Caricatures* (New Jersey and London: A. S. Barnes & Co., 1979).

5. Leonard E. Naylor, *The Irrepressible Victorian: The Story of Thomas Gibson Bowles* (London: Macdonald and Co., 1965), p. 22.

6. Griffin, *Life of Robert Browning*, p. 271.

7. Michael Hancher, "The Beerbohm Caricature of Browning and the Browning Society," *The Browning Newsletter* 9 (Fall 1972): 24.

8. J. G. Riewald, *Beerbohm's Literary Caricatures from Homer to Huxley* (Hamden, Conn.: Archon Books, 1977), p. 52.

9. This photograph is reproduced in Elizabeth Wilson's monograph *Robert Browning's Portraits, Photographs and Other Likenesses*, Browning Interests series (Waco, Texas: Baylor University Armstrong Browning Library, 1943).

10. See caption and comments to Fig. 91.

11. Walter Crane, *An Artist's Reminiscences* (New York: Macmillan, 1907), p. 250.

12. Browning was parodied more often than he was caricatured. One source of early examples is Hamilton, *Parodies*, vols. 5 and 6. Another is Jerrold and Leonard, *A Century of Parody*. A good bibliographical reference is Broughton, Northup and Pearsall, *Robert Browning: A Bibliography, 1830–1950* (Ithaca, N.Y.: Cornell University Press, 1953), Sec. CV, pp. 320–40. One recent parody of Browning is David R. Ewbank's "Friedrich Schlafmacher's Excogitation," a Browningesque version of "Mary Had a Little Lamb" in "Kidding the Victorian Poets: A Collection of Parodies," *Victorian Poetry* 15, no. 1 (Spring 1977): 69–70. For other cartoons and comic commentaries on Browning, see Jerold J. Savory, *Other Likenesses of Robert Browning: The Poet in Caricature, Cartoon and Comic Commentary*, Browning Interests series no. 26 (Waco, Texas: Baylor University Armstrong Library, 1981).

13. P. J. Keating, "Robert Browning: A Reader's Guide," in *Robert Browning*, ed. Isobel Armstrong, Writers and Their Background series (Athens: Ohio University Press, 1974), p. 312.

O IS for Oliver, casting aspersion
On Omar, that awfully dissolute Persian,
Though secretly longing to join the diversion.

P IS for Peter, who hollers "No! No!"
Through the keyhole to Paine,
Paderewski and Poe.

6
A Charivari to Matthew Arnold

IN WHAT MAY BE THE EARLIEST PUBLISHED parody of an Arnold poem, "The Strayed Reveller" becomes "The Strayed Sightseer," a poetic caricature by a pseudonymous author, "Cygnus," in his (or her) 1855 collection of comic commentaries on the Great Exhibition of 1851. Entitled *Crystals from Sydenham: Or, What Modern Authors Say of the Palace* (London: Hope and Co., 16 Great Marlborough Street, 1855), the "edited" book contains several parodies of prominent Victorian writers, including Arnold. A copy of the book is in the Beinecke Rare Book and Manuscript Library at Yale University (Tinker No. 200; Beinecke Call No. Ip.Ar65.F855c), and the poem from pages 25–31 is reprinted here with permission.

Although "The Strayed Sightseer" is more burlesque than parody and doesn't really deal with the *substance* of Arnold's poem, it is a delightful and witty piece and shows that Arnold was popular enough to be ridiculed as early as 1855.

The Strayed Sightseer.
By M. A.

The Terrace of the Crystal Palace—Evening.

A YOUTH. POLICEMAN.

The Youth.

FASTER! faster,
Oh, blue Policeman!

Let the long excursion train,
The gay procession
Of holiday forms
Sweep through my soul!

Thou standest frowning
Down on me; thy right arm,
Raised against thy dewy brow,
Mops thy moist cheek;
Thy left shows, hanging "at ease,"
The broad cuff, duty-cinctured,
Dark blue and white.

Is it then evening
So soon? I see the white mist,
Drifting like beer-foam, dims
The plated buttons
On thy stalwart breast;
The cool night-wind, too,
Blows through the terrace,
Stirs thy hair, "Peeler!"
Waves thy white trousers.

Policeman.

Whence art thou, sleeper?

Youth.

When the grey dawn first
Through the dim window-panes
Of my lodgings, on the third flight
Up at the King's Head,
Came breaking, Peeler,
I sprang up—I threw round me

My dappled shirt.
Passing out from the wet step,
Where a pail stood by the front door,
I snatched up my beaver, my new cane
All tipped with gold,
Came swift down to join
The crowds early gathered
In the station round the Booking-office,
South-Eastern Terminus,
On London Bridge.

Quick we passed, following
The loud engine's steam-track,

Down the branch railway. I saw
On my right, through the window,
This palace, Peeler—
Noiseless, empty.
Wondering, I entered, beheld
The courts all silent,
The bulls sleeping,
On a stall this bottle—I drank, Peeler,
And sank down here, sleeping
On the steps of the terrace.

Policeman (springs his rattle).

Hi, Sir! within there,
Sir Richard Mayne!
Come forth, so please you,
See what the night brings.

Sir Richard Mayne.

Always new prisoners!
Hast then apprehended
Some young, flashy-dressed member
Of the swell mob,
That he sits stroking fondly
His stiff, immaculate collar,
The night breeze ruffling
The long oil-shining locks
That crown his brow,
His waistcoat, half unbuttoned,
Smeared with brown beer stains,
That he sits lounging
So late on the terrace?

Policeman.

Hist! he wakes.
I took him not into custody, Sir Richard—
Nay, ask him.

Youth.

Who speaks? who comes forth
To thy side, Peeler, from within?
What shall I call him,
This stern, plain-featured,
Quick-eyed stranger?

Art thou he whom rogues
This long time dream of—
The knighted Captain of the Blues in
    Scotland-yard?
Art thou he, stranger?
Sir Richard Mayne,
His mother's son?

Sir Richard Mayne.

I am the Baronet,
And thou too, sleeper,
Thy face is brazen.
It may be thou hast followed
Through the streets some fast man—
By life taught many things—
"Bell's Life" and the Prophets,
And heard him delighting
His friends and followers
In the "Coal Hole," and heard his stories

Of "bricks" and heroes;
Of love and cigars,
And billiard tables
In town, or kept
In rustic suburbs.

Youth.

The police are happy.
They turn on all sides
Their shining bull's-eyes,
And see around them
By night and day
The town and men.

They see the Baronet
Strolling, staff in hand,
On the hard, gravelly
Serpentine bank;
His hat thrown back on
The bald, venerable "Head,"
Revolving inly
The doom of London.

They see the Colonels
In the upper rooms
Of Clarendon, in the streets
Where time-killing gossips lounge
At the plate-glass open windows,
With arms relaxed and lips
Curled, gently smoking
The fragrant weed.

They see the "Coster"
Driving, whip in hand,
His frail cart moored to
A spare-ribbed donkey,
Toiling beneath his load upheaped
With large-leaved, white-headed cauliflowers

And the dark cucumber
He piles and packs them,
Driving, driving! round him,
Round his greengrocer cart,
Flock the small housewives,
Their children ring them.

They see the cabman
On the long stand unbuckling
His horse's bit at noon;
He waters his beast there, then makes his meal,
Cold pie and pint
Of half-and-half, fetched from the tap
Of "Truman Hanbury," or the "Noted House
For Barclay, Perkins,
And Co.'s Entire."

They see the heroes
Of midnight brawls,
Singing through the dark streets
In their reckless sky-larking,
Violent spree,
At sunrise nearing
The hapless lock-ups.

The old Inspector
Came strolling in the sunshine
From the crowded palace courts
This way at noon.
Sitting by me, while he brushed
His dusty garments,
He told me these things.

But I, Sir Richard,
Sitting on the warm steps,
Looking over the gardens
All day long, have seen,
Without spectacles, without difficulty,
Sometimes a wild-haired navvy;
Sometimes a cook with ices;
And sometimes for a moment,
Passing through the young shrubs,
Hands in pockets, the beloved,
The renowned, the divine
Sir Joseph Paxton!

Faster! faster!
Oh, blue policeman!
Let the long excursion train,
The gay procession
Of holiday forms
Sweep through my soul!

Over a quarter of a century after this published parody, Arnold had established his reputation as a poet and critic and was frequently the target for caricaturists and parodists in the popular comic press in both England and America. *Punch* was usually at the forefront of gibes from the British side.

Admit that Homer sometimes nods,
That poets do write trash,
Our Bard has written "Balder Dead,"
And also balder-dash.

Thus ran the caption to *Punch*'s "Fancy Portrait" of Matthew Arnold (figure 103). The cartoon, one in a series of *Punch*'s caricatures of well-known personalities of the day, was the offering for 26 November 1881. Shown with his toga, sandals, laurel wreath, "harp of gold," and inspirational bottle of "Sweetness and Light," Arnold is depicted as "Necklong," the subject of the accompanying parody of his own poem, "The Neckan":

Necklong
(After "Neckan"—a reckless, neck-or-nothing attempt.)

Figure 103. Punch's "Fancy Portrait" of Arnold, 26 November 1881.

Figure 104. "Mens Conscia," from a series in Punch *during the 1860s and 1870s featuring a government inspector who clearly resembled Arnold.*

In summer, in Sky-Limbo,
  High o'er PHILISTIA'S throng,
Sits NECKLONG with his harp of gold,
  And thrums a dismal song.

Thick herds, beneath Sky-Limbo,
  The incult dull British P.,
And there Gath's shallow singers chaunt
  Their *Laus Philistiae.*

They sing not of High Culture,
  In pure perfection pale,
Of earth, gross earth, the Gathites sing—
  They have no other tale.

But NECKLONG, in Sky-Limbo,
  Soft pipes a sombre stave,
Sweetness and Light inspire his lay,
  Bland taste and manners suave.

He chaffs the swell Barbarian,
  He chides the stolid clown,
The dull dissenter, BOTTLES,
  JONES, ROBINSON, and BROWN.

Upon the middle classes
  His feather-flail he lays,
And the D. T.'s "young lions" mocks,
  Whose roars to him are brays.

Pooh-pooheth all the Parties,
  Their fuss and fi-fo-fum,
And twitteth their small tweedledee,
  And smaller tweedledum.

He sings how from the Chapel
  Comes nought but narrow pride,
And how the Church's shibboleths
  Pure Reason doth deride.

How Beauty, lone, sits weeping,
  Midst wastes that round her lie,
"PHILISTIA shares my state," she weeps,
  "No cultured mate have I."

How if that fed on Sweetness,
  Exposed to Light's soft rain,
Even the Philistine himself
  True Culture might attain.

He sings how on an evening,
  Beneath the willows cool,
He sat and thrummed upon his harp,
  And wept into the pool.

Beside the pool sat NECKLONG,
  Tears filled his soft blue eye;
On his slow mule, across the bridge,
  The Philistine rode by.

"Why sitt'st thou there, O NECKLONG,
  And thrumm'st thy harp of gold?
'Tis pretty twangling, I admit,
  But finical and cold.

"A soft-curled SAMSON, doubtless,
  Or dandy DAVID, you;
But all your songs and sneers won't dash
  PHILISTIA'S merry crew."

122

The Philistine rode onwards,
  And vanished with his mule;
And NECKLONG, in the twilight grey,
  Wept on into the pool.

He wept: "This earthly blindness
  Would shame the burrowing moles.
By Hecate, I begin to doubt
  If Philistines have souls!"

All Summer in Sky-Limbo,
  Above PHILISTIA'S throng,
Sits NECKLONG with his harp of gold
  And pipes this plaintive song.[1]
                    (26 November 1881, p. 250)`

A line-by-line comparison to Arnold's poem is hardly necessary, but it is amusing to see what *Punch*'s parodist has done with Arnold's version of the tale of the mythic sea-creature who laments the hardheartedness of humans. Arnold is chided as a "Sky-Limbo" poet, hovering "high o'er" the merry but blind and uncultured Barbarians, Philistines, Middle Classes, Parties, and Churches—a fairly comprehensive gathering of earthlings receiving his pooh-poohethings! He is capable of some "pretty twangling" on his harp, but his songs are "finical and cold," full of chaffing, chiding, sneering, and mocking all that goes on in the "throng" beneath him. Although *Punch*'s judgment seems to be that Arnold's poem is "balder-dash" and deserving parody, the lyrics are clearly aimed less at Arnold the poet than at Arnold the social critic. Cast as a weeping dandy, Arnold is caricatured as one whose *Culture and Anarchy* and religious writings, while containing some "pretty twangling," are too somber and cold to have any realistic influence on the "merry crew" of Philistia.

As one of Victorian England's most popular spokesmen for the Philistine "merry crew," *Punch* did not often take kindly to Arnold's outspoken anti-Philistinism. One might expect, therefore, to find the magazine poking occasional barbs at "Our Bard." Since *Punch* itself was inclined to "Pooh-pooheth all the Parties," the "dull British P.," and the Anglican Church's shibboleths, however, there may be just a touch of Arnoldian sympathy for the weeping dandy who pipes his plaintive song over the plodding Philistine on his slow mule. *Punch*'s parody is hardly gentle, but there is enough hinting at clever ambiguity to leave one wondering who is making the ass of whom.

Arnold was a fairly frequent visitor to the pages of *Punch*, seldom, however, as clearly visible as in the "Fancy Portrait" and the "Necklong" parody. During the 1860s and 1870s, for example, the cartoonist Charles Keene did a series of cartoons depicting a government school inspector making his rounds of classrooms. In one (figure 104) the inspector, with increasing anger and frustration, asks the children, "Who signed Magna Charta?!!" Finally a slightly built Dickensian "Scapegrace" nervously answers, "Please, Sir, 'Twasn't me, Sir!!" Another Keene cartoon, from the 15 February 1873 *Punch*, shows the inspector in another situation, the caption for which tells the story. Two years earlier Arnold had been appointed Senior Inspector of Schools, and there seems little doubt that the tall and lean man with hat and umbrella in hand and his back to us is Senior Inspector Matthew Arnold (figure 105). Even if Arnold, or a clear likeness of him, did not appear, *Punch* took frequent delight in "Out-Matthewing Arnold," (figure 106). At times *Punch* would simply take advantage of the currency of Arnoldian phrases to have good-natured fun with their phrase-coining "Civic Monarch":

Sweetness and Light in the City

Could there be a more gallant and graceful compliment than the Lord Mayor paid on Monday, when the Czar lunched in Guildhall, and his Lordship proposed the health of the Royal Family?—

"Of the Princess of Wales and the Duchess of Edinburgh he could not say more than that they were sweetness and light personified."

Which nobody can deny. Said not the Civic Monarch well, MR. MATTHEW ARNOLD? Who but a Philistine as big as GOLIATH can be capable of asking which of the two Royal Ladies is Sweetness and which is Light? Of course the Lord Mayor meant to say that each of them was Sweetness and Light personified in her own person. So the PRINCESS OF WALES is Sweetness, and the DUCHESS OF EDINBURGH is Light; and the PRINCESS OF WALES is Light, and the DUCHESS OF EDINBURGH is Sweetness, and each, by herself, is Sweetness and Light and Light and Sweetness; therefore, they twain are Sweetness and Light jointly and severally, separately and both together. (30 May 1874, p. 225)

The lighthearted playfulness goes at the lord mayor's expense. Arnold would likely have smiled, as he would also at another *Punch* note on the title of another of his poems:

Figure 105. "Penny Wise," Punch, *15 February 1873.*

Is MR. MATTHEW ARNOLD an extreme Land-Leaguer? asks a Correspondent who, having heard the title of one of his poems read out, viz., "Resignation, To Forster,"—wouldn't wait for the remainder. The question is natural: only on referring to the book we found that "Forster" is spelt "Fausta."[2] (30 May 1874, p. 225)

Punch was not the only periodical to provide Victorian readers with parodies, satires, and caricatures of their leading citizens. An excellent series of cartoon caricatures appeared during 1872 in *Once a Week*, a clever weekly published by Bradbury and Evans after they split with Charles Dickens. Among the forty or more cartoons, mostly of prominent literary figures and drawn by Frederick Waddy (as announced in the 13 January 1872 issue), was a marvelous one of Arnold as an acrobat on a flying trapeze (figure 107). Appearing in the 12 October issue of *Once a Week*, the acrobatic Arnold is shown in circus tights, high above the stage and audience-filled boxes, leaping coolly (or "disinterestedly") to the trapeze bar labeled "Philosophy." In

Figure 106. "Out-Matthewing Arnold!" Punch, *18 November 1882.*

the distance the still swinging bars of "Criticism" and "Poetry" suggest that he has just made another agile leap from one to the other. Captioned "Sweetness and Light," the cartoon is accompanied by a brief and generally complimentary biographical sketch that suggests that his more enduring popularity will come less from his poetry than from his "remarkable" prose essays.[3] The caricaturist obviously sees Arnold as a performer in a fairly elite circus held in a theater with a posh interior.

In addition to the *Once a Week* cartoon, the year 1872 also welcomed W. H. Mallock's anonymously published first edition of *Every Man His Own Poet; Or, The Inspired Singer's Recipe Book.* Thanks to Barry V. Qualls and *Victorian Poetry*, Mallock's Oxford undergraduate satire is now available and contains a brief "recipe" on "How to Make a Poem like Mr. Matthew Arnold" that deserves reprinting:

Take one soulful of involuntary unbelief, which has been previously well flavored with self-satisfied despair. Add to this one beautiful text of Scripture. Mix these well together; and as soon as ebullition commences, grate in finely a few regretful allusions to the New Testament and the Lake of Tiberias, one constellation of stars, half-a-dozen allusons to the nineteenth century, one to Goethe, one to Mont Blanc, or the Lake of Geneva; and one also, if possible, to some personal bereavement. Flavour the whole with a mouthful of "faiths" and "infinities," and a mixed mouthful of "passions," "finites," and "yearnings." This class of poem is concluded usually with some question, about which we have to observe only that it shall be impossible to answer.[4]

Since our purpose is to be selective, not exhaustive, we resist the temptation to include more from *Punch*[5] in order to turn next to Victorian England's most popular society journal, *Vanity Fair*.

Vanity Fair's 5 July 1882 issue carried a series of parodies of Tennyson, Arnold, and others, centering on the "Crisis" in Egypt, which sent British forces to Cairo to negotiate and protect English interests there. In what may be one of the best parodies of Arnold's prose, especially his tendency to repeat phrases, *Vanity Fair* offers an obviously exaggerated "Sample Opinion on the 'Crisis' by Mr. Matthew Arnold":

So seeing that the representatives of the middle class, with their crippled sense of justice, their boisterous rejection of refinement, have chosen to approach this question with rudeness and want of calm, it is only fitting that a simple-minded person should remind them of their duty. For their crippled sense of justice and their boisterous rejection of refinement can only be rendered harmless by the simplicity of those who do not approach the question with rudeness and want of calm. How an Englishman with his rudeness and want of calm can be expected to influence the Eastern mind of Arabi is not apparent to any but the Philistine mind. We must get into the air and regard the matter serenely, and not from the point of view of the Engishman with his crippled sense of justice, his boisterous rejection of refinement. Let men be sent from the home of repose, from Oxford; let them be men of simplicity and sweetness; bind them in by no rules framed by thinkers whose aspirations in life are limited to marrying a deceased wife's sister. When these men with their calm and their simplicity present themselves at Cairo, the sensitive Colonels will at once feel the presence of higher souls, and will cease to follow the keen unscrupulous course. Then the middle class with their crippled sense of justice, their boisterous rejection of refinement, will receive their dividends, and will thus be able to afford a marriage with a deceased wife's sister, while the Author of the Mysterious World will see that it is better for Him to be content with Oxford, since He can make nothing sweeter or fuller of light.[6] (5 July 1882, p. 2)

The reference to the "marriage with a deceased wife's sister" is to an issue that Arnold himself enjoyed ridiculing because of its absurdity. "Arminius Von Thunder-ten-Tronckh," in *Friendship's Garland*, speaks of the Liberals' House of Commons bill enabling a man to marry his deceased wife's sister as

Figure 107. "Sweetness and Light," Once a Week, 12 October 1873.

125

just another bit of political "pabulum."[7] With hyperbolic delight, Arnold, in *Culture and Anarchy*, reports his "advantage" at being present when Thomas Chambers introduced the bill with a plea for personal liberty. Another supporter of the bill, Hepworth Dixon, is labeled by Arnold "the Colenso of love and marriage."[8] Bishop Colenso's book on his discoveries of problems in biblical arithmetic among the Zulus had provided Arnold with a vulnerable object for satire. As R. H. Super rightly observes, "Arnold's sense of humor brought him, then, into the heart of the religious controversies of his day, this time in prose, not verse."[9] From his earliest prose until his last, Arnold continued to use the "deceased wife's sister" issue and the Colenso affair whenever a touch of satire was needed. And never was his comic touch better than when he dealt with pettiness in politics and religion.[10]

Contrary to *Punch*'s parodic portrait of Arnold as a weeping dandy with a cold and dismal outlook on life, that Arnold's wit and humor never left him is obvious both in his letters and in nearly all of his prose from the 1863 "The Bishop and the Philosopher" to his final essays of the late 1880s.[11]

At times Arnold's sense of humor must have prompted his amusement at the more mild ridicule he received from such magazines as *Punch* and *Vanity Fair*. Sometimes, however, the popular press went beyond playful parody to downright devilishness and deliberate distortion of his ideas. For example, in response to Arnold's Whitechapel Address of 29 November 1884, *Vanity Fair* printed the following anonymous "poetic" critique of Arnold's art-prating:

> Oh, Matthew! when you prate of Art,
>   Your chatter, like your writing,
> I'm bound to own extremely smart
>   (Though not to me inviting).
> But though of genius you may boast
>   (I don't intend to scoff) it
> Appears to me that you're a most
>   Uncomfortable prophet.
>
> You prophesy a coming change:
>   Society is "rocking":
> It "sways and cracks," you say—how strange!
>   And, if 'tis true, how shocking!
> I really hope you mayn't be right;
>   At any rate we know it
> Is only fair to make some slight
>   Allowance for a poet.

> You think it for the workman's good
>   To stir up revolution.
> Poor devil! what he needs is food,
>   More air and more ablution.
> He who wants this, must work (it seems
>   Most sad); but, you may bet, it
> Is not by listening to your dreams
>   That he will ever get it.
>
> The working man you'd doubtless bid
>   (To shield him from the weather)
> Encase his hands in gloves of kid,
>   His feet in varnished leather;
> With treasures of Japan adorn
>   His room like a Mikado,
> And any garret view with scorn
>   Which hasn't got a dado.
>
> 'Tis thus, I think, your vision runs:—
>   "Away with rank and riches!
> Transfer them to the toiling sons
>   Of gutters and of ditches:
> Away with Fashion's idle reign!
>   With class-distinctions sinful:
> Let every workman quaff champagne,
>   Of turtle swill his skinful:
>
> "On wheels let every workman roll,
>   On cushions loll at leisure,
> And steep his pure aesthetic soul
>   In every sensual pleasure:
> Too long he's had his wrongs to bear,
>   'Tis time with them to grapple!
> The Rough shall revel in Mayfair!!
>   The Peer starve in Whitechapel!!!"[12]
>
> (6 December 1884)

The *Vanity Fair* "Ode," hardly worth noting for its own sake, represents a widespread Philistine mockery of later nineteenth-century "aestheticism" (Oscar Wilde, the public symbol of the "new aestheticism," had been caricatured in *Vanity Fair* only a few months earlier), and the magazine's attack is fairly typical of popular misreadings and, sometimes it would seem, deliberate distortions of positions taken by major critical writers involved in the debates on aestheticism. The *Vanity Fair* writer virtually identifies Arnold as a poor man's aesthete out to create "pure aesthetic soul[s]" through aesthetic hedonism.

While it is true that Arnold does call attention to the need for man's instinct for beauty to be taken seriously in the otherwise dehumanizing drabness of the lower classes, this is by no means his main point in the Whitechapel address. The occasion was the unveiling of a religious mosaic on the East-end's St. Jude's Church, and Arnold's talk was a "lay sermon" on the Christian idealism symbolized in the art's representative figures, "Time, Death, and Judgment." He attacks the avarice and idolatry of upper- and middle-class indifferent isolation from the, therefore, "sacrificed" working class, and he praises the few "saints" who have served at Whitechapel with the vision that access to beauty must accompany economic reform. His main point, however, is not the value of bringing art to the slums. It is rather the need for an enlightened religion to correct idolatries to which both rich and poor are susceptible.

No doubt the social sympathies, the feeling for beauty, the pleasure of art, if left merely by themselves, if untouched by what is the deepest thing in human life—religion—are apt to become ineffectual and superficial.[13]

The real value of the mosaic was not its bringing aestheticism and l'art pour l'art to the East end. Its value was its symbolic role in keeping the Christian ideal of judgment on idolatry before viewers "in a crowded street." And any reader of *Literature and Dogma* would have known that this was by no means Arnold's equivalent of Evangelical "street corner" sermonizing on "the day of doom" or "pie in the sky." The Whitechapel address may not be one of Arnold's better pieces, but it is a good example of his increasing insistence in the later works on the primacy of religion as offering ethical restraints on the kind of decadent aestheticism that was already moving toward its outbreak in the 1890s.

Vanity Fair's was not the only misreading of Arnold's essentially moral-religious aesthetic, nor did such misreadings stop with the end of the Victorian era. But since *Vanity Fair* voiced the popular Philistine sentiment of the day, we think it worth noting that, ironically, Arnold was attacked for representing the very kind of one-sided aestheticism that he himself warned against in his "lay sermon" at Whitechapel.

Vanity Fair writers were often clever in their parodies of Arnold. In 1885 the magazine offered several parodies in the styles of such eminent Victorians as William Morris, John Ruskin, and Matthew Arnold. The issue this time was the rise of the new Tory government and the fall of Gladstone. Using the stanza form and occasional phrases from Callicles' concluding song in "Empedocles on Etna," the

magazine published this parody by "Mr. Matthew Arnold":

Whispers: Opinions on the New Government

Oh! woful departure
    Of sweetness and light!
The Mother of Nations
    Wends fast to the night.

Not here, Oh! Apollo,
    Are haunts meet for thee,
But where tourists to Hawarden
    Go off on the spree.

Great Titan whose musings
    Are classic and pure,
I weep for the trouble
    That you must endure.

The Philistines prosper,
    The Tories are in,
May the gods all forgive us
    Our national sin.

Oh! scions of Hellas
    Return from the shore
Where the shades wander blindly,
    Oh! meet us once more.

Remember my pension,
    And list to my prayer,
Oh! flee to us soon
    From your delicate air.

Oh, then on great Gladstone
    Your exquisite balm,
Bring night with her silence
    And stars with their calm.[14]
                            (18 January 1885, pp. 31–32)

Among the some two thousand different caricatures of prominent personalities appearing in *Vanity Fair* was "Spy's" (Leslie Ward's) drawing of Jesse Collings, the "shrewd, hard-headed, capable, and pugnacious" Parliamentarian with "the gift for mastering dry facts." Collings made his political mark as a Birmingham nonconformist Liberal advocate for agrarian reform, a plank in his platform being "three acres and a cow" for deserving citizens.[15] In 1885 the magazine's "Things in General" column parodied Arnold with an "Arnoldian" paragraph on Collings:

To the mind of a child of Nature the proposals made by the confident reformers who now claim our attention seem to lack measure and proportion. I cannot pretend to fathom the mind of Mr. Jesse Collings, for such a feat would require a strength of vision that few Englishmen possess. But, speaking as becomes a child of Nature, I go so far as to say that a sense of measure and proportion is indispensable to a statesman, and this sense of measure and proportion is apparently denied to Mr. Collings. We may bestow a pig on a citizen, we may give him manure for the soil, we may even grant him a cow. But a pig does not develope Lucidity in its fortunate owner, manure does not imply sweetness, a cow cannot give light. On the contrary, a child of Nature may be pardoned if he deems that pigs, and manure, and cows have no connection with lucidity, and sweetness, and light—that they are inimical to lucidity, and sweetness, and light. A statesman with a sense of measure and proportion cares more for lucidity, and sweetness, and light than for pigs, and manure, and cows, and for that reason I am inclined to say that Mr. Jesse Collings is deficient in the sense of measure and proportion.[16] (14 November 1885, p. 271)

This example, and the one quoted earlier, show how *Vanity Fair* recognized a key element in Arnold's prose style and exaggerated it for comic effect. This technique of "being careful to repeat himself verbally" is one noted by John Holloway as one of Arnold's effective methods of bringing "into a bright light the essential simplicity of his thought."[17] The *Vanity Fair* parodist may not have agreed with this conclusion, but he clearly saw the rhetorical method as characteristically Arnoldian.

Although *Vanity Fair* was often clever in its offerings of verbal parody and satire, the magazine's most noteworthy feature was its weekly offering of a chromolithographed portrait caricature of a well-known person of the day.[18] Of the over two thousand celebrities appearing during its forty-year history it is hardly surprising to discover that the journal's "gallery" contains dozens of individuals either directly or indirectly associated with Arnold's personal and public life. Arnold himself appeared in the issue of 11 April 1871. The drawing (figure 108) is captioned, "I say, the critic must keep out of the region of immediate practice," and the accompanying biographical sketch by *Vanity Fair*'s founding editor, Thomas Gibson Bowles, is worth quoting in full:

The "critical effort," which he somewhat largely defines to be "the endeavour in all branches of knowledge, theology, philosophy, history, art, science, to see the object as in itself it really is," represents, in Mr. Matthew Arnold's opinion, one of the greatest of present English wants. Therefore Mr. Arnold is a critic. Eminently fitted for that vocation by the most extensive literary acquirements in all the important literatures, ancient and modern, by a profound contempt for prejudice and commonplace, and by a courage which impels him to attack them wherever and whenever he finds them, he labours in the field of criticism "to propagate the best that is known and thought in the world." Such labour as his must one day bear fruit among the many, but so far it has only been appreciated, or even understood, by the few. The mass of mankind, as he says feelingly, "will never have any ardent zeal for seeing things as they are," and in England especially men are so exclusively busied in using things as they seem, that nobody as a rule gives a thought

Figure 108. Captioned, "I say, the critic must keep out of the region of immediate practice," this caricature by J. J. Tissot appeared in Vanity Fair, *11 April 1871.*

to the necessity of seeing them as they are. The so-called "practical genius" of the English people has killed in all but a very few all care for that ideal out of which the practical issues, and there is everywhere found a dead-weight of self-satisfied stolidity. This Mr. Arnold has gibbeted, upon a word borrowed from the Germans, as Philistinism, or "Inaccessibility to ideas and impatience of them," and "the man who regards the possession of practical conveniences as something sufficient in itself, something which compensates for the absence or surrender of the idea of reason, is in his eyes a Philistine." This type, of creature he mercilessly pursues with a delicate and delicious sarcasm which, although it makes no impression upon natures inaccessible to any feeling not produced by mere bludgeon-work, is the delight of all who rejoice to behold that self-satisfaction which is retarding and vulgarising castigated, and who look forward to the prospect, remote though it be, of securing some day "a free, disinterested play of mind."

Mr. Arnold holds that creation and criticism should be kept apart. "I say the critic must keep out of the region of immediate practice," he declares; and he illustrates the justice of the distinction. As a critic he is unsurpassed; but although he once filled the chair of Poetry at Oxford, as a Poet he does not attain to his own standard. His poems, tinged though they are, now with the colouring of classic times, now with the force of barbarian legends, and often with too familiar a tone of modern life, lack the "power of so dealing with things as to awaken in us a wonderfully full, new, and intimate sense of them and of our relations with them." With public affairs he deals more successfully. Necessarily an enemy to all confusion, an advocate of system in action, and a believer in the power of the State to systematise many of the forces that now run wild, he calls often and loudly for that "civil organisation" which alone of all modern nations England does not possess, and has not striven to create. Especially does he claim this as a necessity in any attempt to instruct the English people, and, being himself a practical schoolmaster, he must be admitted, even by the Philistine, to be in this respect at least a competent critic.

Other marvelous caricatures of "Arnoldiana" include Thomas Hughes, M. E. Grant Duff, Benjamin Jowett, John Henry Newman, John William Colenso, W. E. Forster, Thomas Carlyle, and numerous others. If Arnold himself were available to offer his own comment on this gallery of fellow Englishmen, our guess is that he would choose the words from George Sand that he quoted in *On the Study of Celtic Literature:*

Nearly every Englishman, however good-looking he may be, has always something singular about him which eas-

ily comes to seem comic;—a sort of typical awkwardness (*gaucherie typique*) in his looks or appearance, which hardly ever wears out.[19]

When Matthew Arnold died on 15 April 1888, many of the magazines that had parodied and satirized him were obviously saddened by his death. "Matthew Arnold was not exactly one of *Punch*'s literary heroes," observes Charles L. Graves. "His urbanity was admitted, but *Punch* slightly resented his intellectual superciliousness. Yet the verses on his death in 1888, cast in the 'Thyrsis' stanza, acknowledge the value of his crusade against Philistinism, and the beauty of his elegiac poetry."[20] *Punch*'s poetic obituary is as follows:

He who sang "Thyrsis," then, shall sing no
    more
    This side the stream that stills all earthly
    notes!
Whilst April wakes the woodland's tardy song,
    On morn's wild breeze the throstle's fluting
    floats
To ears long waiting and attentive long.
    But near the shy Thames shore
Mute lies the minstrel who with mellowest reed
    Piped of its sunny slopes and wandering
    ways.
    Singer of light and of large-thoughted days,
And the soul's stillness, art thou gone indeed?

Great Son of a good father, Laleham's Tower,
    'Neath which thou liest, is not firmlier set
Than thy well-founded surely growing fame.
The budding briers with April drops are wet,
Anon the river-fields with gold shall flame;
    The fritillary flower
Shall spread its purple where thy frequent feet
    Lovingly lingered. For thy Muse's flight·
    The Light of Nature's gift is yet more light,
The Sweetness of Earth's boon is still more
    sweet.

The Python of Stupidity is slain
    By Phoebus' shafts; the Philistine must fall
To lucid wit and lambent irony;
    And hot unreason yieldeth, if at all,
To arms of light. Well, the world owes to thee
    This gospel, and its gain
Perchance is greater than from all the noise
    Of Boanerges. Men at least may turn
    To thee the gracious ways of calm to learn,
High Culture's bland repose and blameless
    joys.

"The night as welcome as a friend would fall,"*
    So didst thou sing, and lo! to thee it came
Like a friend's sudden clasp, and all was still.
Sleep well by that loved Thames; henceforth
    With that of "Thyrsis" blent shall haunt each
        hill,
        Each reach, each islet, all
That spreading scene which CLOUGH and
    ARNOLD loved;
    And men of English mould will love it
Thinking, on silvery flood and verdant shore,
"Here ARNOLD sang, here gentle *Thyrsis*
    roved!"

*"Thyrsis," MATTHEW ARNOLD'S exquisite Monody on the death of his friend, ARTHUR HUGH CLOUGH.[21]

(28 April 1888, p. 195)

Fun (1861–1901), a sometime rival humor magazine to *Punch*,[22] offered a somber poetic lament praising the "sweetness and light" that had become the phrase most associated with Arnold in the periodical press.

One by one they rise and leave us!
    They who teach us to be great;
But their going should not grieve us—
    They have finshed—it is late!
They have given Life more beauty,
    Given humankind their best,
Worked and striven—done their duty—
    It is well that they should rest.

Poet, Thinker—Manhood preaching,
    Foe to ignorance and wrong,
True and wholesome in thy teaching,
    Sweet and tender in thy song,
We could wish thee back among us,
    But the Master knows what's right—
In the land which thou hast sung us,
    There is Sweetness, there is Light![23]

(25 April 1888, p. 7)

However kind *Fun*'s tribute may have been, one may imagine Arnold's turning over in his grave with one more mumble on the increasing "unpoetrylessness" of the times! I might note here, however, that *Fun*'s obituary is one of the rare instances where an English satire magazine acknowledged Arnold's seriousness and his importance. With a few honorable exceptions, the English satirists were almost as blind as the Americans to the significance of his contribution as a man of letters.

Vanity Fair did not attempt the eulogistic versifying of its chief contenders. An extraordinarily un-generous—and inaccurate—paragraph appeared instead, sandwiched in with a dozen other assorted notices of the week:

Mr. Matthew Arnold, whose death at a comparatively early age I regret to record this week, was, as an author, the idol of a clique, but to the general public was scarcely known. He belonged to what may be called the extra-superfine school of literature, and was not endowed with that power of touching the hearts of all classes which makes an author really great. Ten years hence Matthew Arnold will be forgotten, whilst his father, a man whose sympathies were as broad as they were deep, and who was absolutely free from the affectations of the son, will be as famous as he is today.[24] (21 April 1888)

Quite obviously, Matthew Arnold was not forgotten "ten years hence." Indeed, he has been remembered in parody nearly a century "hence" by David R. Ewbank, who offers twentieth-century Arnoldians his remarkable "find" in a false-bottomed hatbox in the sub-basement of the Victoria and Albert Museum. Among the yellowed manuscript poems, one of which, "Mary Had a Little Lamb," he ascribes to one M. Goose, is another, "The Deserted Lamb," daringly attributed by Ewbank to Matthew Arnold:

The sun lies soft upon the sward,
The drowsy air blows warm.
Across the flowered lawn a swarm
Of tireless bees, with random toil,
Improves the sultry hour:
And in the fields, with labor hard,
The steady plower
Tills the heavy soil.

But, ah, how wan and wearisome
The busy hours become
When, through the drear and lonely days,
Languishes desire,
And hopes, deceived by long delays,
Sicken and expire,

Outside, alone, oh absent Mary,
Your lonely lamb repines.
My heart, by faithless love made wary,
Sees naught in Nature's vernal show
To heal my drought embittered soul, or grow
From my parched soul new vines.

Is love, then, a mirage, seen
In a wasted land of want?
Is constancy an empty vaunt
And faith an idle dream?

Are peace and joy and friendship, high
　　endeavor and renown
But sound?

Ah, Mary, leave the straitening school,
The dim and dusky hall.
To fathom what dead sages meant
We forfeit calm and lose content.
He is a wrought and restless fool
Who answers Learning's siren call.

Alas, unheard, unheeded is my moan.
I live alone,
Like a mariner whom mutineers maroon
Upon a lush, uncharted isle.
Always, even in the night, while
Sleep delays its precious boon,
And ever in the brilliant day
He hears the murmurous hum of life,
Alien and near,
The noise of furred and feathered strife—
Grunts of lust, whimpers of fear,
Screams of things at bay.
But human accents never reach his ear—
Except his own unanswered prayer
Dying in the vacant air.[25]

Ewbank's "Deserted Lamb" surely deserves a place
in the long line of Arnoldian parodies and caricatures of the past one hundred years. Unlike so
many of the earlier efforts, this latter day "parody"
is sufficiently strong, especially in its finely "poetic"
ending, as to carry a quite authentically "Arnoldian" charge. Ewbank quite obviously hears the
deep and authentic "feeling" notes in Arnold and
skillfully echoes them in a piece in which the poet
he parodies comes off surprisingly well.

If any generalization might be attempted from
the examples cited in this section of our
"Charivari," it would probably be to note how
rarely the English parodists and satirists of the
1870s and 1880s treated any of Arnold's writing
from these decades. Nearly all of their references
are to either the poetry or the social criticism of the
1860s, as if Arnold had said little that was new
during the last two decades of his life. With few
exceptions, this was true of his treatment by the
British comic press; it was also true of responses to
that event in Arnold's life which prompted more
parody and satire than any other, his American tour
of 1883–84. We turn next, then, to Matthew Arnold, "A Critic (Very Much) Abroad."

THE CHARIVARI, AMERICAN STYLE

Like many other British literary prophets visiting
America, Arnold was saluted by the popular press
in a medley of commentary ranging from the quiet
appreciation of *Harper's Weekly* to the clamorous
hostility of *Judge*. In both 1883 and 1886[26] humorists
were quick to burlesque his phraseology and exag-
gerate his mannerisms; they pounced upon his *faux
pas*, parodied his lines out of context, and reacted
not so much to his actual assessments as to his supposed condemnation of all things American. In its
gentler guise the humorous record is one of persiflage and anecdote; in its more caustic form, one of
bitter satire. On the whole it probably reveals more
about American preconceptions than about the
"apostle of sweetness and light" himself, yet it was
broadly influential in structuring public opinion.

Many of the "Matthewarnoldisms" committed by
the distinguished visitor are apocryphal, as even
contemporary journals hastened to point out.[27]
Some tales, however, had a basis in fact: one such,
originally in the *Boston Transcript*,[28] received wide
circulation in Frank Leslie's *Illustrated Newspaper* on
26 January 1884 (p. 362). The anecdote, contained
in "a private letter from Dartmouth College,"
shows the cultivated Englishman at a loss when
faced with a genuine American "barbarian":

We heard Matthew Arnold here about a week ago. . . . A
curious little incident happened after the lecture. Professor Parker gave him a reception, and during a conversation Arnold was told that this college was founded for the
education of the Indian, and that there was one here at
present. Mr. Arnold expressed a desire to see him, as he
had never seen an Indian. So Eastman, who is a full
blooded Sioux, and a fine specimen of his race, was summoned. He came into the room cool, collected and master of the situation, whereas Mr. Arnold was completely
nonplussed. Whether his fancy had pictured a wild man,
fierce with war paint and tomahawk in hand, is not
known; but at all events he colored up like a boy, held
out his hand, and stammered out—his British egotism
coming up unawares—"Ah! eh! ah! you were there—you
were there. How did you like it?" (referring to his lecture.) It was an amusing sight to see the best representative of English culture so at a loss, and the young
educated Indian standing before him so calm, collected
and even stoical. I believe Arnold has, in some of his
writings, doubted whether the education of the Indian
was practicable.

Another letter, written by E. L. Godkin (the editor of the *New York Evening Post*) to exonerate Arnold from making an uncomplimentary remark about Boston, illustrates the kind of misunderstanding that proved fertile ground for myth. While dealing with a trivial matter—Arnold's geographic preferences—Godkin sounds one of the few conciliatory notes heard through the cacophony of popular protest over the Emerson lecture. On 8 January 1884 he wrote to the editor of the *New York Tribune* to protest a comment attributed to Arnold, that Boston is "a hill covered with granite boulders, with a bleak sea wind always howling among them—a condition of affairs not pleasing to his taste":

The shape in which this remark about Boston has reached you is an excellent illustration of the way in which things sometimes get twisted, in the process of circulation. In its original and correct shape it was made to me a few evenings ago in conversation. . . . What Mr. Arnold said was that the idea he had got out of Boston, from hearing the talk of Americans about it before he came to this country, was that it was on a hill, etc., etc., or rather, if I remember rightly, an "open plain," etc. The impression of the place, obtained from actually visiting it, was on the other hand, he said, very delightful. He thought the city and its suburbs both very beautiful, or in other words, found them a complete and most agreeable disappointment.

A not inconsiderable part of the American response to Arnold's visit was a proliferation of casual editorial comments and puns. Although generally insignificant in their own right, they nonetheless show that Arnold's mannerisms and ideas were familiar to the reading public. One such indirect response was the press's enthusiastic adoption of catchwords and its delight in taking Arnold's name in vain. *Puck*, for example, evokes the "affidavit of M__TTH__W ARN__LD" along with testimonies from other celebrities such as Adelina Patti and the office cat as part of an in-house advertisement touting the magazine's purported circulation of 138,500,000, "the largest in the United Universe":

Matthew Arnold, being duly sworn, deposes and says that he is a poet, essayist, philosopher, and an expert on "Numbers," and that he drove by the *Puck* office in a coupé the other day, and, from observations made at the time, he is quite prepared to verify any statement made by *Puck* with regard to the immensity of its circulation.

(21 November 1884, p. 181)

In addition, Arnold was included, almost as an afterthought, in *Life*'s serial Dantesque spoof, "Letters from Below." In the "Second Letter from Hell" the "author," Bulwer Lytton, reports:

I have been annoyed since my arrival here by the critics who still walk the earth. There's Matthew Arnold, for instance, of whom it is said that he brings "light" everywhere he goes (except Boston, where I understand even he only casts a shadow); he is expected here shortly. There has been a petition signed by all the churchmen in England, except Dean Stanley, requesting that Arnold have a whole gridiron to himself. I hear also that the "Remnant" have been delegated to turn the spit.

(5 February 1885, pp. 74–75)

Educated at Rugby and the author of the *Life and Correspondence of Dr. Arnold* (1844), Stanley would indeed have supported Arnold. A nicely ironic touch is consigning the members of the remnant to hell to roast their creator.

One of the most extensive permutations of Arnold's ideas is found in *Puck*'s 1885 "Unintellectual Life" series, a group of letters modeled after the works of the art critic Philip Gilbert Hamerton. Written by William James Henderson, who eventually became music critic for the *New York Sun* (1902–37), the letters are addressed to typical members of the middle class—"To a Philistine who Liked Steel-Engravings," "To a Philistine who Liked Dickens," "To a Philistine who Disliked Decorative Art," and "To a Philistine who Praised Beethoven"—and are fine examples of the Americanization of Arnold. Henderson's reiterated advice to study and to admit to liking "the best" even if one is in a minority is superficially Arnoldian, but his examples demonstrate his democratic dislike for classical touchstones. Belittling the Philistine for enjoying Dickens, Henderson says: "You like Dickens because you have been told to do so—because it is safe, and the quite eminently proper thing to do." He continues:

My dear boy, that is the very worst form of Philistinism. The man who says Homer is a better poet than Robert Browning, and who prefers Theocritus to Tennyson, does not usually say so because he thinks so. He does it because he has been convinced by rusted old college professors and by the general conventionality of a highly artificial condition of society that it is the proper thing to do. And he does it still more especially—if I may put it that way—because he has read Homer and Theocritus, and has not read Browning and Tennyson.

Henderson is, of course attacking cultural snobbery, but his quite legitimate objection becomes special pleading for contemporary artists:

Haven't you discovered that new stars are rising in the literary firmament? Are you going to read Smollett and Fielding and Sterne and Pope and Abraham Cowley and the rest of them during the remainder of your life, and let the sweet voices of Swinburne and Dobson and Stevenson and all the young singers of the new dawn float away from you forever? (28 October 1885, p. 132)

Beethoven is held up as the musical equivalent of Dickens. Henderson's point that Beethoven's flaws moved Schubert, Schumann, and others to successful musical experimentation has a degree of validity, but again his objection to aesthetic posturing, his prescription to "be independent enough and honest enough to admit that you don't care for classical music" seems, in Henderson's hands, to become not just a demand for a free play of the mind uninfluenced by social climbing, but an irresponsible desire to dispense with the past.

While such responses as Henderson's popularized "Arnoldian" attitudes, others dealt more directly with the Apostle's foibles. Even humorists on the other side of the Atlantic leaped at the opportunity of chaffing Arnold during his American tour. When he confessed to a reporter that he was homesick—"After all, I think there is no place to live in like dear, smoky old London" (*New York Tribune*, 23 October 1883)—*Punch* speculated on the anomaly of a proponent of "light" and "beauty" preferring darkness and soot, and chided "Mellifluous Matthew" for so free a play of mind that he romanticizes a London noted for its pea-soup fogs, inclement weather, mud, and suffocating smoke. What emerges from this versified gibe at Arnold's nostalgia is precisely the spirit of self-criticism he hoped to engender by his lectures: beginning as an attack on the prophet for not practicing what he preaches, the poem becomes a complaint about urban problems.

A Critic (Very Much) Abroad

Oh, Culture's apostle, your notions must jostle,
    Upset by that tossing Atlantic—Atlantic,
Or is it that travel cool reason can gravel,
    And finical judgments drive frantic—drive
    frantic?
To think—oh, good gracious!—that *you*,
    saponaceous

Belauder of Sweetness and Light, are so
    *un*done
As thus to go raising our danders by praising
    That Bogey-hole "smoky old London"—old
    London!

Dear MATTHEW, remember we're close on
    November,
    And fogs foul, pea-soupy, and sooty—and
    sooty,
Are gathering round us to choke and confound
    us,
    And rob us of comfort and beauty—and
    beauty.
And 'tis at this season you, friend of pure
    reason,
    To Yankee reporters go prating—go prating,
In terms eulogistic, but false and sophistic,
    Of London! Pray stick to your slating—your
    slating.

Mellifluous MATTHEW, when on the
    war-path you
    Are noted for slyness sardonic—sardonic;
But drollery cranky that "stuffs" the 'cute
    Yankee
    In this wise is quite *too* ironic—ironic.
What *will* you be saying, your consciousness
    playing,
    With freedom that distance
    enhances—enhances,
About the old City, in which—more's the pity,
    We linger as winter advances—advances.

Wilt chuckle its slime at, and gush of its
    climate,
    And chant its perfections of paving—of
    paving?
Or, laudably humble, sing paeans to Bumble,
    His prowess in sweeping and laving—and
    laving?
Wilt paint rosy pictures, unchequered by
    strictures,
    Of Mud-Salad Market in August—in
    August;
Or pour song's oblations to bleak railway
    stations,
    Saharas of dust cloud and raw gust—and raw
    gust?

Wilt say loving prank meant to *bless* the
    Embankment
    With smoke-reek that savours of Tophet—of
    Tophet?
Nor launch satire's bolt on sleek STIFF and
    shrewd DOULTON,
    The potters who turn stink to profit—to
    profit?

Wilt deem him a pessimist who Lambeth's
    messy mist,
      Streaming away o'er the river—the river,
Considers a scandal from which he'd command
    all
      The Bigwigs JOHN BULL to
      deliver—deliver?

Oh, come, now you're joking! It's really
    provoking
      To Cockneys half-choked and
      neuralgic—neuralgic.
Why should you talk rot so? Or if it is not so,
    You *must* be extremely nostalgic—nostalgic.
Discourser on "Dogma," a true London fog
    may
      To one who is home-sick, or
      sea-ditto—sea-ditto,
Seem almost pleasant; yet were you here
    present
      You'd vote it atrocious, and we ditto—we
      ditto.

It's just *aberglaube* you're diddled, I trow, by,
    But sage though you be you shan't fiddle
      us—fiddle us.
Not *you* plus COLERIDGE! A home-sick mole
    her ridge
      Might esteem worthy of
      Daedalus—Daedalus.
But we assure you one week here would cure
    you
      Of bosh about Fogdom's
      deserving—deserving;
You'd soon cut your lucky to Maine or
    Kentucky,
Or start to far 'Frisco with IRVING—with
    IRVING!

                    (3 November 1885, p. 206)

Both the *Boston Globe* and *Life* introduced Arnold
to their readers in an unflattering but comic light.
The *Globe* included him in its series of mock "telephonic interviews" in 1883; his rhetoric is unwieldy
and his supersubtle philosophy incapable of han-
dling the prosaic reality of railroad schedules and
fish balls. A sketch of a youthful-looking Arnold
holding a telephone receiver accompanies the "interview" (figure 109).

TELEPHONIC INTERVIEW WITH M. A.

M.A.—Hello, Globe office!
Globe—Hello!
M. A.—I desire to be interviewed.
Globe—Who is it?

M. A.—M. A. of England.
Globe—One moment, please, until I call the telephone
editor. Now, if you are ready.
M. A.—All ready.
Editor—Mr. A., how do you like this country?
M. A.—My dear sir, I'm not an opera singer.
Editor—I am well aware of that.
M. A.—That's the question you always ask them;
sometimes even before they leave their state-rooms.
Editor—But you have been here long enough to form
an opinion.
M. A.—So far as I have observed, Boston is the only
city worthy of the name.
Editor—Thanks, on behalf of its citizens. How did
you come to lecture?

Figure 109. "Telephone Interview with M. A.," Boston
Globe, *27 November 1883.*

M. A.—In a coupe.

Editor—Why did you choose the subject of "Numbers"?

M. A.—Did you hear my lecture?

Editor—No, but I have read it.

M. A.—I requested the press not to publish it, but of course they disregarded my entreaty. If you had reflected—

Editor—Beg your pardon, Mr. A., but will you please speak a little louder?

M. A.—As I was saying, one thing that struck me very forcibly as I passed through your principal thoroughfares was the numbers of street cars I saw waiting for passengers, particularly in the business portions of the city. Beg pardon?

Editor—I was only coughing.

M. A.—I thought you spoke.

Editor—The cars you saw were not waiting for passengers. It was a blockade.

M. A.—But I have seen it every day when in the city.

Editor—Very true. It is of daily occurrence.

M. A.—As I saw so few passengers in them, I thought they must have been waiting for a load, especially as I watched them for over an hour one day, and they made no visible progress. So I thought to myself, what numbers of strange people there must be in this city to give up their principal streets almost entirely to street-cars. If you had read my lecture understandingly you would have seen my ulterior object was to express my surprise at that very peculiarity.

Editor—It is very annoying to many of our business men. Could you suggest a remedy?

M. A.—It would take a long study of your local laws, but I might in time. I would suggest, however, meanwhile, that a circulating library be established, supported by the street car companies, to furnish reading material for the improvement of the time spent by the passengers during these blockades. Of course, there should be all of my works, and such others as John Stuart Mills' [sic] "Essays," Gibbon's "Roman Empire," Fox's "Martyrs," etc., as the mind would have plenty of time to digest the most ponderous platitudes of theological or political dogmatics during such sequestration. The doctrine of the remnant by which I meant to infer those endeavoring to cross the street at imminent danger of their lives and those obliged to walk, being in a hurry would be to idealize the fanaticism of preponderating cynics who object to widening your great thoroughfares at the risk of slicing a portion from that palladium of your liberties you call "The Common."

Editor—Your views are very lucid for a non-resident.

M. A.—I am surprised at the apathy of patriotism that allows the wheels of commerce and consequently of prosperity to be thus blocked.

Editor—You mentioned our Common. You have visited it, then?

M. A.—Oh yes; I have passed across it several times on my way to the Vendome, as well as your Public Garden.

Editor—What is your opinion of them?

M. A.—They are lovely spots in the centre of the city, surely, and in season, I should judge the gardens would be a most delightful resort. The beauty of the flower-bed designs struck me, particularly the large one in the centre crossed by a bridge. The ideas seemed very novel to me, both its being sunken instead of raised, as is usual, and its being crossed by a bridge from which to view its beauties. I think I shall recommend the plan for adoption in my own country on my return. It semed particularly rich ground in this bed, and I suppose only very choice plants are raised there. Beg pardon?

Editor—It is only my cough again. You have made a slight mistake. That is not a flower bed. It is, or rather was, a pond that has been undergoing a process of cleaning for some time.

M. A.—Oh! I thought it rather singular, don't you know?

Editor—What is your opinion of the products of this part of the country?

M. A.—I find your table amply supplied with all known delicacies. One of your culinary products in particular I admired greatly.

Editor—Pray, what was that?

M. A.—At an admirable breakfast in a private family one Sabbath morning, a charming dish of baked beans was my especial favorite, accompanied by a certain kind of bread I had never before chanced to find on my travels. These, together with a peculiar combination of marine and vegetable products, by some means unknown to me prepared in shape not unlike billiard balls, but of a beautiful shade of seal brown on the outside, constituted our breakfast. My modesty prevented my inquiring the appellation by which they were designated, but I have since since [sic] learned their vulgar cognomen to be simply fish balls. I am really surprised that such a pleasing edible should not be honored by being more aesthetically denominated. I presume, however, my host, having discovered the peculiar appropriateness of the combination of the two principal viands of our breakfast, desired to keep the gratifying secret in his own family.

Editor—Why, sir, the dishes you mention form the staple Sabbath breakfast of at least four-fifths of the population of New England.

M. A.—You surprise me greatly! Your people, then, must be far more advanced in practical aesthetics than I had imagined, for surely a more practical and yet thoroughly poetic coalition of ingredients for a delightful breakfast was never concocted.

Editor—Have you visited any of our theatres yet?

M. A.—My time has been so occupied with social duties outside of my lecturing hours that I have had time to visit but one. A young friend of mine at Harvard

College took me the other evening to a theatre, or rather "Museum" he called it. But I could not see any collection of curiosities there, as one would expect in a Museum, if we except the performers, some of whom were curiosities indeed. I suppose it is one of your local peculiarities in calling it a Museum.

Editor—Did you not see the large hall of curiosities?

M. A.—No; it was a small theatre up stairs. I saw no large hall. The audience seemed to me to be of rather a different type from those I have seen at my lectures, although my Harvard friend said it was patronized largely by the students. I think he called it "The Boylston," or some similar name. Beg pardon, did I hear you laugh?

Editor—Oh, no! It was my cough. I have a slight cold.

M. A.—I notice a great deal of coughing in my audience here. Every other person seems to be suffering from chronic cold.

Editor—How do you like our audiences in Boston?

M. A.—Very much, indeed. It struck me as rather singular, though, that so large a proportion should be from out of the city.

Editor—How did you know they were?

M. A.—By so many leaving as the close of the lecture approached. I understand it is the same at all public places of amusement in Boston. Can't your railroads change their times of leaving to a little later? It's very annoying, don't you know, for so many to leave to catch their trains.

Editor—It is annoying indeed, and very impolite.

M. A.—I had always heard Boston mentioned as the centre of culture, and I am surprised to find such evidence of impoliteness.

Editor—Is it true, Mr. A., that you are the author of "The Bread-Winners?"

M. A.—Professional secrets, sir, I never divulge.

Editor—Do you know who the author is?

M. A.—If I were called upon for my shrewdest guess, I should reply it was by the author of "Beautiful Snow."

Editor—I see you are discreet. Have you written any new poems lately.

M. A.—I have. If you wish and can spare the time I will read you my latest.

Editor—I shall be delighted to hear it. May I publish it?

M. A.—In proof of the pleasant regard I have for *The Globe* and its many readers you shall not only be the first to hear, but the exclusive publisher of my latest. Listen. I call it

UNKNOWN

Among the crowds that throng the street
Is one I almost daily meet,
 Whose pleasant face

And charming grace
It always gives me joy to greet.

Unknown to me her name and rank,
And yet—one smile so sweet and frank
 As her's would be,
 If 'twas for me,
Would any other smile out-rank.

In vain I ask among my friends,
Distance alone enchantment lends.
 None seem to care,
 Or know the fair
That fate across my pathway sends.

So fair and bright she seems to be—
Like summer blossoms on a tree,
 Content I'd live
 If she would give
Her friendship only unto me.

(27 November 1883, p. 2)

Arnold's "discreetness" in attributing "Bread-Winners" to the author of "Beautiful Snow" and implying that he is that author involves him in a controversy of the day: "Bread-Winners" is a short story that was published anonymously in the *Century*, and "Beautiful Snow" a poem by John Whittaker Watson published by the *Chicago Tribune* under another contributor's name. The saccharine verse that Arnold claims at the end of the "interview" may in fact itself be borrowed from a popular writer as yet unidentified.

Life, in "Triplicate Philosophy" published on 20 December 1883 (pp. 314–15),[29] supposes that Arnold in fact never left his library, but instead hired three "sad-eyed and intellectual men of lean habit" to deliver his lectures (figures 110, 111, and 112). The satire is pointed directly at Arnold's need for money, a theme that aroused considerable antagonism in the American press, partly because his indictment of the "Hebraistic" equation between salvation and economic success could not be reconciled with his own apparent money-grubbing. R. Kemble, the London correspondent for *Harper's Weekly*, was one of the few to view the unremunerative nature of Arnold's position as philosopher-at-large sympathetically; about the £250 pension that Gladstone offered Arnold, he writes, "it is hardly likely that a man of his character would have applied for the grant unless he stood in need of it. . . . For my part, I only regret that a man who has written so much, and on the whole so well, should stand in need of any subsidy of the kind" (6 October

Figure 110. "Triplicate Philosophy" series from Life, *20 December 1883.*

Figure 111. "Triplicate Philosophy" series from Life, *20 December 1883.*

Figure 112. "Triplicate Philosophy" series from Life, *20 December 1883.*

1883, p. 631). In general, however, *Life*'s picture of a slyboots entrepreneur hiring three impersonators at £4 a week to fulfill speaking engagements in the United States, Australia, and India, and then enjoying his spoils—"the gold of three continents heaped upon his library table"—seemed to satisfy public expectation.

Life also indirectly attacks Arnold for a supercilious manner and for failing to prepare his lectures thoughtfully. He is portrayed with "a cold smile [which] played over his lips" as he decides to dupe the Yankees; when he addresses his impersonators, he says, "since you strikingly resemble me, I may safely call you gentlemen." Even worse, he is made to confess his own ignorance:

I have prepared three lectures, which I wrote when I was an undergraduate; the first being upon a subject of which I know very little and the world knows nothing; the second on a subject of which the world knows very little and I know nothing; and the third is upon a subject of which neither I, nor the world know anything whatever.

Far from being jejune productions, the lectures were, of course, products of mature experiences:

"Literature and Science" was delivered as a Rede lecture at Oxford on 14 June 1882 and then revised for American consumption; "Numbers" was an elaboration of an idea that appeared in the 25 March 1876 review of Adolphus Ward's translation of Curtius; and "Emerson," written during the tour, was in final proof form less than two weeks before its first presentation on 1 December 1883.[30]

Although Arnold had given all three lectures at least once by the time "Triplicate Philosophy" was published, only "Numbers" and "Emerson" are dealt with directly. One impersonator delivers a talk on "Lubricity" in Sidney, Australia; his attention to his "printed notes" is characteristic of the portrait sketched by a *New York Herald* reporter, who while stressing Arnold's deliberateness of address in the first "Numbers" lecture, nonetheless describes him as holding "his manuscript in his left hand, nearly level with his face" and speaking "extemporaneously" only a few times.[31] In addition, *Life's* parodic newspaper, the *Sydney Boomerang*, reports, "We are requested not to publish the lecture; and cheerfully refrain from doing so." The *New York Tribune* was, in fact, asked by its London correspondent, George W. Smalley, not to publish the lecture so that Arnold's next reading would not be preempted; to Smalley's chagrin, a summary did indeed appear.[32] A second impersonator purportedly goes to Calcutta, where, according to the nonexistent *Calcutta Times*, he delivers a talk "full of brilliant ideas" but "so obscure, that we cannot but think the leaves had not been numbered and that the lecture had been shuffled wrong." Aside from what may be a sly allusion to "Numbers," the passage contains no identifiable reference to any other lecture. It does, however, suggest that Arnold "lunches upon a glass of whiskey and a cigar," perhaps a gibe at his cosmopolitanism.

The third impersonator is sent to Boston, the "Modern Athens," where he astonishes his "cultivated and refined audience" by his appearance in "pink tights and a single eye-glass" quite as much as Arnold is popularly supposed to have horrified the Boston grandees by his refusal to accord greatness to Emerson. As the *Boston Herald* reports, the impersonator gives an "inferior exhibition" of "Sleight of Hand or Spiritualism Unmasked," a turn of phrase that may suggest that Arnold "unmasked" Transcendentalism. The section ends by implying that Arnold's sharp criticism is tantamount to "eating glass and swallowing swords." Portraying the impersonator as a mountebank may be an oblique reference not only to D'Oyly Carte's sponsorship of the tour but to Barnum's rumored support as well;[33] moreover, since Arnold in "Numbers" notes that the Athenian state fell because the saving remnant was too small, *Life's* sobriquet for Boston—the "Modern Athens"—is hardly the praise it seems to be: it is, rather, of a piece with the New York magazine's constant sniping at what it considered to be Boston's intellectual snobbery.

Four months later *Life* again attacked Arnold for trading his genius for cash; he is revealed not only as a circus curiosity, a kind of human Jumbo, but also as a posturing "intellectual giant" who attacked Emerson unjustifiably.

Pater's Divine Dialogue
INTERLOCUTORS—PROFESSOR AND DAUGHTER (18).

D.—Is not Mr. Arnold a great teacher and leader in thought?

PROF.—Yes! He assumes to be—or it is assumed for him—that he is a modern Moses in literature, leading his people out of the bondage of ignorance into a land of culture. He is especially the apostle of sweetness and light.

D.—Why did he come to America?

PROF.—Probably to make money!

D.—Then the curse of the money-getting spirit fell on him too?

PROF.—It would seem so.

D.—Does he want to found a chair of sweetness and light—or perhaps a college?

PROF.—Not exactly, my dear! He wants to pay off the debts made by his son, who has been sowing a crop of uncivilized oats—at the university.

D. (pauses)—Oh, I see. Was he invited to come, just as Dr. Waldstein was to deliver his lectures on Greek Art, by some professors and literary men who wanted to know more about sweetness and light?

PROF.—No! A popular manager of English Opera Bouffe brought him out.

D.—And placarded him all around like a circus clown?

PROF.—Well—yes!—No!—Perhaps!—Not exactly! But something in that line, only in a more refined and gentlemanly way.

D.—Then people went to see him as they do Jumbo, who is also large and English? out of curiosity, did they?

PROF.—Oh, no! They went to hear him lecture!

D.—Ah! I see. He told them all about his theories of life, and his beautiful thoughts of sweetness and light, and gave them a grand new doctrine and noble ideas. He availed himself of this opportunity to unfold the rich treasures of his intellect, and he made it the occasion of teaching this great and growing young nation his lovely new philosophy, and, true to his principles, he has left behind him a glorious inheritance of thought for them to ponder over and enrich their lives with. He told them how to study and what to study. He pointed out a shining new path, where it would be ecstacy to tread. Oh! I see it. I see it all. How superbly proud and happy an intellectual giant must feel to give of his strength to the world, and to know that at every turn he has left behind him rays of sunshine. How I yearn to do that! And all this he did, papa, did he not?

PROF. (hesitating)—Well, hardly.

D.—What did he tell them, then? Certainly very much. Perchance more and better things than my poor wits can suggest.

PROF.—Well, he delivered for the most part one lecture on Mr. Emerson, the gist of which was to say that he ought not to be placed on a very high pedestal.

D. (with vigor)—Oh, impossible! For shame! And he preached about *nothing else?*

PROF.—No! I might justly say, nothing else!

D.—But, papa, does not that derogate immensely from his name as a great thinker and leader in thought?

PROF.—Perhaps it does.

D.—And will he not lose all prestige as a man of letters after he has been willing to lower himself, just for a few paltry dollars to the level of a Punch and Judy show?

PROF.—I do not know that we have all looked at it in that light, my dear.

D.—Then his American tour was a total and disastrous failure?

PROF.—Intellectually and morally speaking, I suppose we must admit that it was, but financially it was a success.

D.—Well, for my part I would rather play five-finger exercises before 5,000 people and play them well, than to be a man of such calibre, and present such a spectacle to the world, and I am going now to the library to turn all his books with their backs in, and I am going to pin a paper over them in the shape of a headstone, and write on it, "Sacred to the memory of £s. and d., one who was killed by the curse of the money-getting spirit." (24 April 1884, p. 228)

Probably *Life's* best expression of paranoia in this respect is Oliver Herford's 1886 cartoon, "The Modern Argonauts with Their Golden 'Fleece'" (figure 113); Arnold, portrayed with a bilious, distrustful mien, has a prominent place. In clockwise order, beginning with Arnold, the figures in the ship seem to be Canon Frederic William Farrar, Oscar Wilde, Henry Irving, W. S. Gilbert, and Lily Langtry. The figure lurking between Wilde and Irving is too indistinct to recognize, but the top

Figure 113. "Modern Argonauts," dedicated to W. S. Gilbert and others who "Have been pillaged right and left" by Americans. Life, *11 March 1886.*

hat and monocle may identify him as a generic British tourist like Sir Lepel Griffin; the "argonaut" leaning over the gunwale has not yet been identified. The cartoon appeared with the following commentary:

The more we think of it the more we pity those poor pillaged Britishers, so feelingly alluded to by Mr. W. S. Gilbert.

There was the poverty-stricken Oscar Wilde, who came over with a few other emigrants shortly after Messrs. Gilbert and Sullivan had saturated us with musical advertisement of his peculiarities. Mr. Wilde came here with nothing but his clothes and hair. Of these the American pirate robbed him even to the last vestige of his pauperism. So thoroughly stripped of all he had was he that in self-defense he went home and got married, so that he should have some visible means of support and keep him from vagrancy.

Then there was Henry Irving, absolutely pelted out of the land with seventy-nine cent dollars.

Canon Farrar, too, went home loaded to the muzzle with depreciated American currency, which the pickpocket American public left in his trousers by mistake.

Mrs. Langtry came among us, confiding her sweet presence to our care, and actually left a hundred thousand dollars' worth of mortgages on New York real estate. Poor pillaged thing!

Matthew Arnold lost several carloads of sweetness and light to these American bandits without receiving any more than some fifty thousand dollars.

As for Gilbert & Sullivan, whose operas have carried desolation into so many homes, they are the worst sufferers of all. It is said that Mr. Gilbert never received a penny from the elevated railroad patent, while Sullivan's request for a share of the Madison Square Garden receipts have [sic] always been treated with silent contempt. (11 March 1886, p. 145)

Like *Life*, *Judge* maintained that Arnold was a foreign profiteer taking advantage of a gullible public;[34] also like *Life*, *Judge* offered commentary on specific lectures. One poem, expressing disappointment in "Numbers," contains a modicum of self-criticism:

To Mr. Matthew Arnold:
Upon Hearing his First Lecture in the U. S.,
"Cherish That Remnant"

Yes, it was orthodox, the proper thing,
After your exodus from the land of bondage,
To give no "Numbers"—though poor
    Chickering,
Is scarce deemed Canaan, even in this fond age,
The tendency of which is in a fine way
To mix the muse and beer in such *a Stein way*,
That you may change your views on our
    economy,
Before you're well advanced in Deuteronomy.

Surely more seemly it would be, should you
Assume the name, as well as *role*, of Moses,
And quote the ten commandments in Hebrew,
To aid your hearers in the diagnosis.
But advertise no "remnants," nor compare
Our too provincial "States" to Chatham
    Square;
For though we know full well we're crudely
    pious,
Our minds and noses are not all cut bias.

So warmly have we felt your agile pen
Infuse its force throughout our social statics,
A vague regret crept o'er our pleasure, when
We saw our Matthew, and heard mathematics.
Meanwhile, our palates, palled by such light
    lunches,
Await a finer zest in your Hub punches—
Your kindly heart will find, here naught of
    treason,
So prithee, spare our rhyme, nor spurn our
    reason.

(22 December 1883, p. 10)

The poem elaborates on Arnold's implied conceit: he is a Moses, traveling out of an English Egypt to an American promised land, delivering as he goes a lecture-circuit Deuteronomy about the duties of the remnant. He is, moreover, viewed as unexpectedly optimistic. Having criticized the American social order so vigorously (presumably in the earlier "A Word About America"), he is taken to task for providing a "light lunch" of mathematics, raising hopes of an American remnant, for example, instead of dashing them. While the author looks forward to a more toothsome experience in the Hub (a nickname for Boston, where Arnold's Emerson lecture certainly evoked a spirited response), he himself assumes the burden of criticizing the age, not only by punning on the rhetorical confusion between drinking beer and playing the piano in the phrase *Stein way* but by suggesting that Americans are so hebraised that Arnold must use a special language (ll. 11–12). Nevertheless, he defends his compatriots, albeit anti-Semitically (l. 16), against the accusation of too rigid an adherence to duty and closes by assuring Arnold that an appeal to reason would indeed be successful.

Like *Judge*, *Punch* celebrated Arnold's first lecture in rhyme, similarly ascribing a prophetlike stance to the Apostle:

Matthew Arnold on "Numbers"*

[The lecturer dwelt on the errors of majorities, especially in morals and politics.]

Nothing so good as a merry minority,
    Very few people are sure to be right;
Down with the power of the tyrant majority,
    Wanting in sweetness and lacking in light:
This is the creed, in that far Western land,
ARNOLD has preached, and they won't
    understand.

Though you belong to a feeble minority,
  You can look up and be bold with the best,
Nor should a feeling of inferiority
  Ever arise in your militant breast;
Take up an ARNOLD'S ineffable song,
Truly the multitude's sure to be wrong.

Who shall be sure that he's in this minority,
  So that he's truly among the elect.
Let him dissent from all men in authority,
  Scoffing at everything others respect:
That's how the ethical trick can be done—
MATTHEW'S minority's just Number One!

*Mr. MATTHEW ARNOLD'S first lecture was listened to, in conse-
quence of the Poet's ineffective delivery (according to the report), with
the greatest attention; and he was occasionally asked to "Speak up!" He
began by lecturing on "Numbers;" but, if he goes on like this, will he
end by lecturing *to* Numbers? Some are asking if he is going through
the entire Pentateuch.

(10 November 1883, p. 221)

While *Judge*'s author implies that he is part of the
saving or saved remnant by allowing a free play of
his critical faculty over the American scene, *Punch*
is bound by no such personal chauvinism; in an
even freer play of mind—or humor—it ridicules the
"merry minority" itself as feeble, inferior, and militant, and elevates the multitude into the guardian of
taste (ll. 15–16); its attack on elitism, though
tongue-in-cheek, is the selfsame democratic stand
one might expect from an American periodical. A
comment similar to *Punch*'s footnote about Arnold's
unpopularity was reprinted in *Judge* (23 January
1884, p. 7) from the Boston *Transcript:* "Matthew
Arnold had but 150 listeners to his lecture in Balti-
more. It is not strange that Mr. Arnold should say
that the majority is usually in the wrong, when it is
the majority that neglects to buy tickets to his lectures."

Other humorous, direct attacks appeared. One of
the most successful is Francis Attwood's "Souvenir
for Mr. Arnold" (*Life*, 31 January 1884, p. 61)
(figure 114), which depicts the progress of an un-
mistakably large-headed and supercilious Arnold
on his lecture circuit. As a "Missionary," the Apostle arrives on the shores of America with a large roll
of lectures prominent among his bundles and a
palm frond in his hand; the trees in the background
bear coconuts embellished with dollar signs. Attwood's amusing drawing of the worshipful delega-
tion of American barbarians dressed in frock coats
and adorned with feathers makes use of the same
cultural pun—this time visually—that occurred to
the observer of Arnold and the Indian at Dart-

Figure 114. Life's "*Souvenir For Mr. Arnold,*" 31 January 1884.

mouth. Again, Arnold figures as the sun, cheer-
lessly shedding sweetness and light, and as "The
Mountain in Labor" (which proverbially brings
forth a mouse), exhibiting the same nearsighted attention to his notes that newspaper reporters generally complained of. When Attwood records Arnold's Boston experience, however, he relies for
humor on the contrast between the exaggeratedly
disdainful expression on Arnold's face and the be-
nevolent smile on Emerson's. Arnold significantly
has his back to Emerson and Hawthorne, both se-
curely ensconced on their pedestals; he operates a
"patent" telescope that offers a reduced rather than
a magnified image because the lens is serving as an
eyepiece.

While the Hub is subtly chided for idolizing its
sages, Washington is taken to task for its bad manners; Attwood's drawing refers in part to the
aftermath of Arnold's 17 December presentation of
"Literature and Science," when William Chandler,
then secretary of the Navy, turned the gathering
into a political brouhaha by inviting his friends in

141

the audience to respond to Arnold's remarks. The historian George Bancroft, with whom Arnold dined, is fifth from the right, and while the enthusiastic handshaker (third from the right) might logically represent Frederick Douglass, who astonished Arnold by moving a vote of thanks for the lecture, he bears a passing resemblance to Edward Everett Hale, who spoke at Chandler's request. The rotund, disapproving figure standing third from the left has the side-whiskers affected by Chester Arthur, who entertained the Arnolds on 25 December.[35]

Later, *Life* speculates about Arnold's own evaluation, comparing his published and unpublished "impressions":

From Matthew Arnold's Aftermath

With an uncanny and almost regretful hesitation I plucked up my courage to explore the wilds of America and to mix with the uncultured throngs that bid fair to drown the sweetness and light of letters with the hum and grime of new and tirelessly busy factories.

* * * * *

I thank the Giver of Light for America! The keen appreciation of its in-dwellers for all that is broad and fine, the calm reflection over adverse criticism, the majestic breadth and generosity even of their Philistinism, and their graceful habit of ascribing to me all that any Arnold ever wrote, are traits enough to challenge even an Englishman's respect and love.

From "The Private Diary and Business Correspondence of the lamented Matthew Arnold"

Mr. D'Oyle Carte has guaranteed me a round sum for a lecturing tour in America. I do not feel quite satisfied with his financial responsibility, but he is certainly good for all expenses, at least, so I shall have a free excursion—shall advertise my books, and peep at the ultra-marine, double-dyed Philistines.

* * * * *

The Rubicon is passed. Our expenses were light. I spent 112 days in America, and was invited to 197 dinners and receptions. Accepted 148 and live to tell the tale. I met but one Englishman—alas! his mal addresse—and he was a tallow-Chandler. Deposited in bank £4008 17s 4d as the net profits of the trip. (17 April 1884, p. 214)

While *Life* suggests that the Apostle's fine phrases mask a commercial spirit, the satire is nonetheless good-humored; the *New York Tribune*, however, presents Arnold as an irreclaimable pessimist. Making use of the public expectation that Arnold would publish his disapproval of American customs with undue haste, the *Tribune* printed parodies that purported to represent Arnold's coldly disdainful evaluation of American philistinism. "Matthew Arnold: His Marked Disapproval of the Solar System and Things (An Unverified Interview)" features a highly respectful reporter interviewing an Arnold whose unbounded cynicism is impossible to reconcile with any view of the philosopher as a touchstone in the "pursuit of perfection":

The fact that Mr. Matthew Arnold lately furnished "The Nineteenth Century" with his candid—but by no means candied—opinion of America might well have prompted some enterprising reporter to find out how the rest of creation appeared as seen through the same double convex pessimistic lenses. But although this is so we feel in duty bound to add that the interview that follows, conceding that it is stamped with truth, had not been verified when we went to press.

Reporter—Mr. Arnold, would you mind telling me how the sun strikes you?

Arnold—I distinctly disapprove of the sun. Its admirers are constantly obtruding the fact that it is the centre of the solar system. The trouble with such people is that they glorify the average sort of centre. I never do, I keep my enthusiasm for the really superior. The sun is by no means a satisfactory planet. Either it underheats or it prostrates with what the French—I distinctly disapprove of what the French—call a coup de soleil. Besides, the sun does not appeal to the lovers of the beautiful. There are unaesthetic spots on its face. So while I commend the sun for abstaining from placing esq. after its name I distinctly disapprove of it.

Reporter—And the Moon, Mr. Arnold?

Arnold—I distinctly disapprove of the Moon. I never could endure a plagiarist, and Luna, as you are aware, shines by a reflected light. Moonshine is simply a feeble dilution of sunshine. I have no patience with those that glorify dilutions. Moonshine is responsible for many a sentimental, ill-considered marriage, for quantities of silly verse, for dog-baying and cognate nonsense. The ancient assertion that the moon is made out of green cheese, while possibly incorrect, regarded as a specific statement of its essence, certainly goes to prove that Luna's origin was low. However, to her praise be it said that she never tacks Esquires to her name.

Reporter—And the Stars, Mr. Arnold?

Arnold—I distinctly disapprove of the Stars. They arrogate to themselves the title of "the heavenly bodies." Why heavenly, forsooth? A true conception of heaven is that of a state of sublimated being rather than a high material place. Heavenly is what heavenly does. An able apostle of sweetness and light—I will not mention names—is my idea of a heavenly body. Some of these so-called heavenly bodies are fixed, some of them shoot, some of them affect long tails. But to be eternally fixed like an ultra-conservative, or to wildly shoot, or aimlessly to swing a long tail is not to perform a celestial function.

Reporter—And the New Jerusalem, Mr. Arnold?

Arnold—I distinctly disapprove of the New Jerusalem. It is given out that its streets are of gold and its gates of pearl. Such things are repugnant to my ideas of true urban simplicity. I will not countenance the ornate in building material. A well-laid pavement of granite blocks and gates of iron—rendered secure against rust by the patent McComber process—are more to my taste. Furthermore I dislike the name "New" Jerusalem. I have a prejudice against the new. One reason why I decline to condone the United States is because its civilization is so new. Leave me old Greece and old Rome and let who will be satisfied with your New-Jerusalem and your New-York.

Reporter—If I may further trespass on your kindness, Mr. Arnold, will you please give me your candid opinion of the Four Seasons?

Arnold—I distinctly disapprove of the Four Seasons. Spring is damp and fickle, Summer is hot and dusty, Autumn depresses with its tokens of decay, Winter completes the desolation. The quartette is a failure.

Reporter—What about Day and Night, Mr. Arnold?

Arnold—I distinctly disapprove of both. Day is a trifle too garish, too deficient in repose, to commend itself to the artistic eye. Then again it lays bare much that were better hidden. Night, on the other hand, although not garish, is so dark as to furnish opportunity for burglars and chicken-thieves, and processions that carry malodorous torches. By day I long for night, by night I long for day; when high noon strikes I project my aspirations forward to the twilight.

Reporter—What is your attitude towards the North and South Poles and the Equator?

Arnold—I distinctly disapprove of all three. They are imaginary without being imaginative. If, like myself, they were imaginative without being imaginary I doubtless would think better of them. Poles and Equators, like civilization, must be regarded as failures unless they are interesting. The South Pole certainly is not interesting, it has never inspired any great deed. My writings can be searched in vain for a series of sonnets dedicated "To the South Pole." The same thing is true of the Equator. As for the North Pole, it not only is uninteresting, it is a positive nuisance, since it is responsible for costly expeditions, whose end is vanity frappe—vanity as chilly as some of the audiences that attended my lectures in America.

Reporter—Mr. Arnold, which, pray, do you prefer, the three-quarters of the earth's surface composed of Wa-

ter, or the remaining quarter composed of Land?

Arnold—I distinctly disapprove of both. Water and Land. The three-quarters are responsible for a dire and incurable affliction known as seasickness and the other quarter is cursed by earthquakes. The ocean is treacherous and wet. The Land being of dirt is dirty and it is inadequately supplied with caves that can be utilized as cyclone cellars. I can tolerate the Water only when I am on the Land. And when I am being tossed on the billows, then only I find joy in contemplating real estate.

Reporter—Do you indorse either Time or Eternity, Mr. Arnold?

Arnold—I distinctly disapprove of both Time and Eternity. Time, as an American poet, Longshanks or some such name, has remarked (I distinctly disapprove of Lonshanks) Time is fleeting. And, obviously that which in its nature is fleeting is not to be taken seriously by a man of exacting stamp. Eternity, on the other hand, has the glaring defect of the average epic poem—it is too long.

Reporter—Mr. Arnold, in a word, what is your candid opinion of the Heavens above, the Earth beneath, the Waters under the Earth, inclusive of their varied contents?

Arnold—The question is rather an ample one. And while not attempting to answer it in detail I may say that I have not distinctly disapproved of the proposition that whatever is is wrong. (8 April 1884, p. 12)

A second, more widely publicized parody appeared in the *New York Tribune* on 6 April 1884 (p. 4) and was immediately pirated by the *Chicago Tribune* as a factual report. "Mr. Arnold in Chicago: His Observations of Society, A Solid Basis of Philistinism—A Varnish of Culture" represented Arnold not as he was but as the American press had stereotyped him: tactless, chauvinistically British, and above all, eager to belittle American achievements. The parodic Arnold excoriates Chicagoans for pretending to be cultured:

This affectation of concern for the things of the spirit, which may very easily be seen to be nothing more than an affectation, is chiefly observed in its aesthetic aspect. Of ethical culture there is hardly any pretence. . . . it would be safe to say that the condition of trade in tinned meats, or in port or in grain, has the largest share of their thoughts even during the hour of ostensible devotion.

He laughs at them, moreover, for confusing Herbert Spencer and Hibbard Spencer, a merchant in the "iron business," and for attributing to him Thomas Hughes's *Tom Brown at Rugby* (a composite title adapted from *Tom Brown's Schooldays* and *Tom*

Brown at Oxford) and Edwin Arnold's *Light of Asia*. He takes their unfamiliarity with "Obermann" as a gauge of their lack of culture:

I gave myself the pains to ask a large number of the apparently cultivated people with whom I came in contact whether they had read "Obermann." As the result of these inquiries I must state the melancholy fact that to all but one of those questioned, the name was wholly unfamiliar, and this one understood me as referring to a gentleman of that name who is the proprietor of a chemist's shop in Chicago. I do not know of any other little thing connected with my stay in America which gave me such a sense of the crudeness of American culture. What another alchemy was that of the author of "Obermann," than the art practised by the Chicago chemist in his daily dispensations!

Finally, he concludes that "a society that has lived in the flesh, so to speak, for so long, cannot at once and naturally come to live in the spirit. . . . Nor, I fear, will the sweetness and the light of cultured life come to Chicago at the beck of the rich man."

The spurious article caused a furor, which the *Chicago Tribune* encouraged by inviting comments from leading citizens. The *New York Tribune* reprinted the parody a week later along with a selection of editorial responses from other newspapers under the general heading, "The Agony that Followed": the responses carried such headlines as "Still Another Wicked Author," "Did They Nourish a Viper?", "A Shedder of Nitric Acid and Chinese Musk," "A Podsnappian Crusher," and "He Should Visit Oshkosh." Apparently the claim that the *New York Tribune* published the fraudulent article in an attempt to expose the *Chicago Tribune*'s unethical newsgathering practices is itself a myth. While Arnold himself denied authorship, the damage to his American reputation was undeniable; as Super notes, "there was some disposition, even in Chicago, to believe that this was what Arnold would have said if he had written about their city."[36]

Apparently the one comment that particularly rankled was that which arraigned Chicagoans for their philistinism because they did not recognized "Obermann." *Puck*'s response to the affair was to claim that "Obermann" was a blundering typesetter:

THE QUESTION of the day seems to be: Who is Obermann? Obermann we take great pleasure in stating, was a typesetter on a comic paper which has been dead some years. Obermann was noted for his knowledge of metaphysics and his rare skill in making blunders which perverted the author's meaning. One day Matthew Arnold walked in with a poem on "Spring in England." It was full of tender allusions to hop-vines, vetches, mavises, merles, pimpernels, etc. He had a pretty picture of the Lady Alice feeding the swans and guinea-pigs out on the mall of Lord Walter's spacious demesne. Obermann secured the copy and succeeded in making the Lady Alice feed the swans and "gunnybags." Then Matthew came in and waxed wroth, and girded up his loins to thrash Obermann, who remained in a beer saloon until Matthew left. Then the poet wrote him up, and sarcastically called him a German metaphysician. Obermann has murdered our copy, too, and made us writhe with agony; but we never called him a German metaphysician. We simply said we wanted to speak to him. And when he left the office a sadder and a sorer man, it was difficult to say which he needed most, a new shirt or a new set of features. (28 May 1884, p. 195)

To be sure, the humor is heavy-handed; yet the treatment of Arnold as one who is a victim of a careless perversion of meaning conveys little impression that the hoax accurately reflected if not the letter then the spirit of his remarks. *Life*'s comment is even briefer: "Mr. Arnold may have entranced Boston, but the delirious whirlwind of enthusiasm he has awakened in Chicago must ever be one of his most delightful recollections" (24 April 1884, p. 226).

Once Arnold did publish his own evaluation of the United States in 1888, the popular press stood condemned of adding to the unsolved "human problem" and the country as a whole of lacking the distinction conferred by "elevation" and "beauty." That his essay "Life in America" was immediately pirated by a Boston firm[37] adds witness to Arnold's testimony as does *Puck*'s complaint (published on 18 April 1888 without mention of Arnold's death three days before) that he is an "ill-bred foreigner who tells us that we must be vulgar because some of our towns have vulgar names." The original remark is, of course, unfortunate, but one poetaster found a good-humored way to answer it:

An Arnoldian Ode

Of Briggsville and Jacksonville
    I care not now to sing.
They make me sad and very mad,
    My inmost soul they wring.
I'll hie me back to England,

144

And straightway I will go
To Boxford and to Swaffham,
To Plungar and Loose Hoe.

At Scrooby and at Gonerby,
At Wigton and at Smeeth,
At Bottesford and Rumcorn
I need not grit my teeth.
At Swineshead and at Crummock,
At Sibsey and Spit Head,
Stoke Pogis and Wolsoken
I will not wish me dead.

At Wissey and at Kegworth,
At Cockshut and Winkfield,
At Chorley and at Horley,
I'll wander far afield,
And think me not of Briggsville,
At Pinchbeck when I am
At Cobham, and at Chobham [*sic*]
I will not care a d——n.

At Horbling and at Skidby,
At Chipping Ongar, too,
At Botterel Stotterdon and Swops,
At Skellington and Skew,
At Piddleton and Blumsdown,
At Shanklin and at Smart,
At Gosberton and Wrangle
I'll soothe this aching heart.

At Cockerton and Lytchet,
At Harbottle and Slurk,
At Charley and at Horley
I'll sit me down and smirk;
At Dorking and at Smarden,
At Leighton Bussard I
Will soon forget those Yankees
And their low vulgaritie.

Then to Askrigg and Wivelsfield,
To Diddlebury, O!
To Petherton and Cowfold,
And to Foulness I will go.
So, ho for merry England,
Its 'am and mutton pies,
Its ale and swipes, the which are types
At which no gorge doth rise.
(*New York Times*, 11 April 1888, p. 5)

The American charivari, as polyphonic as the British version, made Arnold dance to many a comic tune. While some of the parody published at his expense is vicious, much of it is either good-natured sparring or an excuse for discussing domestic concerns, such as the danger that "anglomania" presented to national identity. Disappointment that

Arnold should need to "sell" his talents is a recurrent note; irritation at his critical judgments, however, is usually coupled with admiration for his honesty. On the whole, the parodic response to his visit probably reveals more about American philistinism than about Arnold himself, but that he was adopted at all by the press as a comic touchstone shows the extent of his popularity. Even William Robbins in *The Ethical Idealism of Matthew Arnold* could not resist a touch of verbal caricature in a memorable description that seems appropriate here:

Figure 115. St. Nicholas *magazine, in its December 1930 Calendar, featured numerous literary figures born during the month, including Matthew Arnold, born on Christmas Eve 1822.*

Figure 116. As late as 1946, Max Beerbohm continued to play pencil games by making "incomplete copies" of photographs of famous faces. His "amended view" of a whiskerless Arnold provided readers of The Listener *of 19 September 1946 with a more "actual image" of Beerbohm's literary idol.*

Figure 117. From Beerbohm's The Poet's Corner *(1904), this famous caricature shows Arnold with his niece, Mary Augusta (later Mrs. Humphrey Ward).*

Roped in by dogma, padlocked by logic, shut up in a dark metaphysical cupboard, he would always escape Houdini-like, stroll back to the footlights, and urbanely tell the audience that such conventional bonds were child's play to a supple man of culture.[38]

A verbal magician, Arnold triumphs over the not-always-melodious voices of our "Charivari" as well.

Well into the twentieth century, Arnold has continued to appear in cartoon and caricature. *St. Nicholas* magazine, in 1930, celebrated his Christmas Eve birth (fig. 115), and, as late as 1946, Max Beerbohm was still playing pencil games with Arnold's familiar visage (figure 116). Speaking of Beerbohm, no Arnoldian charivari would be complete without our inclusion of his famous caricature of the poet with his niece, Mary Augusta (later, Mrs. Humphrey Ward), a drawing (figure 117) that offers new enjoyment in the light of Park Honan's biography, *Matthew Arnold: A Life*.[39]

NOTES

1. "Necklong," *Punch*, 26 November 1881, p. 250.

2. "Sweetness and Light in the City," *Punch*, 30 May 1874, p. 225.

3. "Matthew Arnold," *Once a Week*, 12 October 1872, pp. 320–23.

4. Barry V. Qualls, "W. H. Mallock's *Every Man His Own Poet*," *Victorian Poetry* 16 (1978): 184. Mallock's 1877 work, and the one that brought him public notice, was *The New Republic*, a series of responses to the Victorian debate over religion in a scientific age. Along with various fictionalized portraits of such prominent figures as Huxley, Jowett, and Pater, Arnold is also represented, as "Mr. Luke," the "great critic and apostle of culture." Book-length parody and satire fall beyond the scope of our present collection from periodicals, but we might note that Mallock himself was caricatured in the 30 December 1882 issue of *Vanity Fair*. The brief accompanying letterpress noted his contribution of "one of the cleverest squibs of modern times."

5. *Punch*, alone, is loaded with references to Arnold, several others of which we deal with later. Other samples include one "Brian Boroimhe O'Buggaboo," who invokes Arnold's defense of English poets with a "Celtic dthrop in them" in *Punch*, 27 July 1867; *Punch* cartoonist Linley Sambourne, who offers a full-page drawing of the "Royal Academy Banquet at Burlington House" (*Punch*, 7 May 1881) in which Arnold (possibly Edwin, rather than Matthew?), difficult to identify in the packed portrait of some sixty faces, is described as having been "all Mouth and Moaning on this Jaw-ful occasion"; and a "report" of an Inaugural Address at "A College for the Higher Education of Lower Class Left-Off'uns," entitled "Criticism for the Million" and delivered by "Mr. M-TTH-W A-N-LD" (*Punch*, 14 October 1882). The rather lengthy report concludes that "the meeting then terminated in some confusion"! One poem that also plays on Arnold's plea for "lucidity" does so with a Gilbert and Sullivan swing that bears noting:

A Lesson to the British Lion

To Matthew Arnold hark
  With both ears all avidity;
That Matthew—a man of mark—
  Says, "Cultivate Lucidity."

"Civil Courage" the Germans lack;
  (Query—what can mean that quiddity?)
But England's especial drawback
  Is a certain want of "Lucidity."

In "Morality" France most fails
  To exemplify rigidity;
The defect that England ails
  Must be owned to be "Lucidity."
The Salvation Army shines
  In devoted intrepidity;
But the fault of its valiant lines
  Is the foible of no Lucidity.

The Puseyite phalanx glows
  With a most intense calidity;
But the heat of the movement throws
  Not a gleam or spark of Lucidity.
There is genius, love, charm, no doubt,
  In Ritualistic floridity,
But what would have snuffed it out
  Would have been a ray of Lucidity.
Roast beef is excellent meat,
  Of most extreme sapidity;
Plum-pudding is nice to eat,
  But it doesn't produce Lucidity.
John Bull is a worthy old wight,
  Though he sometimes behaves with stupidity,
Uninspired with Sweetness and Light,
  And, in short, nearly void of Lucidity.

(*Punch*, 14 October 1882)

6. "Sample Opinion on the 'Crisis,'" *Vanity Fair*, 5 July 1882, p. 2.

7. Super, ed., *Complete Prose Works (CPW)*, 5:45, 313–18.

8. *CPW*, 5:205–6.

9. R. H. Super, *The Time-Spirit of Matthew Arnold* (Ann Arbor: University of Michigan Press, 1970), p. 76.

10. Examples are numerous throughout *Complete Prose Works*, but a good collection is John Bertrand Lott's unpublished Harvard University dissertation, "Matthew Arnold as Satirist," Ann Arbor: University Microfilms 61-2317, 1961.

11. Again, we recommend Lott's collection of examples which include the obviously satirical *Friendship's Garland*, the "vivacities" of *Culture and Anarchy*, the Shaftesbury Trinity, and the quarrel between the admirers of Milton and those of Eliza Cook. Arnold's response to the Colenso affair demonstrated his skill at satire in religious matters, and his religious books, especially portions of *God and the Bible* where he responds to "The Author of *Supernatural Religion*," are alive with oblique satire through biblical allusion.

12. *Vanity Fair*, 6 December 1884.

13. *CPW*, 10:252.

14. "Whispers: Opinions on the New Government," *Vanity Fair*, 18 January 1885, 31–32.

15. *CPW*, 9:259 and 410.

16. "Things in general, By Eminent Hands," *Vanity Fair* 14 November 1885, 271.

17. John Holloway, *The Victorian Sage* (New York: W. W. Norton, 1965), 226.

18. For general information on the *Vanity Fair* cartoons, see Savory's publications, especially the introductions and bibliographies in *The Vanity Fair Lithographs: An Illustrated Checklist* (New York: Garland Publishing, 1978) and *The Vanity Fair Gallery: A Collector's Guide to the Caricatures* (New Brunswick, New Jersey: A. S. Barnes,

1979). In the total collection of over two thousand drawings, nearly every prominent individual during Arnold's lifetime was caricatured in the magazine, including his friends among the clergy, politicians, and men of letters.

19. *CPW*, 3:361.

20. Charles L. Graves, *Mr. Punch's History of Modern England*, 4 vols. (London: Cassell, 1921–22), 3:322.

21. *Punch*, 28 April 1888, 195.

22. The most extensive study of *Fun* is Edward Stewart Lauterbach's unpublished 1961 University of Illinois dissertation, "*Fun* and its Contributors: The Literary History of a Victorian Humor Magazine," Ann Arbor: University Microfilms 61-1636, 1961.

23. *Fun*, 25 April 1888, 7.

24. *Vanity Fair*, 21 April 1888.

25. David R. Ewbank, "Kidding the Victorian Poets: A Collection of Parodies," *Victorian Poetry* 15 (1977):67–69. Quoted with permission.

26. Arnold visited the United States 22 Oct. 1883 to 8 Mar. 1884 and 30 May to 4 Sept. 1886.

27. *Harper's Weekly* 28 (1884): 295, attempted to discredit a remark Arnold was rumored to have made about the dreariness of the Lowell household.

28. This and other anecdotes and satires are reprinted by Chilson Leonard, "Arnold in America: A Study of Matthew Arnold's Literary Relations with America and of his Visits to this Country in 1883 and 1886," Diss. Yale 1932, pp. 103–4. This important study is at long last available from University Microfilms.

29. "Triplicate Philosophy" is reprinted in Fraser Neiman's *Essays, Letters, and Reviews by Matthew Arnold* (Cambridge: Harvard University Press, 1960), pp. 386–90.

30. Super, *CPW*, 10:464, 498, and 505.

31. The reporter's remarks are reprinted in Harriet Holman, "Matthew Arnold's Elocution Lessons," *New England Quarterly* 18 (1945): 480.

32. Super (*CPW*, 10:499–500) discusses Smalley's request.

33. A reference to Barnum's involvement is in Leonard, p. 109.

34. See also *Judge's* "Harvest Ground," 17 Nov. 1883, p. 2.

35. Among the accounts of Arnold's Washington experience which aid readers in identifying Attwood's caricatures are Leonard, pp. 166–70, and McCallum, pp. 374–75, as well as the other Attwood drawings which appear in almost every early issue of *Life*.

36. Super, *CPW*, 11:492. Leonard reprints the *Tribune* article in full, pp. 336–40.

37. Super, *CPW*, 11:487.

38. *The Ethical Idealism of Matthew Arnold: A Study of the Nature and Sources of his Moral and Religious Ideas* (London: William Heinemann, 1959), p. 140.

39. Park Honan, *Matthew Arnold: A Life* (New York: McGraw-Hill, 1981). Honan has done an especially fine job with Arnold's relationships with the women in his life.

Q IS the Queen,
  Most noble and true.
For further particulars, pag 22.

R IS for Rubenstein, playing that old thing in f
  To Rollo and Rembrandt, who wish they were deaf.

7
Oscar and the "Brief Bard"
Wilde, Swinburne, and the Aesthetes

If you're anxious for to shine in the high
    aesthetic line, as a man of culture rare,
You must get up all the germs of the
    transcendental terms, and plant them
    everywhere.
. . . .
Though the Philistines may jostle, you will
    rank as an apostle in the high aesthetic band,
If you walk down Piccadilly with a poppy or a
    lily in your medieval hand.
        And everyone will say,
        As you walk your flowery way,
"If he's content with a vegetable love which
    would certainly not suit *me*,
Why, what a most particularly pure young man
    this pure young man must be!"

THE WELL-KNOWN GILBERT AND SULLIVAN lines from *Patience* (1881) paint an exaggerated portrait of the new breed of late nineteenth-century "aesthete." His tastes and poses, exemplified in the character of Bunthorne in the play and in the persons of Oscar Wilde, Algernon Charles Swinburne, and James Whistler in actual life, were quickly seized upon for caricature, parody, and satire in the popular comic press. This chapter, therefore, focuses upon several of the most likely candidates for Bunthorne's model, various writers and artists who were repeatedly attacked as "Mighty Masters" of what *Punch* called a "perverted form of aestheticism." What Gilbert and Sullivan did with amusing libretto and light-hearted spoofing, the satire magazines often did with a vengeance. An 1882 issue of *Punch*, for example, declared that the magazine would "persistently attack to the bitter end" this peculiar new movement.

The word "Aestheticism" has been perverted from its original meaning; *i.e.* the perception of all that is good, pure, and beautiful in Nature and in Art, and, as now vulgarly applied, it has come in a slang sort of way to stand for an effeminate, invertebrate, sensuous, sentimentally-Christian, but thoroughly Pagan taste in literature and art, which delights in the idea of the resuscitation of the Great God Pan.

Punch's specific reference in this case was to Swinburne (frequently labelled "Swineborn" or "The Brief Bard" by *Punch*), but the attack was similar when directed toward Wilde and others whom *Punch* found among the "Mighty Masters." When *Patience* moved to American performances followed by Wilde's 1882 American tour, the aesthetes rapidly became open game for comic cartoonists and satirists on both sides of the Atlantic. Although Wilde was the most frequent victim, Swinburne and others were also mocked with regularity during the last two decades of the century. The poetry and painting of Dante Gabriel Rossetti, the art of Edward C. Burne-Jones and Aubrey Beardsley, the livs and works of others of the Pre-Raphaelite and Aesthetic movements—all became whipping boys for the predominantly "Philistine" comic press satire on whatever countered the more moralistic, utilitarian, and evangelical spirit of conventional Victorianism.

When Oscar Wilde left for his American tour, *Punch* personified aestheticism as a grief-stricken woman waving him farewell (figure 118). "Ariadne in Naxos; Or, Very Like a Wail" read the caption. "Design by our own Greenery-Yallery-Grosvenor-Gallery Young Man, in humble imitation of the picture by Professor W. B. Richmond, symbolizing 'the grief of Aestheticism at the departure of her Oscar.'" In a mock "interview" accompanying the cartoon, Wilde gives his "aesthetic" opinion of various poets.

Alfred Tennyson is a prolific, though somewhat old-fashioned writer. . . . Swinburne, though in some respects in sympathy with myself, has, I fear, contracted a fatal taint of Bohemianism, perhaps from living in an unaristocratic neighbourhood. Browning is a conscientious, though somewhat uneven writer. As to Morris, his verses are prosy, but his wall-papers are eloquently poetical. (3 November 1883)

The American *Puck* offered a full-page illustrated "Aesthetic Fantasy" on extracting St. Jacob's Oil

Figure 118. "Aestheticism" waves farewell to Wilde as he leaves for his American tour. Punch, *3 November 1883.*

from sunflowers (figure 119) and recommended several hair styles for the aesthetes (figure 120). *The Spectator* presented "The Session of the Poets" by "Caliban," in which a gathering of Victorian bards are shocked by Swinburne's railing, "All Virtue is bosh! Hallelujah for Landor!/ I disbelieve wholly in everything!—there!"

> With language so awful he dared then to treat
> em,—
> Miss Ingelow fainted in Tennyson's arms,

Figure 119. "*Aesthetic Fantasy*" *from* Puck, *6 April 1882.*

Poor Arnold rush'd out, crying
  "Soecl'inficetum!"
    And great bards and small bards were full of
      alarms;
Till Tennyson, flaming and red as a gipsy,
    Struck his fist on the table and uttered a
      shout:
"To the door with the boy! Call a cab! He is
      tipsy!"
    And they carried the naughty young
      gentleman out.

Punch also gathered various champions of "King Cultchaw" in a comic vignette in its 7 January 1882 issue:

Clowning and Classicism.
A Suggestion for the Season.
Being the Opening Scene of a New and Original
Great-god-Pan-tomime, entitled,
Harlequin King Cultchaw;
OR, THE THREE CHAMPIONS OF PAGANISM AND THE
SLEEPING BEAST.

CHARACTERS.

KING CULTCHAW *(a Modern Evil Genius).*
SWEETNESS, INDIGESTION,   *His*
  LIGHT, UPHOLSTERY, BAD   *Attendant*
  FORM, INDECENCY,   *Sprites.*
  SENTIMENT, IMPUDENCE,
  and LEMPRIÈRE ....
MR. A. C. SW-NB-RNE *(afterwards*   *The Champions.*
  Clown).....................   *Creatures of*
MR. P-T-R *(afterwards*   KING CULTCHAW.
  Harlequin) ....
MR. B-RNE-J-N-S *(afterwards*
  Pantaloon) ....
MR. OSC-R W-LDE *(a Spirit of the Hair, afterwards*
  Columbine).
THE GOOD FAIRY R-SK-N.
PROFESSOR C-LV-N *(his faithful Sprite, afterwards*
  Policeman X).
MR. C-M-NS C-RR *(a Would-be-if-he-could*
  Nymph).
SIR C-TTS L-NDS-Y *(a Bond Street Magician).*
SCENE I.—*The Realms of Gimcrack Æstheticism.*
      KING CULTCHAW *discovered surrounded*
      by his attendant Sprites.
King Cultchaw. What ho, my Sprites! Once
    more the hour draws near
  When Christmas, vulgar season, calls for
    cheer.
  So Cultchaw, who, though equal to the
    times,
  Cannot descend to common Pantomimes,

153

A *Great-god-Pan*-tomine might take in hand.
What, to the notion, says my trusty band?
(*They nod their heads and dance round him, in sign
    of acquiescence.*)
    'Tis well. Too long, in quiet humdrum ways
The Modern World has passed its decent
    days.
A relish we must give Society
For sixth-form scraps of impropriety—
A dished-up, dainty, dull, and prurient feast!
But how to serve it?
The Three Champions, Mr. A. C. Sw-nb-rne,
    Mr. P-t-r, *and* Mr. B-rne-J-n-s, *rise
    through a trap, clinging on to the back of a
    Publishing and Advertising Dragon.*
Mr. A. C. Sw-nb-rne. Wake the Sleeping Beast!
King Cultchaw. A good idea! But how?
Mr. A. C. Sw-nb-rne.   A simple task:
    Since Modern Cultchaw gives us all we
        ask—
    The stinging stripes that toy with sensuous
        taste;
    The utter sprawl of the Unwashed,
        Unchaste—
    The beastly beauty of a schoolboy's smirch,
    That, all unbeaten, battens on the birch;
    The windy wash of words that bend and
        bound,
    The seething swell of surging, senseless
        sound;
    The slimy swamp of Scholarship begot
    By probing Liddell and by searching Scott;
    The languor hailing, with blind blinking
        cheek,
    The knock-kneed manhood of the
        Neo-Greek.
All this shall Cultchaw yield the sacred
    three,
Of whom the Sunrise Singer view in me!
[*He kicks* Mr. P-t-r *and* Mr. B-rne-J-n-s *off the
    Dragon's back, and stands in a limp classical
    attitude on one leg.*
King Cultchaw. That's nicely put, Sir Poet. And·
    your use is?—
Mr. A. C. Sw-nb-rne. To start the mysteries of
    chaste Eleusis.
    With moist and meretricious metre, I
    To godless gush will school the public eye.
Mr. B-rne J-n-s. And I, within the limits of my
    frame,
    Will, patient pagan, play the same small
        game,
    Till verse and canvas our new creed disclose,
Mr. P-t-r. And I am stamped Apostle of its
        prose!

*The Three Champions are about to depart, when the
    Scene opens, and reveals the Good Fairy
    R-sk-n, who descends amidst a shower of unsold
    numbers of an excellent but unpopular
    Magazine.*
*The Good Fairy R-sk-n (driving back the Three
    Champions with his wand).* Hold! Impious,
    bumptious, brazen-faced boys!
    'Twas I first woke the world to Grecian joys,
    Led it, in holy, reverent attitude,
    To worship Art, not gloat upon the nude.
    The gold, and not the dross. I brought to
        men,
    Minerva-crowned; not wallowing in his den,
    The goat-brute Pan; *Pallas Armigera,*—
    Not on all fours!
Mr. A. C. Sw-nb-rne   Like *Fors Clavigera?*
    Still, aged Fairy, Pan shall breathe our bliss.
    We'll wake him.
The Good Fairy R-sk-n. Never! for, unless a kiss
    Some nymph imprint upon his horned brow,
    He'll wake no more, but sleep. For, mark
        me, now
    With thorough third-class Muse, yet not
        afraid
    To handle themes that genius but degrade,
    There lives no Spirit such a task to dare!
King Cultchaw. Ah! you forget the *Spirit of the
    Hair!*
            (*The Sprites express satisfaction.*)
    What ho, there! portly Nymph! for I must
        trouble you.
    Peri of Pimlico! Arise, *O. W.!*
(Mr. Osc-r W-lde *rises through the Stage,
    reclining in a roomy flower-pot in the midst of
    pale lavender fire.*)
You're equal to the work of waking Pan?
Mr. Osc-r W-lde. Give me a *Lemprière,* and I
    think I can.
(*A Lemprière is handed to him over the top of the
    flower-pot.*)
    Of things that I know little much I speak;
    'Tis here I pick up all *my* Neo-Greek!
            (*He turns over several pages.*)
    Yet, much to classic vesture I have owed:
    For, fancies fitter for the Mile End Road,
    If reared on Attic soil, somehow go down,
    And neither sicken, shock nor scare the
        town,
    But place one on a pinnacle! A fact,—
    Secure too even from Lord Campbell's Act!
            (*Holding up Lemprière gracefully.*)
    With this,—and *vellum*—I've avoided failure!
King Cultchaw. You have, my pippin! Look out
    Lupercalia.
    We mean to try *that* next in Piccadilly.

(Mr. Osc-r W-lde *pulls out a pocket rhyming dictionary and becomes gradually absorbed in reference.*)

So, to your work:

The Good Fairy R-sk-n. Nay, Cultchaw, you grow silly!

But though I crowned you King, no more I'll try you.

False, Pagan, perjured Cultchaw, I defy you!

[*He again waves his wand, on which Sir* C-tts L-nds-y, *and Professor* C-lv-n, *apparently much surprised, float in on a rainbow of quiet, subdued, and carefully selected High-Art colours, and, sliding artistically to the ground, join in a long, serious, and very earnest conversation with the* Good Fairy R-sk-n, *in a corner. While nobody is paying the slightest attention to them,* King Cultchaw *gives the signal for departure, upon which the Three Champions, preceded by the now bounding Nymph, Mr.* Osc-r W-lde, *enter the Realms of Professional Beauty, and continue their journey through a succession of unedifying adventures, to wake the Sleeping Beast, till, by some mistake they instead only manage to arouse the* Great-stick-god Mr. Punch, *who intervenes, most effectively, at the eleventh hour, with a quite unexpected, but startling severe Transformation.*

(7 January 1882)

Even the master mockers themselves were parodied in *Punch*'s issue of 20 September 1890. With apologies to Gilbert and Sullivan, the magazine presented its own version of the song of the aesthete from *Patience*, howbeit with a decidedly more caustic tone than that of the original!

DEVELOPMENT.
(With acknowledgments to the Author of "Patience.")

["Even a colour-sense is more important in the development of the individual than a sense of right and wrong."—Oscar Wilde.]

If you're anxious to develop to a true hedonic "swell," hop on a pinnacle apart,
Like a monkey on a stick, and your phrases quaintly pick, and then prattle about Art.
Take some laboured paradoxes, and, like Samson's flaming foxes, let them loose amidst the corn
(Or the honest commonplaces) of the Philistines whose graces you regard with lofty scorn.
  And every one will say,

As you squirm your wormy way,
"If this young man expresses himself in terms that stagger *me*,
What a very singularly smart young man this smart young man must be!"

You may be a flabby fellow, and lymphatically yellow, that will matter not a mite,
If you take yourself in hand, in a way you'll understand, to become a Son of Light.
On your crassness superimposing the peculiar art of glosing in sleek phrases about Sin.
If you aim to be a shocker, carnal theories to cocker is *the* best way to begin.
  And every one will say,
  As you worm your wicked way,
"If that's allowable for *him* which were criminal in *me*,
What a very emancipated kind of youth this kind of youth must be."

Human virtues you'll abhor all, and be down upon the Moral in uncompromising style.
Your critical analysis will reduce to prompt paralysis every *motor* that's not vile.
You will show there's naught save virtue that can seriously hurt you, or your liberty enmesh;
And you'll find excitement, plenty, in Art's *dolce far niente*, with a flavour of the flesh.
  And every one will say,
  As you lounge your upward way,
"If he's content with a do-nothing life, which would certainly not suit *me*,
What a most particularly subtle young man this subtle young man must be!"

Then having swamped morality in "intensified personality" (which, of course, must mean your own),
And the "rational" abolished and "sincerity" demolished, you will find that you have *grown*
With a "colour-sense" fresh handselled (whilst the moral ditto's cancelled) you'll develop into—well,
What Philistia's fools malicious might esteem a *vaurien* vicious (*alias* "hedonic swell").
  And every one will say,
  As you writhe your sinuous way,
"If the highest result of the true 'Development' is decomposition, why see
What a very perfectly developed young man this developed young man must be."
With your perky paradoxes, and your talk of "crinkled ox-eyes," and of books in "Nile-green skin,"

That show forth unholy histories, and display
the "deeper mysteries" of strange and
subtle Sin.
You can squirm, and glose, and hiss on, and
awake that *nouveau frisson* which is Art's
best gift to life,
And "develop"—like some cancer (in the
Art-sphere) whose best answer is the silent
surgeon's knife!
And every *man* will say,
As you wriggle on your way,
"If 'emotion for the sake of emotion *is* the aim
of Art,' dear me!
What a morbidly muckily emotional young
man the 'developed' young man must be!"

This time readers would not have to speculate on the subject of the satiric stab. It was Oscar Wilde.

OSCAR WILDE

No literary figure ever left himself so open to critical commentary, or, indeed, invited derision as did Oscar Wilde. Those nineteenth-century periodicals directed to the middle-class audience seized upon Wilde's affectations and nailed him to a cross of public ridicule. Although he was lampooned without mercy in print, he may also have been a satirical subject of *Patience*. Whether he was Reginald Bunthorne, the "fleshly poet," or Archibald Grosvenor, the "idyllic poet," or neither of these, is a matter for speculation. For the most part Wilde took the ridicule good-naturedly, for he probably realized that it kept his name, his talents, and his aesthetic doctrines before the public.

Of all the popular journals, *Punch* was the forerunner, as well as the most consistent, in attacking both the aesthetes and Wilde personally. Beginning in 1880, a series of caricatures was introduced featuring two aesthetes, Postlethwaite and Maudle, who typified the affectations associated with the group. In some of these cartoons by George Du Maurier, the central figures were given many of Wilde's postures and resembled him somewhat in appearance. At this time, however, Wilde had not yet been identified individually by the journal. *Punch* was attacking the aesthetes not only in drawings, but also in verse.

A Philistine.

Take away all your adornments aesthetical,
Plates of blue china and bits of sage green,

Though you may call me a monster heretical,
I can't consider them fit to be seen.
Etchings and paintings I loathe and abominate,
Grimly I smile at the name of BURNE
JONES,
Hating his pictures where big chins
predominate—
Over lean figures with angular bones.

Buy me what grinning stage rustics call
"farniture,"
Such as was used by our fathers of old;
Take away all your nonsensical garniture,
Tapestry curtains and borders of gold.
Give me the ancient and solid mahogany,
Mine be the board that will need no repairs;
Don't let me see, as I sit at my grog, any
Chippendale tables or Sheraton chairs.

Hang up a vivid vermillion wall-paper,
Covered with roses of gorgeous hue,
Matching a varnished and beautiful hall-paper,
Looking like marble so polished and new.
Carpets should all show a floral variety,
Wreaths intermingling of yellow and red,
So, when it enters my home, will Society
Say, here's a house whence aesthetics have
fled.

(20 November 1880, p. 237)

Punch continued its series of attacks upon the aesthetes in general up to the publication date of Wilde's *Poems* in June 1881. From that time forward he became the primary target of ridicule. Although he was not identified by name until after June 1881, he was well known in London and might well have been the object of satire in this poem and in the following one.

A Maudle-In Ballad.
To His Lily.

My lank limp lily, my long lithe lily,
My languid lily-love, fragile and thin,
With dank leaves dangling and flower-flap
chilly,
That shines like the shin of a Highland gilly!
Mottled and moist as a cold toad's skin!
Lustrous and leper-white, splendid and
splay!
Art thou not Utter? and wholly akin
To my own wan soul and my own wan chin,
And my own wan nose-tip, tilted to sway
The peacock's feather, *sweeter than sin*,
That I bought for a halfpenny, yesterday?

My long lithe lily, my languid lily,
  My lank limp lily-love, how shall I win—
Woo thee to wink at me? Silver lily,
How shall I sing to thee, softly, or shrilly?
  What shall I weave for thee—which shall I
    spin—
    Rondel, or rondeau, or virelay?
Shall I buzz like bee, with my face thrust in
Thy choice, chaste chalice, or choose me a
    tin
  Trumpet, or touchingly, tenderly play
On the weird bird-whistle, *sweeter than sin*,
  That I bought for a half penny, yesterday?

My languid lily, my lank limp lily,
  My long lithe lily-love, men may grin—
Say that I'm soft and supremely silly—
What care I, while you whisper stilly;
  What care I, while you smile? Not a pin!
While you smile, while you whisper—'Tis sweet to
decay!
  I have watered with chlorodine, tears of
    chagrin,
  The churchyard mould I have planted thee
    in,
  Upside down, in an intense way,
  In a rough red flowerpot, *sweeter than sin*,
    That I bought for a halfpenny, yesterday!
                (9 April 1881, p. 161)

It is significant that the phrase *sweeter than sin* is italicized in each verse, because the next year *Punch* issued a statement about aesthetic sinfulness.

During 1881 *Punch* offered several amusing parodies of Wilde's poems under the names of Ossian Wilderness and Oscuro Wildegoose. In May, "La Fuite de la Lune" turns into "La Fuite des

Oies," or peace of the moon into peace of the geese; "Theoretikos," which appeared in November, follows more closely the original poem and retains its central ideas.

More Impressions
By Oscuro Wildegoose

La Fuite des Oies.

To outer senses they are geese,
  Dull drowsing by a weedy pool;
  But try the impression trick. Cool! Cool!
Snow-slumbering sentinels of Peace!

Deep silence on the shadowy flood
  Save rare sharp stridence (that means
    "quack"),
Low amber light in Ariel track
Athwart the dun (that means the mud).

And suddenly subsides the sun,
  Bulks mystic, ghostly, thrid the gloom
  (That means the white geese waddling
    home),
And darkness reigns! (See how it's done?)
                (28 May 1881, p. 242)

Theoretikos
By Oscuro Wildegoose
(Put into plain English for the benefit of Philistia.)

This mighty Empire seems in a bad way!
  Of all that may a languorous bard delight
  Our little Island is deserted, quite.
What now is left ME, but the moon to bay?
Loll on the hills, and cry, "Oh, lackaday!"?
  Who prates of Progress? Oh, come out of it,
  My most superior Soul! Thou art not fit

Figure 120. "Coiffeur of the Aesthete," Puck, *25 January 1882.*

157

For virile conflict or for manly play,
The Forum's toil, the labours of the Mart.
   Nasty rude people rage with impudent cries
Against the worship of dead centuries.
   It mars my calm! In dreams of moony Art
And Maudlin Cultchaw I will stand apart,
   Since Providence proceeds not as I please!
               (26 November 1881, p. 242)

It was not until June 25 that the identified caricature of Wilde appeared as one of *Punch*'s "Fancy
Portraits" (figure 121). Linley Sambourne's drawing probably influenced several other caricaturists
in their satirization of the poet. It shows Wilde as a
large sunflower with lilies on either side. An open
cigarette case is propped against the vase with the
familiar walking stick beside it, both items being
Wilde trademarks. A wastebasket figures prominently so that the reader is immediately conscious
of its presence. Oscar is looking downward, supposedly reading from one of his odes. The cartoon
was prompted by the publication of Wilde's *Poems*,
published during the same month. One must reason
that the wastebasket symbolized the value of the
book in *Punch*'s judgment, and the appended verse
makes the meaning of the cartoon distinctly clear.
Actually, the reviews of *Poems* were mixed. Oscar
Browning, whom Wilde had requested to review
the book, wrote "we lay down this book in the con-
viction that England is enriched with a new poet."[1]
In an unsigned review appearing in *Dial*, the author
commented that "most readers of poetic taste will
agree that there is something in this young man
from Dublin not discovered by the caricaturist of
Punch."[2] On the other hand, an unidentified reviewer in *Spectator* expressed the opinion: "Mr. Oscar Wilde is no poet, but a cleverish man who has
an infinite contempt for his readers, and thinks he
can take them in with a little mouthing verse."[3]
Saturday Review wrote that "the book is not without
traces of cleverness but is marred everywhere by
imitation, insincerity, and bad taste."[4]

Harry Furniss created two cartoons of Wilde that
were based on actual paintings. The first of these
appeared as one of "Mr. *Punch*'s 'Mother Hubbard'
Fairy Tale Grinaway Christmas Cards" in the 24
December 1881 issue (figure 122). The drawing is
entitled "The Sleeping Beauty," showing Wilde
and the other characters soundly napping with Oscar asleep on his feet. Furniss modeled his caricature after the Briar Rose series by Burne-Jones,
which was based on the story of the Sleeping

Figure 121. Punch's *"Fancy Portrait,"* 25 June 1881.

Beauty, painted between 1871 and 1890 (figure
123).[5] In this case, the cartoon is turned into one of
the Lily series, for all clues identify the Sleeping
Beauty as Lily Langtry, the actress. The vase holding the lily is labeled "Jersey," and instead of
Burne-Jones's briars and draperies as a background,
Furniss decorated his drawing with large and
numerous L's, peacock feathers, and sunflowers.
Wilde's play, *Vera; or the Nihilists*, had been sched-
uled for production in December but had been can-
celed; the invitations scattered on the floor probably
had been designated for special friends whom he
wanted to attend. His play and book of poems fallen to the floor, in combination with the sleeping
figures, suggest an ennui caused by boredom.

Up until this time the reasons for *Punch*'s vitriolic
forays had not been explained. In January 1882,
however, a statement of editorial policy concerning
aestheticism was included. It was not, according to

Figure 122. "The Sleeping Beauty," Punch, *21 December 1881.*

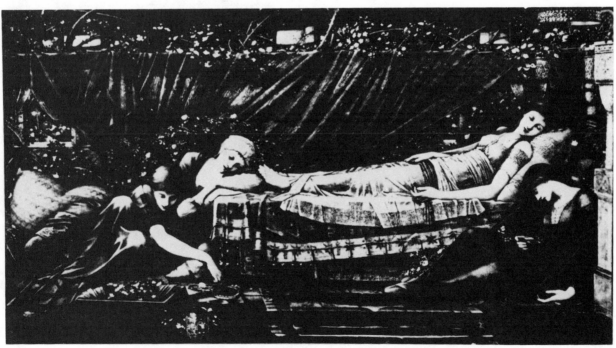

Figure 123. A panel from Briar Rose *series, 1871–90, by Edward Burne-Jones.*

the statement, opposition to aestheticism that was responsible for *Punch*'s stand, but rather opposition to the perverted and paganistic brand of aestheticism preached by Swinburne, Burne-Jones, Wilde, and others.

In Earnest

Let us be clearly understood. The word "Aestheticism" has been perverted from its original meaning; i.e. the perception of all that is good, pure, and beautiful in Nature and in Art, and, as now vulgarly applied, it has come in a slang sort of way to stand for effeminate, invertebrate, sensuous, sentimentally-Christian, but thoroughly Pagan taste in literature and art, which delights in the idea of the resuscitation of the Great God Pan, in Swinburnian songs at their highest fever-pitch, in the mystic ravings of a Blake, the affectation of a Rossetti, the *Charmides* and revolting pan-theistic *Rosa Mystica* of Oscar Wilde, the *Songs of Passion and Pain* and other similar mock-hysterical imitations of the "Mighty Masters." Victor Hugo, Ouida, Swinburne, Burne-Jones, have much to answer for.

This Aestheticism, as it has gradually come to be known, is the reaction from Kingsley's Muscular Christianity. Exaggerated muscular Christianity, in its crusade against canting and whining religion, in its bold attempt to show that the practice of true religion was for men, as well as for women, trampled on the Christian Lily, emblem of perfect purity; and what Athleticism trod under foot, Aestheticism picked up, cherished, and then, taking the sign for the reality, paid to it the extravagant honours of a Pagan devotion; and the worship of the Lily was substituted for the veneration paid to the sacred character, in whose hand Christian Art had originally placed it. To this was added the worship of the Peacock Feather. It is this false Aestheticism which we have persistently attacked, and will persistently attack to the bitter end, and henceforward those who misunderstand us do so wilfully, and it may be maliciously. (7 January 1882, p. 12)

Several drawings under the caption "Sketches from 'Boz'" (figure 124) were included in February. One of these depicts Wilde leaning languidly on a mantle, as Harold Skimpole, the unproductive dilettante from Dickens's novel, *Bleak House*. From the character he portrays, the conclusion may rightly be reached that this is *Punch*'s deliberate comment on his value.

On the same page as the above cartoon, the aesthetes are called clowns in a satiric letter supposedly addressed to the magazine:

DEAR MR. PUNCH,

A LETTER from "AN OLD CLOWN," which recently appeared in your Contemporary, is all nonsense. Clowns, if they wish to keep their place upon the stage, must go with the times. They must become AEsthetic. A long-haired Clown, a flabby Harlequin, an intense Pantaloon, and a Burnes-Jonesian Columbine, would be a great success. Fancy a lugubrious Clown singing the following version of HOT CODLINS.

> Some foolish young people, quite famous they
>   got
> By posing, and talking—rot, rot, rot!
> They made themselves Guys, not fit to be seen,
> And they painted their walls a sad sage green;
> They worshipped in silence their white and
>   blue,
> And their friends all said they were quite—
>   Da-do, daffodilly, silly-billy,
>   Sunflower, Botticelli, quite Too-too!

Oscar Wilde as *Harold Skimpole.*

Lord Alfred Paget as *Captain*

Sir Wilfrid Lawson as *Mark Tapley.*

J. G. Biggar, M.P., as *Quil*

Figure 124. "Sketches from Boz," Punch, 4 February 1882.

These foolish young people, they cared not a
    jot;
They thought they knew what was what, what,
    what!
They painted poems they averred were good;
They sang sweet pictures that none
    understood.
And though it was said they had no common
    sense,
Everyone declared they were much too—
    Da-do, daffodilly, silly-billy,
    Sunflower, Botticelli, quite Too-too!

Would not that be splendid? I may inform you, in the
strictest confidence, that Mr. E. L. Blanchard is going to
write, for the Drury Lane Annual next season, *Harlequin
Dado and the Sighing Sunflower; or, the Languorous Lilies of
Limpshire*, in which there will doubtless be an ample field
for the display of the talents of

Your obedient Servant,
A YOUNG CLOWN.
(4 February 1882, p. 49)

In spite of the fact that Oscar was no longer in
England, having sailed for his American tour on
Christmas Eve 1881, he continued to be the subject
of numerous verses, articles, and cartoons. One of
the cleverest pieces is to be found in the 11 March
1882 issue and is called "Ossian (with variations):
The Son of Ia-Cultcha" (figure 125), an appropriate
title, since Ossian was the son of Fingal, one of
Oscar's names. Its author treats his subject's departure from England and his visit in America, very
much in the style of MacPherson's translation of
Ossian's poem "Carthon." In fact, both pieces begin
with the same line: "A tale of times of old!" The
language is very similar; at times the same phrases
are used, such as "beam of light," or nearly identical, as with "car-borne Carthon" and "car-borne
Sone of Erin." In other instances events are
switched to suit the situation. Clessammor remained in Reuthamir's halls for three days; the Son
of Cultcha stayed in the ship for three days. In
Ossian's work "The son of a stranger came"; in
Punch, "The son of Cultcha has gone to the land of
Strangers." The end result is a satiric but poetical
treatment of Wilde.

The accompanying caricature shows Oscar aesthetically clad, floating through the air with a
manuscript of his lecture in one hand and the ubiquitous peacock feather in the other. The effect is
both ethereal and aesthetic, with Oscar representing the Son of Higher Culture.

Figure 125. "Ossian," Punch, *11 March 1883.*

Ossian (with Variations)

The Son of Ia-Cultcha.

I

A TALE of the times of old! Where art thou, beam of
light? Why, thou bearer of the Lily, thou wanderer unseen, hast thou left these shores? No sound of thy song
comes now. I hear but the roaring blasts. Strike the harp
and sound the song! The son of Cultcha has gone to the
Land of Strangers. Can I forget that beam of light, that
breeze of the valley, the long-lock'd sunbeam of love? I
have heard the mournful tale. When the hero left these
shores, three days he stayed in the ship unseen—alone. It
is dark. The meteor of night is dim. The sea darkly
tumbles beneath the ship. Slowly, with unequal steps,
he ascends the deck. Unfrequent blasts rush through his
hair. Grief is dwelling in his soul. The song is faint on his
lips. His face is like the darkened moon. His arms hang
disordered by his side. His hair spreads wide across his
face. With trembling steps he nears the edge—He feels

Figure 126. "Private Frith's View," Punch, 12 March 1883.

the unseen foe! See Cultcha's mighty hero fails!! Thrice he sighs over the dark billows. Thrice they echo back the mournful sound! He bends his head above the sable surge!! Then with a bursting sigh, he pours his signs on night!!! Unhappy youth of Love, let me forget that dreadful sound. The hero resumes his soul. He gains the upper deck. He pours the song "My soul, O lambent maiden, lies far away in thy bower; but my corse is on this all-too-rolling ocean. Never more shalt thou flop with Ia-Cultcha's chosen son, nor sweetly sigh over a new 'Depression.' I am light as the feather of our love, yet my limbs support not this airy form. How long will ye roll around me, O darkly tumbling ocean!" Near, two sailors receive his words, SWAB'EM of decks, and STARNO, foe of strangers. They rose in their wrath. "SWAB'EM, lay that wanderer low," said STARNO, in his pride. SWAB'EM heaves his marlin-spike. He follows it with words. The hero ducks. The shaft falls rolling on the deck. STARNO turns away in wrath. The hero's song is heard no more. Rolled into himself, he departs. Pleasant is the joy of grief.

II

The Chief steps on the stranger's shore. Soon the feast of shells is spread. The joy of the hero is great. Again he resumes his soul. He forgets the dark-rolling ocean. It is in Fila-Delfia's Hall. The strangers come like a stream. His fame has reached their shores. They fill the hall. Sixty youths come in. Each bears the Flower of the Sun. The robe of each descends to his knees. They fill the foremost seats. Behold! he comes, the Son of Fame! He bears the long, bending Lily. His face is like the broad, blank moon in the skirt of a cloud, before the storms arise! He sees the youths. A cloud grows on his soul. He pours the song, and calls forth all his steel. The sons of the stranger yawn. His eye is like a green meteor. His face without form, and dark. He tosses his wandering hair. A voice is heard in the mist, "O, cut it, Son of Cultcha!" The hero's wrath arose. His lips are trembling pale. He shakes the dreadful Lily. He speaks, amidst his darkening joy. From thought to thought rolls along his Kosmic Soul. The sons of the stranger flee away. Like mist they melted away. One stranger Chief remains. He lifts his voice:—"Son of a distant land, where thou dwellest in a field of fame, there let thy song arise, but visit us no more!" The Son of Love is alone! He hides the big tear with his disordered locks, and turns admist his crowded soul. In wrath he leaves the Hall. His voice is heard in the mist, "Awake my soul no more! I am come too soon!!"

III

Why art thou sad, O Son of Songs? The vanquished, if brave, are renowned. Soon hast thou set, O beam of light! but thou shalt rise like the beam of the East, amongst thy friends, where they sit in the Dadoed Hall and the Chamber of Yallery-green. Return! Return! for thou hast left us in darkness. Thy voice has been heard. Thou has sung of the Inexpressible. Thou hast strung the harp in Bostona. Thou art one amongst a thousand foes! Thou art not understood! Come, O come away, that joy may return to my darkened soul! For shall I live, and the Son of Cultcha low? Return! Return! for we will wither together, O car-borne Son of Erin! (11 March 1882)

There were no more cartoons of Wilde in *Punch* during 1882. In issue after issue, however, there were satiric pieces about him and the aesthetes. One of these, published shortly after he sailed for America on 14 January, is an amusing but blistering fictional interview with Oscar upon his arrival here. A part of the interview is quoted below:

Figure 127. William Powell Frith (1818–1909): The Private View at the Royal Academy, 1881.

Figure 128. Detail of figure 127.

"Oh, yes! I speak most languages; in the sweet honey-tinted brogue my own land lends me. *La bella Donna della mia Mente* exists, but she is not the Jersey Lily, though I have grovelled at her feet; she is not the Juno Countess, though I have twisted my limbs all over her sofas; she is not the Polish Actress, though I have sighed and wept over all the boxes of the Court Theatre; she is not the diaphanous Sarah, though I have crawled after her footsteps through the heavy fields of scentless Asphodel; she is not the golden-haired Ellen, more fair than any woman Veronese looked upon, though I have left my *Impressions* on many and many a seat in the Lyceum Temple, where she is the High Priestess; nor is she one of the little Nameless Naiads I have met in Lotus-haunts, who, with longing eyes, watch the sweet bubble of the frenzied grape. No, Sir, my real Love is my own Kosmic Soul, enthroned in its flawless essence; and when America can grasp the supreme whole I sing in too-too utterance for vulgar lips, then soul and body will blend in mystic symphonies; then, crowned with bellamours and wanton flower-de-luce, I shall be hailed Lord of a new Empery, and as I strain my lips in the bleeding wounds of the Pomegranate, and wreathe my o'ergrown limbs with the burnished disk of the Sunflower, Apollo will turn pale, and lashing the restive horses of the Sun, the tamer chariot of a forgotten god will make way for the glorious zenith of the one Oscar Wilde." (14 January 1883)

The idea for the second Furniss cartoon (figure 126) appeared in the 12 May 1883 issue and was taken from "The Private View of the Academy," a painting by William Powell Frith in 1881 (figures 127 and 128).[6] It was appropriate for Furniss to use this painting, since one of the artist's aims was to satirize the aesthetic movement. The original work shows many eminent persons from all walks of life, but the focal point is Oscar Wilde holding a catalogue of paintings on display and surrounded by a group of admirers. No doubt, Oscar is giving his opinion rather freely concerning the merits or demerits of the exhibit. Furniss's conception of the gathering is a meeting of the Salvation Army with Wilde leading the prestigious group in spirited hymn singing. The idea is not so far fetched as might at first appear, since many of these persons were zealous evangelists for one cause or another. Wilde was, of course, the self-appointed apostle of beauty, while Millais, Marks, and Leighton ardently espoused the Pre-Raphaelite cause. Ellen Terry, Lily Langtry, and Henry Irving were responsible through their efforts for raising the drama to its rightful place among the arts. Eminent politicians and scientists such as Gladstone and Huxley, who were devout disciples of their respective areas, are also included in both painting and cartoon. The following explanation accompanies the cartoon:

Mr. Frith's Private View. The Artist is, of course, as much entitled to his private view as is Mr. BRADLAUGH, or General BOOTH, or as we are ourselves. Like *Daniel* in the celebrated Newdigate poem—

And when we saw the picture on the wall,
At first we couldn't make it out at all.

But a few moment's reflection will help the spectator to the Artist's meaning. It is clearly this:—A number of celebrities have joined the Salvation Army and having hired a room in the Academy for a Sunday Camp Meeting, have brought their hymn books, and the majority of them are joining heart and soul in a hymn, which is being led by the aesthetic Mr. OSCAR WILDE, while Mr. SALA, having lost his place in the book, is giving echoes in the background. Mr. MILLAIS, only half converted, feels uneasy, and is rubbing himself sideways against the corner of a frame. Mr. MARKS is anxiously waiting for the hymn to be finished, in order to preach on his own conversion, and point to himself as a Frightful Example. Mr. HENRY IRVING looks pale and nervous; he is probably about to yield to inspiration, and to address them in the unknown tongues. The prominent members are of course Generals, Captains, and Lieutenants, while "Private" View himself is modestly at the back taking notes.

The distinctive mark of this Corps of the Salvation Army is the shape of their hats; they have all been compelled to observe uniformity in this respect, and have, no doubt, all dealt with the same hatter. The President's,

Sir F. LEIGHTON'S, clothes will give his tailor fits. May the tailor do the same for Sir FREDERICK!

On the old system adopted by the stage-managers of the Elizabethan era, who called a spade a spade, and wrote up "This is a House," "This is a Tree," and so forth, Mr. FIRTH [*sic*] has most considerately placed the names of celebrities represented underneath, so that, after the first ten minutes, there is no possibility of mistaking Sir FREDERICK for Mr. IRVING, ELLEN TERRY for NELLY FARREN, Mr. GLADSTONE for Mr. TENNIEL, or Sir W. V. HARCOURT for Mr. W. AGNEW, M. P., and so on. It will be a most valuable picture long after the Salvation Army craze is forgotten, and most interesting when all photographs of the persons here represented shall have faded away, and their likenesses everywhere been destroyed,—excepting always those in *Mr. Punch's* unique collection which will ever exist to answer doubts, decide bets, restore certainty, and correctly teach history. (12 May 1883)

The second time *Punch* compared Wilde to a Dickens character was occasioned by the publication of *Dorian Gray* in 1890. He is parallel to the Fat Boy in *Pickwick* in that he startles the conventional Mrs. Grundy with his sensational book (figure 129). Oscar is portrayed as the Fad Boy, an iconoclast who is interested only in the shock value upon morality. The character is gross, as Wilde was to become in later years, leering at the respectable Mrs. Grundy as he offers her a copy of *Dorian* (19 July 1890, p. 25).

Wilde's second "Fancy Portrait" appeared 5 March 1892, a few days after the opening of his play *Lady Windermere's Fan* (figure 130). It caricatures the author's unorthodox behavior and curtain speech at the close of the first performance. The author came on stage smoking a cigarette and gave the following speech.

Ladies and Gentlemen, I have enjoyed this evening *immensely*. The actors have given us a *charming* rendering of a *delightful* play, and your appreciation has been most intelligent. I congratulate you on the *great* success of your performance, which persuades me that you think *almost* as highly of the play as I do myself.[7]

Punch could not resist renaming the playwright Shakspeare Sheridan Oscar Puff and captioning the cartoon appropriately "Quite Too-Too Puffickly Precious!!" The actors are depicted as mere puppets controlled by Oscar, since they were in fact not given much credit for the play's success.

The cartoon is accompanied by a take-off on the play itself, at the end of which is a parody of the much-discussed author's speech:

Author. Ladies and Gentlemen, it is so much to the fashion nowadays to do what one pleases, that I venture to offer you some tobacco while I enjoy a smoke myself. (Throws cigars and cigarettes amongst the audience à la Harry Payne.) Will you forgive me if I change my tail-coat for a smoking jacket? Thank you! (Makes the necessary alteration of costume in the presence of the audience.) And now I will have a chair. (Stamps, when up comes through a trap a table supporting a lounge, and a cup of tea. Another table appears through another trap, bringing up with it a tray and a five o'clock set.) And now I think we are comfortable. (Helps himself to tea, smokes, etc.) I must tell you I think my piece excellent. And all the puppets that have performed in it have played extremely well. I hope you like my piece as well as I do myself. I trust you are not bored with this chatter, but I am not good at a speech. However, as I have to catch a train in twenty minutes, I will tell you a story occupying a quarter of an hour. I repeat, as I have to catch a train—I repeat, as I have to catch a train—

Entire Audience. And so have we! (Exeunt. Thus the play ends in smoke.) (5 March 1892)

Bernard Partridge's cartoon in the 9 July issue (figure 131) is a humorous rendering of Wilde as an overweight but abject French soldier, complete with a manuscript of his play *Salome* protruding from his knapsack. Wilde's threat to become a French citizen if the Lord Chamberlain refused to license his play for performance turned out to be an idle one but one filled with promise for the cartoonist.

Punch for the first time offered Wilde praise for *A Woman of No Importance* after its opening in April 1893. While critical of his ability to construct a plot without melodrama, the reviewer in "A Work of Some Importance" went on to say that Wilde's merit lay in the quality of his comical material and in his timing. The play was recommended for "the Christy-Minstrel epigrammatic dialogue," and *Punch* based a cartoon on this idea (figure 132). Wilde is portrayed as the leader of the Christy Minstrels, with Beerbohm Tree, who played Lord Illingworth, Henry Kemble as the archdeacon of Brancaster, and Rose Leclercy in the role of Lady Hunstanton (6 May 1893, p. 213).

Figure 131. "A Wilde Idea," Punch, 9 July 1892.

Figure 133. Wilde by Beerbohm, Pick-Me-Up, 22 September 1894.

Figure 132. "Christy Minstrels of No Importance," Punch, 6 May 1893.

Max Beerbohm, a personal friend of Oscar's, drew him in several caricatures, none of which Oscar could bear. The example included here was first published in *Pick-Me-Up*, 22 September 1894, a year prior to the trial (figure 133).[8] Beerbohm later related how he had found it on the wall of the police inspector who arrested Wilde. It is striking for its simplicity, yet at the same time it manages to catch the essential Oscar with relatively few strokes. As Lynch points out in his book, Beerbohm emphasized the peculiarity of Oscar's hand, which in this particular caricature resembles a crab.[9] It also illustrates his grossness which, according to the artist, became more pronounced with success, both in body and in his relations with people.

The *Vanity Fair* caricature by Carlo Pellegrini appeared in the issue for 24 May 1884, a matter of weeks before Wilde's marriage to Constance Lloyd (figure 134). Unlike any other drawing up to that time, Pellegrini shows the new Oscar, the one who had cut and curled his hair like Nero's and who had replaced his knee breeches with long pants. He now took on the look of a fashionable and successful man-about-town, though somewhat foppish in pose. It is interesting that the visible hand is similar to that of Beerbohm's caricature in that the fingers are curled in an almost identical position.

Prior to Oscar's visit to America, *Puck* began satirizing his aestheticism and materialism in the "Hugo Dusenbury" column. Hugo, a poet, wrote the following letter to the editors on 21 September 1881:

Editor Puck—Dear Sir:

I must again ask you to allow me some of your valuable space for advertising purposes, taking it out in trade, as usual. Please do not forget that the Fall rates for poems are a little higher than usual this year, on account of a wide spread epidemic of malarial fever among the Muses. My own has suffered severely.

The announcement I am about to make I might really ask you to publish as news, if you had any soul in you for the concerns of the literary world. I wish you would credit my a/c with any increase of circulation resultant upon the publication of the following.

Copartnership notice.

Notice is hereby given that we, V. Hugo Dusenbury, of New York, and Oscar Wilde, of London, have this day formed a copartnership for the purpose of carrying on a first-class poetical business in New York, under the firm name of Dusenbury, Wilde & Co.

V. Hugo Dusenbury, P. P.
Oscar Wilde, Aesthete-at-large.

Sept. 15th, 1881.

Yes, Oscar Wilde and I are partners. It had to be. There could be but one Dusenbury, and it was not desirable that there should be two Wildes. We were brought together by a syndicate composed of Charles Algernon Swinburn, Martin Farquhar Tupper and Baron Rothschild. We shook hands. The two greatest business poets of this or any other age are now one firm. There is no divided empire. Orders addressed to either party will be promptly filled by the new firm.

. . . .

Here I want it distinctly understood that the firm name is Dusenbury, Wilde & Co. When signing for the

Figure 134. Wilde by "Ape," Vanity Fair, *24 May 1884.*

firm I shall not sign P. P. There is no "Co." at present; we are looking out for a capitalist. Ocky wanted to have his name first; but I pointed out to him that people would take my name for an adjective, like his; and would say that our poems were wild and dusenbury. He saw the force of the objection, and yielded.

We are now prepared to receive and fill all orders; and have an exceptionally fine line of Fall samples on hand. . . .

Very truly yours,
Dusenbury, Wilde & Co.,
Professional Poets.
(21 September 1881)

"Fitznoodle in America" appeared regularly in *Puck*, supposedly written by the affected and lisping Fitznoodle character. A displaced Englishman, Fitznoodle had choice comments to make on a variety of subjects and persons currently in the news. In the 28 September 1881 issue several months prior to Wilde's visit, the column was devoted to the topic of aestheticism, in which he mentions the poet's name.

Aestheticism.

Ya-as faw a verwy long time there has been a considerwable amount of talk in Gweat Bwitain on the subject of aesthetics.

Numerwous fwiends of mine have witten to me about it, and I have observed aw in the London *Punch*, a widiculous comic journal, ye know, some verwy curious engravings tweating on the mattah. They are, I believe, by some fellow who dwaws, and his name is aw DuMaruwiah. I must say that I nevah saw anything in them specially to laugh at, although when some of the men I know see them they positively wo ah, and wemark that I wesemble some of the individuals that are wepwesented in the aw cuts.

The peculiarwity about this system of aestheticism is that the people who pwactice it dwess themselves up in an odd sort of way, decorwate their houses in a stwange mannah, use a vocabularwy understood only by their own twibe, and indulge in a super-wefined and ware kind of aw literwature.

They pwofess also an extwaordinarwy admirwation faw all descwiptions of flowahs, although they show a pweferwence faw lilies and sun-flowahs. They wear their hair long, and their attitudes are invarwiably classical; but, to my mind, not excessively gwaceful. In fact, aw I look upon the whole business as aw outwageous tomfoolerwy.

There will, Jack Carnegie says, always be persons who will exaggerwate, and wun into the gwound things in which there may be something weally good, which, if

carwied out in a moderwate mannah, will be all wight.

No one, faw instance, would accuse Mrs. Fitznoodle of being cwazy on the question of art decorwation, and yet she has made our wesidence look much pwettiah by ornamenting and filling it with verwy desirwable and attwactive *bwic-a-bwac*, some of it of the same charwactah as affected by the aw aesthetics. So that they have done some twifling amount of good aftah all.

This aw weminds me that I was induced to wandah the othah evening into a theatah called the Standard, where an aesthetic operwa called "Patience" is being played. It is said to be new and orwiginal, and it is by the two fellows whose names, I believe, are Gilbert and Sullivan. They are, I believe, also wesponsible faw an operwa called "Pinafore."

This "Patience" tweats of this aesthetic cwaze in quite a clevah and amusing mannah. One charwactah in it, Jack says, is supposed to wepwesent a fellow at home named Oscar Wilde, who is said to belong to the aesthetic twibe, and who has wecently published a book of poetwy, some of which I have had gweat difficulty in compwehending. If I were to cwiticise it myself, I should decidedly charwacterwize it as wubbish.

The operwa met with my appwoval, and it quite merwits it. I smiled severwal times, and expwessed my satisfaction to those arwound me, and wapped faw encores. The chorwus of wapturwous, maidens sang in a pwaiseworthy mannah, and appeared awfully classical, while the dwagoon guards looked verwy naturwal in their pwopah uniforms—besides, they were tall, stwapping fellows. I like "Patience," I think it will have a run aw. (28 September 1881)

During the 1882 lecture tour of the United States, there were many cartoons of Wilde illustrating the American brand of satire. Unlike their British counterparts, several American artists saw a common theme in his aestheticism, that of materialism. In the January issue of *Puck*, for instance, there appeared a full-page cartoon of "Oscar, the Apostle," American style, with a money bag labeled "lecture receipts" and a comical "dream" collage of an "aesthetic future" (figure 135). The artist's conception of Wilde is entirely different from that of other drawings. An almost unrecognizable figure dominates this cartoon, the legs disproportionately elongated and the nose prominently emphasized. The long hair and rather thick lips are characteristic, but were it not for the caption and the abundance of aesthetic symbols, the poet would not be easy to identify with certainty.

In addition to satirizing Oscar in cartoon, the next week *Puck* also ran the following verse:

The Philistines to Oscar

Philistines we, and earth-worms every one,
And yet we would be glad at thine advent
And bid thee welcome, had we but the call
Upon the racket upon which thou'rt bent—
And stake our shekels all on the event.
But, as the game now stands, we can but say
We're glad thou'rt here, and hope thou meanst
    to stay
And teach us to be utter. Will it pay?
We're shouting, Oscar, will the business pay?
                            (18 January 1882, p. 314)

The newspapers too saw a mercenary purpose to the apostle's sermons on beauty. The *New York Daily Graphic* carried this cartoon and poem in its 11 January issue (figure 136).[10]

Figure 136. "Aestheticism as Oscar Understands It," New York Daily Graphic, *11 January 1882.*

Figure 135. "Oscar the Apostle," Puck, *11 January 1882.*

Taken out of chronological order for the purpose of dealing with theme, a most interesting cartoon was published in the 22 November 1883 issue of *Life* (figure 137) without the benefit of explanatory text. The contemporary audience was probably familiar with the characters appearing in the drawing, but nearly a century has obscured their identities for the modern reader. The cartoon was probably intended to show Wilde's place in the procession of European notables who had enjoyed successful American tours. Leading the procession is Richard D'Oyly Carte, producer of Gilbert and Sullivan's operas, under whose auspices Wilde came to this country. The foreground includes, from left to right: Wilde, Christine Nilsson, Etelka

Figure 137. "The Land of Promise and Pay," Life, 22 November 1883.

Gerster, Adelina Patti, Nicolini, Lily Langtry, and Freddie Gebhardt. Nilsson was the Swedish operatic soprano who had made several U.S. tours during the 70s and whose final appearance here was in 1884. It was reported by the *New York Times* that she would receive $2,400 for each performance during her farewell tour. Actual receipts, however, did not quite reach this figure.[11] Etelka Gerster was a Hungarian opera star and rival of the great Patti. Gerster's initial visit to America was in 1878, followed by additional tours from 1883 to 1887. Adelina Patti, the Italian soprano, who was herself caricatured several times by *Puck* and other periodicals, is depicted carrying Nicolini, the tenor whom she was to marry in 1886. Next to Patti, Lily Langtry carries her Freddie Gebhardt, the wealthy young man who followed her devotedly during her 1882 American tour. Langtry, by the way, had an advanced sale in Cincinnati alone of $3,500. It is interesting that both Freddie and Nicolini are caricatured as canine pets of the prominent female performers. While all of these are gathering money that grows as sunflowers, Oscar emerges dripping wet from the river carrying a monogrammed satchel. To judge from his expression, the satchel is not filled with lecture proceeds, for he seldom spoke to capacity audiences.

The Judge published what was probably the most

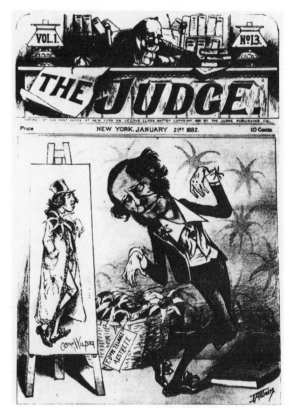

Figure 138. "Prominent Evangelist Imitating Oscar," by J. A. Wales, Judge, *21 January 1882.*

comical of the Wilde cartoons in the 21 January 1881 issue; certainly it is one that captured the essence of Oscar and the aesthetes in general (figure 138). DeWitt Talmage, the clergyman, editor and lecturer whom some called a pulpit clown, decides that he must change his style and become aesthetic according to Oscar's instructions. Having read *How to Be Aesthetic*, by Oscar Wilde, and modeling himself after a portrait of the author, Talmage appears adorned in aesthetic garb and looks just as foppish and foolish as Oscar.

When Oscar appeared before the Boston audience that included sixty Harvard students, a part of his speech was picked up by *The Harvard Lampoon* and made the subject of one of its cartoons (figure 139). Oscar commented about his visit to the college and noted that he was favorably impressed with both the art and athletics of the school. It would not be inappropriate, in his opinion, for a Greek sculpture of an athlete to be placed in the gymnasium. If the gift would be accepted he would like to present the students with such a statue.[12] The cartoon shows Oscar dispensing replicas of classical Greek sculpture, including the Discus-thrower and Aph-

rodite, while the students reach eagerly to receive his contribution.

Another cartoon of Wilde appeared in the same periodical in December when Lily Langtry left Oscar behind in New York to complete her tour, taking Freddie Gebhardt with her (figure 140). In "The Transit of Venus" Oscar is depicted as a large aesthetic sunflower, similar to the original caricature in *Punch*, and Langtry is shown as Venus. The sunflower in this cartoon is also representative of the sun, the center of the solar system, around which Venus revolves. Since Venus is the most brilliant of planets, and signifies both love and beauty in mythology, one can assume that her departure left the poet in despair (15 December 1882, p. 55).

Puck was opposed to the nomination of Samuel Jones Tilden as Democratic presidential candidate

Figure 139. "*The Aesthetic Image-Vender,*" Harvard Lampoon, *9 February 1882.*

Figure 140. "*The Transit of Venus,*" Harvard Lampoon, *15 December 1882.*

OL. X.—No. 258. FEBRUARY 15, 1882. Price, 10 Cents.

"What fools these Mortals be!"
MIDSUMMER-NIGHTS DREAM

Puck

PUBLISHED BY
EPPLER & SCHWARZMANN. NEW YORK OFFICE No. 21 - 23 WARREN ST
TRADE MARK REGISTERED 1878
ENTERED AT THE POST OFFICE AT NEW YORK, AND ADMITTED FOR TRANSMISSION THROUGH THE MAILS AT SECOND CLASS RATES.

Figure 141. "The Great 'Patience' Candidate," by Gillam, Puck, *15 February 1882.*

in the 1884 election. Its cover for the 15 February 1882 issue turned Tilden into a Bunthorne or Wildean character in knee breeches, demurely posed, holding a sunflower with 1884 on its petals (figure 141). The significance of the barrel of money lies in the fact that Tilden was extremely wealthy, so wealthy that he was investigated for personal income taxes for a number of years. The maidens represent the states who are looking to him as their leader, and the accompanying verse makes *Puck*'s position clear. For Wilde, the connotations are not favorable.

The ever-present sunflower, the knee breeches, and the pointed shoes identify Oscar as the subject

of his most unique caricature (figure 142). In "A Few Canine Cuts" from *Puck*, he is a dog, probably a hound of some type, with long flowing ears that resemble his own long hair (3 May 1882, p. 135). Even as an animal, his pose is characteristic and somewhat effeminate.

One of Wilde's 1882 lecture topics was "House Beautiful"; it concerned itself with identifying that which was considered aesthetically pleasing in household furnishings. After seeing a goodly portion of America, Wilde felt qualified to speak out on some of the atrocities he had seen on his tour. In what was to have been his farewell address 11 May in New York, he had this to say:

"I found everywhere I went bad wall papers horribly designed and colored carpets, and that old offender, the horse-hair sofa, whose stolid look of indifference is always so depressing. I found meaningless chandeliers and machine-made furniture, generally of rosewood, which creaked dismally under the weight of the ubiquitous interviewer. I came across the small iron stove which they always persist in decorating with machine-made ornaments, which is as great a bore as a wet day or any other particularly dreadful institution."[13]

Thomas Nast drew the following cartoon for *Harper's Weekly* 9 September 1882, in which the denounced cast-iron stove anthropomorphically assumes the capability of returning Wilde's scorching criticisms (figure 143). Its reply is, "I can stand it if you can." In addition to tolerating the put-down, perhaps the artist also intended to imply that it could adjust to its new aesthetic sunflower decoration as well.

Though the following cartoon from *Puck*—*Puck*'s "Pyrotechnics-Fourth-of-July Fireworks Free to All"—was not devoted entirely to Wilde, he is part of the July 4th fireworks display. He appears in the upper-right-hand corner as the "aesthetic flyer" (figure 144). Again he is shown as a combination sunflower and lily (5 July 1882, pp. 284–85). Since he was quite vocal in criticizing the American way of celebrating this holiday, it is ironic for him to be included here.

SWINBURNE

"The Brief Bard" was one of *Punch*'s favorite labels for Algernon Charles Swinburne, the poet introduced in the following lines as he steps into the "Battle of the Bards" for the laureateship in 1896:

Figure 142. "Canine Cuts," Puck, *3 May 1882.*

And first advances, as by right supreme,
With frosted locks adrift, and eyes a-dream,
With quick short footfalls, and an arm a-swing,
As to some cosmic rhythm heard to ring
From Putney to Parnassus, a brief bard.
(In stature, not in song!) Though
       passion-scarred.

Like Alfred Austin, Swinburne was a favorite of caricaturists because of his tiny physical stature. *Unlike* Austin, however, he was a writer of some poetic stature, and he was recognized as such by many who caricatured and parodied him.

"A True Poet" was Frederick Waddy's caption for his 1872 *Once a Week* cartoon of Swinburne (figure 145), and the editorial commentary accompanying Carlo Pellegrini's 1874 *Vanity Fair* lithograph (figure 146) called him "the only modern poet of the flesh" and gave more weight to his strengths than to his weaknesses.

In an age of hypocrisy the path he has chosen is a dangerous one, but he has trodden it with boldness and success. Yet he has made the mistake of leaving this path, which he knows, for that of politics, which he knows not, and for which his organisation peculiarly unfits him. He does not reason, he sympathises. Rejecting the common fash-

Figure 143. "Red Hot Stove," Harper's Weekly, *9 September 1882.*

Figure 144. Wilde as "Aesthetic Flyer" in Fourth of July celebration, Puck, *1883.*

all in all, he is the figure of a man interesting, wonderful and admirable because he is quite unlike all other men.

However "wonderful and admirable" *Vanity Fair* may have found Swinburne in the early 1870s, by the early 1880s he was increasingly classed as one of the "Mighty Masters" of the regularly mocked aesthetes. Throughout the 1880s and 1890s, until his death in 1909, Swinburne, himself the author of a collection of parodies in his 1880 *Heptalogia*, appeared fairly frequently in caricature, cartoon, and comic commentary in the periodicals. The 1880 Christmas number of *Truth* contained an extensive series of cartoons and parodies on several poets,

Figure 145. Swinburne by Waddy, Once a Week, *23 March 1872.*

ions, yet incapable of touching with his finger the realities of things, he lands after all upon a fashion uncommon and pretentious yet none the more real. His notions of public policy are those of an enthusiastic schoolboy. He believes in Massini. He has grand ideas of Liberty; none of Law, which has yet to find a singer. Personally he is nervous, excitable, explosive, rebellious, graphic, and ready in revolt against all revealed religions and moralities; and just as no punctuation can hold his luxuriance of speech, so no social laws can control his acts. Admirable in many great things he is lamentable in many small; sometimes merely a poet, he is often a seer and a revealer of deep-lying truths; and, taking him for

Figure 146. Swinburne by "Ape," Vanity Fair, 21 November 1874.

The air I breathe is cloyed with cloves and
    nard;
  I lurk and linger in the satyrs' haunt;
To caprid hordes I chaunt my Lesbian lays—
    The joy that stings, the lethal love that kills;
The bliss that blasts, the beauty that betrays;
    The hope that blights, the threnody that
      thrills;
The poet's bay with noxious weeds I twine,
    And through the mud I drag a gift divine."

Truth may have presented Swinburne as Pan, but Chicago's *Figaro* literally "panned" him in a mock "horror" drama "The Blisters" by "All-Chin-On Snarls Skinburn." Swinburne's play, "The Sisters," had been printed in its entirety (complete with illustrations) on the first two pages of the second section of The Chicago Sunday *Tribune* of 15 May 1892. On the following Saturday *Figaro* ran its parody, in response to "the Swinburne tumult in the Sunday Times," with the Dilstons becoming the "Swillsomes" and with Reginald Clavering becoming "Reginald Clattertongue."

(Vide the Swinburne Tumult in the Sunday Tribune.)
THE BLISTERS.
A HORROR.
BY
ALL-CHIN-ON SNARLS SKINBURN.

Sir Transport Swillsome . . . . . . An Amiable Old Gent.
Crank Swillsome . . . . His Son.
Reginald Clattertongue . . . . .A Dude.
Anne Swillsome and Mabel Swillsome
                Country Belles and co-heiresses.

Act I. *Clattertongue Hall, Northbummerland.*

Anne: 'Tis spring again and wintry weather yet.
Is it not tough, dear sister? For I wot
Such beastly weather saw we ne'er before.
Mabel: Talk of face-powder, bleaches, matinees,
Or any mortal thing on this green earth,
Except the weather—
Anne: Rats!
Mabel: Say rats again,
And as I am your sister, I will pull
Your bangs out by the rootlets—
Anne: Pshaw! go to!
This persiflage, but ill becomes us, dear;
There's something else much dearer to our hearts.
Now, Reggie—
Mabel: That name cometh very pat,
From *you*, considering that he is *my*
Betrothed, and not—not yours.
Anne: O, cheese it, dear,

including Swinburne. Swinburne is caricatured as Pan (figure 147), who identifies himself with the lines

"I am the founder of the fleshly school—
    The lips that bite like flame, the kiss that
      scorches,
The blood-red mouth; flanks smelling of the
      south;
    The clinging clutch; the tongues like flaming
      torch
The throats like towers and the breath like
      wine—
    All are *my* phrases—every one is mine!

I am alliteration's artful bard—
    The arch-priest of a Muse lenocinant;

*Figure 147. Swinburne as Pan in the Christmas Number
of* Truth, *December 1880.*

All's fair in love and war, the poet saith,
And, as for me, I fancy Reggie too.
What's more, I'm fairer—
Mabel: Pooh! you tawny puss,
Sister of mine, altho' you be, I'll swat
You o'er the jowl if you do not at once
Relinquish Reggie—
Anne: Tush! I fear you not,
And I will scratch your pasty face—
Mabel: Have at
Thee!
*(They fight. Enter Reginald and Crank, smoking cigarettes
and scanning the illustrated sporting papers.)*
Reginald: How now! I fear—
Crank: That things—
Reginald: Are wrong. Yes, wrong.
That sisters should so very fiercely scrap;
Shoo, girls!
Crank: Yes, fight it out in the alley.

(Exeunt Girls.)
Reginald: Beats the old Harry, don't it, hebe Crank,
How girls will fight and scratch, and fight again,
For love of such a sorry wight as I?
Dont it?—
Crank: It do, indeed. I cannot see

Why they should fancy such an ugly mug
As yours—
Reginald: Peace, loon! I've writ a play.
(Enter Sir Transport, who overhears)
Sir Transport: My God!
Reginald: Yes, and what's more, I surely do propose
To read it to you!
*(Sir Transport commits suicide on the spot, and is borne out
by a game-keeper.)*

ACT II. *In the back yard.*

CRANK AND MABEL

Crank: I may not say what any jay may say?
Mabel: To me? You give me pains, you do indeed.
Sweet Crank, there's just one little thing that I
Would ask of you—
Crank: Then spit it out, and let's
Have no more monkeying. What is't—
Mabel: Just this:
Is it my sister Anne or I, on whom you're mashed?
Let's have no further shilly-shallying.
But tell the truth—
Crank: Well, since you press me, dear—
Mabel (blushing.) I havn't pressed you; no, at least not
yet;

Though very willingly would I submit
To just a squeeze or two from—
Crank: Me? I knew
I'd won you, for you gave yourself away
By that sweet blush. I do believe I love
You—
Mabel: I knew I would knock out that green-eyed
Anne.

                    (They kiss.)

Crank: There, there, now, that will do; please do not
eat
Me up—
Mabel (sobbing for joy.) God reward
You, Frank!

ACT III.

REGINALD AND MABEL.

Reginald: No wonder both these girls on me are soft.
I'm but a dude, but yet a nervy dude,
For did I not attend the chicken-fight
At fair Milwaukee? Yea, and bet my roll
Just like the toughest sport in that tough gang?
Ho! Ho! Here's one of 'em!

                    (Enter Mabel.)

Mabel: Yes, I'm here, young man,
And hearken, please, to what I have to say:
When in the hottest of the chicken-fight
Who was't you thought of? Answer me.
Reginald: My God!
She's got me now! Well, say, since you must know,
I did not think of anyone. The fight
Was so exciting. For the game birds fought
Like furies. How could I have time to think?
I had no time, for I was drawing pictures
For the Police Gazette.
Mabel: Ha! Artist, too,
As well as sport. Now scan me well, I say,
And see if you can not detect a blink
In my left eyeball, that might mean I loved
You!
Reginald: My love! Mabel! What can I?
Mabel: Say
Just that again.
Reginald: Go slow now, here comes Crank.

                    (Enter Crank.)

Crank: What's this I see before me?
Reginald: Only this
That you are not deuce high in this small game.
In other words, you are not in it, see?
Crank: Mabel—
Reginald: Loves me. You'd better chase yourself.
Crank (lighting a cigarette.) Well, I can stand it.
Mabel (offended)   Are'nt you going to weep?
Crank: Not I, i'faith, for I would just as soon
That Reggie have you, he, the doughty dude—
The hero of a hundred chicken-fights.

I'll now go off and bet a bone or two
On the suburban, and thus win enough
To buy you both some snide old wedding-gift.
Eh, Reggie—
Reginald: Stow your gabble! Here comes Anne.

                    (Enter Anne.)

Anne: I think you both have got a pile of nerve.
Didn't you know, you puss, that I was struck
On Reggie—
Mabel: That's what I did, but I have gotten there
With both feet, as it were, while you have got
Anne: (beginning to cry) The mitten!
Mabel: Aye!
Anne: But I shall be revenged;
I'll give you both a dose will make you sick,
See if I don't.
(Goes into kicking hysterics. Crank and Reginald discuss the American Derby odds while Mabel douses her prostrate sister with a bucket of water from the well.)

Figure 148. Swinburne dines in Punch, *5 June 1897.*

Reginald: Say, Mabel, I am feeling far from well.
Mabel: And I am feeling squeamish too.
Reginald: Wow! wow! I'm knocked out I'm afraid.
(Falls on the grass.)
    Mabel: (*also sinking*) Reggie, dear, I know what ails us.
Reginald: What?
Mabel: You know that bread and butter that we ate
At breakfast?
Reginald: Aye!
Mabel: Anne buttered it with rough on rats! *(Dies.)*
Reginald: I'll never see another chicken-fight *(Dies to slow music.)*

          (CURTAIN.)   *H.R.V.*
                     (Figaro, 21 May 1892)

During the remainder of the 1890s, Swinburne continued to receive more than his share of barbs from the periodical press, especially from *Punch.* In an 1897 issue of *Punch,* the Brief Bard is shown indulging in a new poetic diet (figure 148). The envious poet must learn to cultivate his talents on beef and beer because it is "no longer considered a sign of genius to live on lilies." Therefore,

> If you'd know the precise apparatus
> To produce the poetic afflatus,
>   You need, it is clear,
>   But a pint pot of beer
> And a big plate o' beef an' pertatus!

Beef and beer were not enough, however, to gain Swinburne the Laureate's crown, and *Punch*'s Almanack for 1907 finds the Brief Bard turning from poetry to golf (figure 149) in a cartoon by Bernard Partridge.

Unlike Wilde, whose bizarre and controversial life seemed to overshadow his actual writings in the eyes of the satirists, Swinburne was frequently acknowledged, even by those comic magazines that poked fun at him, as an accomplished poet. Despite *Punch*'s playfulness with him during his lifetime, the obituary verses in the 21 April 1909 issue, for example, left little doubt about the magazine's high regard for the poet:

IN MEMORIAM.
Algernon Charles Swinburne.
BORN 1837. DIED APRIL 10TH, 1909.

WHAT of the night? For now his day is done,
    and he, the herald of the red sunrise,

Leaves us in shadow even as when the sun
    Sinks from the sombre skies.

High peer of SHELLEY, with the chosen few
    He shared the secrets of Apollo's lyre,
Nor less from Dionysian altars drew
    The god's authentic fire.

Last of our land's great singers, dowered at
    birth
    With music's passion, swift and sweet and
    strong,
Who taught in heavenly numbers, new to
    earth,
    The wizardry of song—

His spirit, fashioned after Freedom's mould,

Now it is AL-GER-NON's turn. He is cross be-cause so. one has giv-en ALFRED some Lau-rels for writ-ing Po-et-ry. What a Shame Ne-ver mind: he has gone in for Golf now, and is go-ing to win the Cham-pi-on-ship. Look, he has just done the Long Hole in On

Bernard Partridge

Figure 149. Partridge's version of Swinburne, Punch, *17 January 1907.*

Impatient of the bonds that mortals bear,
Achieves a franchise large and uncontrolled,
Rapt through the void of air.

"What of the night?" For him no night can be;
The night is ours, left songless and forlorn;
Yet o'er the darkness, where he wanders free,
Behold, a star is born!

O.S.

ARTISTS AND OTHERS

Among the aesthetes, Wilde and Swinburne
were the most frequent victims of the pens of the
caricaturists and satirists. Others, however, especially those associated with the art of astheticism
and "decadence," were sometimes mocked and
copied by the comic press. Rossetti, for example,
was parodied in both poetry and art. The typical
Rossetti female figure and profile are drawn by Linley Sambourne (figure 150) for an 1880 *Punch*
parody of Rossetti's "Troy Town," in which
"Heavenborn Helen, Sparta's Queen" becomes
"Kent-born Helen, England's Pride," and the
typical Rossetti parenthetical refrain is changed
from "(O Troy's down,/Tall Troy's on fire!)" to "(O
London Town!/ Fashion's thralls ne'er tire!)"

KENT-BORN HELEN, England's pride,
 (O London Town!)
Had a waist a world too wide
For the height of her heart's desire.
Vinegar she in vain had tried.
 (O London Town!
  Fashion's thralls ne'er tire!)

HELEN knelt at Fashion's shrine,
 (O London Town!)
Saying, "A little boon is mine,
A little boon, but my heart's desire.
Hear me speak, and make me a sign!
 (O London Town!
  Fashion's thralls ne'er tire!)

"Look! my waist is in excess.
 (O London Town!)
I would die to have it less.
Shape it to my heart's desire.
Fit for fashionable dress.

 (O London Town!
  Fashion's thralls ne'er tire!)*

"It is moulded like a Greek's,
 (O London Town!)
One of Nature's spiteful freaks.
Pinch it to my heart's desire:
I am full of pains and piques.
 (O London Town!
  Fashion's thralls ne'er tire!)*

"See BELL FANE's, how slim it is!
 (O London Town!)
Eighteen inches at most, I wis!
Poisons the cup of my heart's desire.
O that *I* should suffer this!
 (O London Town!
  Fashion's thralls ne'er tire!)*

"Yea, for straitness here I sue!
 (O London Town!)
Antifat I find won't do;
Give me, give me, my heart's desire,
Three inches less, or at least full two.

Figure 150. "London Town" (after Rossetti), Punch,
24 April 1880.

(O London Town!
Fashion's thralls ne'er tire!)

"BELL to outrival were *so* sweet!
   (O London Town!)
E'en if my heart could hardly beat;
Heart-room is not my heart's desire,
But to bring hearts to my feet.
   (O London Town!
     Fashion's thralls ne'er tire!)

"I have rivals two or three:
   (O London Town!)
Sylph-like, slim of waist they be;
I'm forlorn of my heart's desire.
What thou hast given them give me.
   (O London Town!
     Fashion's thralls ne'er tire!)

"I am girthed like MILO's Venus;
   (O London Town!)
(Could Greek sculptors but have seen *us!*)
O my rivals! my heart's desire
Is to win in the fight between us."
   (O London Town!
     Fashion's thralls ne'er tire!)

Fashion looked on HELEN's waist,
   (O London Town!)
Looked and frowned with sore distaste,
Saw the sense of her heart's desire,
Said "This must be changed, with haste."
   (O London Town!
     Fashion's thralls ne'er tire!

Fashion looked on HELEN's face,
   (O London Town!)
Said, "'Tis clear you must tight-lace,"
And gave her there her heart's desire,
A corset new that should give her grace.
   (O London Town!
     Fashion's thralls ne'er tire!)

Fashion looked on HELEN's breast.
   (O London Town!)
"Ne'er Anaconda more tightly prest
Than this new corset, thine heart's desire.
Take it and wear, it shall bring thee rest!"
   (O London Town!)
     Fashion's thralls ne'er tire!)

HELEN took the proffered boon,
   (O London Town!
The first appliance made her swoon;
But what are pangs to the heart's desire?
She was one inch less than her rival soon!
   (O London Town!
     Fashion's thralls ne'er tire!)

HELEN turned upon her bed,
   (O London Town!)
Turned in pain on her bed, and said,
"Death at heart, with the heart's desire,
Is better than being outrivalléd."
   (O London Town!
     Fashion's thralls ne'er tire!)

Rossetti is also the victim of the American *Life*'s illustrated version of his poem "The Blessed Damozel," ridiculously rendered as "The Cussed Damozel." Since *Life*'s "poet-artist" even made an attempt to copy the Rossetti manner of incorporating poetry and art, we include this one as it appeared on the page in the magazine (figure 151).

There were, of course, other "stars" in the late nineteenth-century galaxy of aestheticism. Along with caricatures and parodies of the poetry of Swinburne, Rossetti, and Morris, comic periodicals also played games with various artists whose works and

Figure 151. "The Cussed Damozel," Life, *1890.*

and artist in a materialistic and money-grubbing generation . . . . That he will ever live to see his opinion adopted or even seriously entertained is not to be expected; but by those who have not bowed the knee to the modern Baal he will be gratefully remembered as one preaching in the wilderness the abandonment of the grosser things of life and the realisation of the Ideal." *Vanity Fair*'s commentary was accompanied by an excellent 1872 cartoon by Adriano Cecioni (figure 152). "Art Criticism" was the caption for another 1872 Ruskin caricature, this one by Waddy in *Once a Week* (figure 153). Shown flying with angel wings over the "world of art" and

Figure 152. Ruskin by Cecioni, Vanity Fair, *17 February 1872.*

words were either directly or indirectly a part of the aesthetic movement and the so-called Decadent 1890s. Rossetti and Morris were satirized as artists nearly as frequently as they were as poets; and throughout the 1890s and early twentieth century, caricatures of and by Max Beerbohm and numerous drawings in the style of Aubrey Beardsley make mock appearances in popular magazines. So also was the era's foremost art critic, John Ruskin, a frequent visitor in the journals.

"There is, perhaps, no harder fate in store for a man than to be irredeemably at variance with the spirit of the country and the times in which he lives," said *Vanity Fair* of Ruskin. "And it is Mr. Ruskin's great misfortune to be an incurable poet

Figure 153. "Art Criticism," Ruskin by Waddy, Once a Week, *25 May 1872.*

Figure 154. "Mr. Narcissus Ruskin," by Sambourne, Punch, *18 December 1881.*

Figure 155. Beerbohm by Walter Sickert in Vanity Fair, *9 December 1897.*

toward the star of "high art," Ruskin scatters the "flowers" of his writings to the world below, and Waddy comments, "There is no more honoured name in contemporary English literature than that of John Ruskin. In his books, he has discharged the noblest functions of a writer; but it were enough to make him famous in his generation had he done no more than teach our Philistine art-critics what is the true standard to which art criticism should be raised." *Punch* did not treat Ruskin so kindly. In an 1880 "Fancy Portrait," he is "Mr. Narcissus Ruskin" (figure 154), admiring his own reflection with the words, "Who is it that says most? Which can say more, than this rich praise,—that *You* alone are You!"

One of the finest of all English caricaturists was Max Beerbohm, and one of the finest caricatures of Beerbohm himself is the 1897 drawing by W. R. Sickert (figure 155). An "amiable young fellow,"

said *Vanity Fair.* "He has insulted more people than any other boy of his years; and he is full of affectations, of which unruffled assurance is the chief. He has been guilty of ideas; he thinks that he can dress; and his friends say that he knows his way about. He likes to be called 'Max,' even by his enemies; who are many." So numerous are Beerbohm's delightful drawings of literary and artistic personalities that we simply include here what seems a most appropriate one, "Some Persons of the Nineties" (figure 156), picturing among others, Sickert, Le Gallienne, George Moore, John Davidson, Oscar Wilde, William Butler Yeats, Aubrey Beardsley, and Beerbohm himself.

Figure 156. "Some Persons of the Nineties," by Beer-bohm, 1925.

Finally, a small offering of Beardsleyana from the British *Punch* and the American *Life* seems a fitting conclusion to this chapter. *Life* had a field day with such drawings as "The Waltz" by "our first Au-breybeardslist" (figure 157), An Evening Party" (figure 158), "Showing the effect upon our artist of a prolonged study of The Yellow Book" (figure 159), and an illustration to a comical vignette "In the Bor-derland (A Drama of the Coming School)" (figure 160):

In the Borderland
(A Drama of the Coming School.)

A tropical night—yellow. A moonbeam, cold as a bone. Clouds like continents. A terrace. A settee of wrought steel. A woman in a hat. A youth with a face like a desert full of air.

He (*resuming a lute*): Listen. (*Sings in a voice like a tinkl-ing cymbal*).

> Your lips are like the vines of night,
> Like tortured ivies, twisted tight,
>   Like tangled eels that turn and twine,
>   Like trampled mess of eglantine,

> Beneath your hat
> They're just like that.

She (*sobbingly*): But your hair! Your hair! Your hair!
He: My hair! Ah, ah—Hully——
She: Whose fault is it?
He: His! Himmel—his'n! I'm symbolized.
She: Is he dead?
He: Is it better to be dead——
She: He lives—lives. You are avenged. Is it better to have hair like that or to be dead? Is it better to be—What is one more reason for the heathen to be happy?
He: They miss such nights as ours—such talks—such——. Listen.
She: Again? Ah——
He: Listen. (*Resuming a lute, sings.*)

> The bigger bugs look for their pickin's;
> The murdered ones shriek like the Dickens!
>   The mortified moon,
>   A skull-white balloon,
> Swoops over some little dead chickens.

Is not the night like that?

Figure 157. Life cartoon spoofing the style of artist Au-brey Beardsley.

Figure 158. Another Beardslesque Life *cartoon, "An Evening Party," borrowed from the* Pall Mall Bulletin.

SHE: Oh yes, the night is quite like that! That's the sort of a·night it is. But the others do not tinkle.

HE *(waving his chin):* Listen. It is like that. It is like that. It is like that. Here's some more. *(The moon withdraws.)*

SHE: You go on—on. Ah! I could——. Again?

HE: Listen. *(Sings.)*

> The muskiness thickens and thickens,
> The stagger-bat dizzies and sickens,
>   Soft, supple and slight,
>   The jewelish night
> Sees little boys getting their lickin's.

SHE: And I—oh—ah! I thought I had known trouble!

HE: Listen. I will sing on—on.

SHE: You *will. (Falls screaming upon the settee.)*

HE: Listen. *(Resuming a lute.)* Hush.

SHE: *(springing to her feet with one hand and stifling a sob with the other):* More like that?

HE: Listen. *(Falls writhing upon the terrace.)*

SHE: Listen. Hush. *(She stands over him waving the settee.)* Curtain.

Another *Life* spoof on "Suppressed Chapters" from "The Callow Book" stars "Henri du Bodleyhead" and "Rosamund Newera" (figures 161 and 162).

THE CALLOW BOOK.

"I'm tired of everything," said Henri du Bodleyhead, as he stretched himself on his pale green divan, and placed his noble head on a saffron colored pillow.

"Then my dear Henri, you are in the right mood to become a contributor to *The Callow Book*," said Rosamund Newera, his mental affinity, who had dropped into his study to smoke a cigarette with him.

"I've thought of that as a last resource," said Henri. "I've tried every respectable Magazine in London, but they all return my stories and poems with the remark that they are 'overcrowded,' etc., which means they are afraid of the British Matron."

"You know, of course," said Rosamund, "that *The Callow Book* is meant to defy that prudish old lady. And the publishers have discovered that she likes to be defied. So all of us are doing our best to keep shocking her. It's great fun!"

"I'm afraid I should tire of that also," yawned Henri. "One can't always interest oneself in simply being shocking. It isn't Art you know. After all, I've lived these awfully long twenty-four years simply for Art. I'm hoping it will keep me alive till I'm twenty-five. Then I'll die happy, like a lot of other geniuses."

"Don't die," pleaded Rosamund. "There is plenty for you to live for yet. Beardsley has never yet illustrated one of your stories. You can't die happy without that."

"I've often thought of that also," said Henri pensively, "but I can't think of a plot wicked enough to appeal to so great an artist. Oh, my dearest Rosamund, why can't I be as wicked as the really great writers of France! I've tried to make my good old Yorkshire name look like something French; I drink absinthe, I read Maeterlinck and Verlaine, and occasionally I smoke opium. But it's no use. Way down in my heart I know that I'd rather be playing cricket or riding a good hunter, or reading Thackeray. I can't lie to you any more, Rosamund, and that's the solemn truth."

"Poor, dear fellow," said Rosamund, stroking his fair curly hair, "I did not know that your case was as hopeless as that. I fear that after all *The Callow Book* editors would discover that you are a hollow sham, and keep you out."

"My last hope is in you, dear Rosamund," whispered Henri. "Teach me what true wickedness is, and I will try to acquire it."

"I think that I have put our creed in a poem," said Rosamund, "and if you really grasp its meaning you are saved. Listen:

"To hate virtue, to despise truth, to love another's wife,

To doubt your bosom friend—yes, that is best in life!
To write as though the world were evil at the heart,
And full of hypocrites—Yes, that is ART!"

"It's a hard creed" sighed Henri. "Perhaps, I'd better

Figure 159. Life's version of another Beardsley drawing.

Figure 160. Life's illustration to a comic vignette, "In The Borderland."

185

Figure 162. Illustration to Life's *"The Callow Book."*

Figure 163. Punch's *"Danby Weirdsley"* contributes to an issue of April 1894.

Figure 164. *"Britannia à la Beardsley,"* in Punch's *"Almanack"* for 1895.

remain a despised British Philistine, and go back to the old Yorkshire farmhouse."

"Then," said Rosamund severely, "our love is at an end. You need never hope to be a contributor to *The Callow Book*. Farewell, false one! Farewell!" and she swept through the turquoise portières and vanished in the fog.

Droch.

Punch, also, had its fun with Beardsley with one of its many commentaries on the Aesthetes (figure 163):

Oh, The Muddle of It!
(Overheard at an Amateur Pastoral Pantomime.)

He. Well, Angelina, I see nothing in it. I think I must be
going, in a minute!
She. You're bored? To you it seems a little mystic,
But still, you'll own it's awfully artistic!
He. I don't quite enter into Pierrot's wrongs.
She. Then listen to the Incidental Songs.

Song I.—*Crocuses,*
High diddle diddle,
The cat and the fiddle

(Fragrance and Colour and Sky,
Almond and Husk,
Cedar and Musk),
O, what a good boy am I!
   II.—*Carnations.*
Little Bo-peep,
Has Lost her sheep
(Poppies and Heather and Sun,
Moonlight and Shade,
Blossom and Blade),
And so the poor dog had none!
   III.—*Heliotrope.*
Little Jack Horner,
Sat in a corner
(Rainbows, and Lilies and Laughter,
Silence and Fears,
Heartsease and Tears),
And Gill came tumbling after!

She (enthusiastic). Isn't it beautiful? So fresh and quaint!
He (sulky). Some people may admire it, others mayn't.
She. Well, if you don't I take it as a sign
   That you are quite a hopeless Philistine!
   Why, EDWIN, surely you're not going yet?
He (rising). I *must* go out, and have a cigarette. [*He goes,*
   and returns no more.]

Finally, probably the finest of *Punch*'s Beardsley-esque offerings is a full-page "Britannia A La Beardsley" (figure 164). The drawing, "By Our 'Yellow' Decadent," features the lion-guarded Britannia overlooking her isled domain, carefully watched by her court jester, Mr. Punch!

NOTES

1. Oscar Browning, "Oscar Browning on *Poems*," *Academy*, 30 July 1881, p. 85; reprinted in *Oscar Wilde, the Critical Heritage*, ed. Karl Beckson (New York: Barnes & Noble, 1970), p. 42.

2. "The Poetry of an Aesthete," *Dial*, August 1881, pp. 82–85; reprinted in Beckson, *Oscar Wilde*, p. 42.

3. *Spectator*, 13 August 1881, pp. 1048–50; reprinted in Beckson, *Oscar Wilde*, p. 47.

4. *Saturday Review*, 23 July 1881, p. 118; reprinted in Beckson, *Oscar Wilde*, p. 37.

5. Timothy Hilton, *The Pre-Raphaelites* (New York: Abrams, 1970), p. 198.

6. William Gaunt, *The Restless Century, Paintings in Britain 1800–1900* (London: Phaidon Press, 1972), pl. 144.

7. H. Montgomery Hyde, *Oscar Wilde* (New York: Farrar, Straus & Giroux, 1975), p. 137.

8. Riewald, *Beerbohm's Literary Caricatures*, p. 159.

9. Bohun Lynch, *Max Beerbohm in Perspective: With a Prefatory Letter by M. B.* (London: William Heinemann, 1921), p. 119.

10. "Aestheticism as Oscar Understands It," *Daily Graphic*, 11 January 1882; reprinted in *Oscar Wilde Discovers America (1882)* by Lloyd Lewis and Henry Justin Smith (New York: Benjamin Blom, 1936), p. 53.

11. "Nilsson to Sing with Mapleson," *New York Times*, 5 September 1884, p. 1.

12. Lewis and Smith, *Oscar Wilde Discovers America*, p. 346.

13. Ibid.

S IS for Swinburne, who, seeking the true,
    The good and the beautiful, visits the Zoo,
Where he chances on Sappho and Mr. Sardou,
And Socrates, all with the same end in view.

T IS for Talleyrand, toasting Miss Truth
    By the side of her well, in a glass of vermouth,
And presenting Mark Twain as the friend of his
    youth.

8
From Stage to Page

TO JUDGE ONLY BY THE AMOUNT OF PARODIC material available, readers in the late nineteenth century were avid theatergoers. That many of the periodicals in question were addressed to urban audiences is one reason for the bias; *Punch*, for example, was published in London and *Life* in New York, both cities lively centers for the arts. Another reason is, of course, that a number of the theatrical figures who appeared again and again were not just playwrights or actors, but outspoken commentators on the manners of the times. The pronouncements of Bernard Shaw and William S. Gilbert thus achieved a life of their own quite outside of the works themselves. Other personalities, noteworthy for their stage presence, took innumerable curtain calls in the press as well; the reading public apparently delighted in Sarah Bernhardt's coffin, Lily Langtry's French fashions, and Henry Irving's bowed legs. In addition, the pages of the press provided a forum in which theatrical conditions were discussed. Humorists tried to shame their female readers into removing elaborate hats in the theater and their fellow writers into eliminating gothic stage machinery; they lampooned adapters, ticket speculators, and advertisers; they produced enough parodic playbills to fill a book. The spirited comments, both visual and verbal, created another stage on which many a reputation flourished—and perished.

An important facet of theater criticism is the humorous review; allusive and uninhibited, it often reveals by the broadness or delicacy of its wit the taste of the public to which it appeals. In *Fun*, for example, "The Round of the Theatres" is a versified composite review of theaters and offerings. In the aggregate the plays are burlesques and light-hearted extravaganzas; the Christmas season and the reviewer's own taste combine to highlight "family" viewing. The reviewer, who dislikes didactic plays, probably caters to the preferences of his readers:

> At the Lyceum we have good QUEEN
>   BESS,[1]
>   Hight *Queen Elizabeth of England*—she
> Is a tremendous monarch and no less,
>   And Essex acts his part Essex-ively,
> And altogether—well, I rather guess
>   It is a thing a party ought to see,
> That is, if parties like such things. I am a
> Feeble supporter of historic drama.

What he does enjoy is a trip to the Haymarket to laugh and cry at a revival of James Robinson Planché or to Sadler's Wells for a slapstick pantomime.[2]

> But at this season, as the season's due,
>   *The Fair One with the Golden Locks* replanned

190

Returns, to show how deftly PLANCHE
    drew,
    And laid his colours with how light a hand!
I need not bid you go—you're sure to go, so
Give my respects to good King Lachrymoso.

    Lo! at the Wells holds pantomime its sway
      (This year there are not many, you'll take
        note)
The Maid of Merry Islington, a play
      Of local interest, which yet you'll vote
A pleasant bit of fooling in its way,
      With comic business whereon children
        dote—
(And grown-up people too—I hold my sides
At red-hot-poker jokes and butter-slides).
               (15 January 1870, p. 187)

Unlike *Fun*, *Life* preserved a serious mission behind its humor: the development of its readers' critical faculties.[3] It published many of its reviews in the form of parodic playbills or playlets, a large number directed against the playwrights, critics, and managers for engaging in "anglomania" to the detriment of native talent. For example, John Kendrick Bangs, writing as "Arthur Penn," lambastes "Mr. Wallack's Imported Company of Cockney Comedians" in parodic playbills for "The Cape Snowball" and "The Silver King." The first is a composite review of Clement Scott's *Cape Mail* and Sydney Grundy's *Snowball*, British plays that ran concurrently at Wallack's Theatre in New York in May 1883. Bangs, taking issue with the *New York Times* reporter who praised Scott for his "delicate and fanciful dramatic sense,"[4] attacks both plays for their triteness and "imported character" and for being "sickly and hyper-sentimental rubbish, full of machine-made pathos and patent leather emotion." The playbill gives the last word to an unsophisticated "Old Lady from the Country," an alter ego to the "Cynical Escort" or "Enquiring Young Man" Bangs usually includes in his scenarios: as she says, "'I suppose them shows is all alike. They're big on promisin' an' mighty slim in performin''" (10 May 1883, p. 227). The second review in question, "The Silver King," is a playlet narrated by "The Imported Mr. Osmond Tearle," a popular British actor who joined Wallack's company in September 1880. According to the playlet, "The Silver King" presents the improbable adventures of a reformed drunkard, who, chloroformed by thieves, believes that he has committed a murder and so exiles himself to America, where in three years he becomes a millionaire and is forgiven by his long-suffering wife and children (8 March 1883, pp. 118–19). The comments reflect Bangs's grudging admiration of Tearle's "fine acting" as well as his suspicion that Tearle does not exert himself for an undemanding American audience that is satisfied with blatant melodrama. Most important, however, Bangs implicitly attacks Lester Wallack's penchant for staging British plays with British talent; throughout its long career, *Life*—despite its gentle treatment of Queen Victoria—attempted to uphold its masthead motto, "Americanus Sum," by attacking "anglomania" wherever it appeared.

Part of *Life*'s reminder to its readers that they, as Americans, should develop a native drama, was couched in terms critical not only of stage managers who made fortunes by importing foreign talent, but also of the low quality of American vaudeville, which it characterized as "pink piffle." The versifier Edward F. Coward adopts the persona of a typical stage manager giving an interview to a newspaper reporter:

> "Yes, there is no doubt, and again I say,
> Th' American drama has come to stay.
> I'm glad to see that the public here
> Wants native plays. . . .
> But, incidentally, you might note
> That while I was over in London town
> I paid important royalties down
> For Pinero's latest and Jones's best;
> And one by Hicks that stood the test.
> I also got from Sims and Raleigh
> A melodrama red and gory.
> Yes! Quote me strong, for again I say,
> Th' American drama has come to stay.
> Oh! by the bye, if there is no hitch
> I'll probably do a play by Fitch."
>   (6 September 1906, p. 250)

All of the names mentioned would have been familiar to readers on both sides of the Atlantic. By the time the poem was published, the *New York Times* had reviewed Arthur Wing Pinero's *His House in Order*, playing at the St. James's in London (4 September 1906, p. 9, col. 1), and Henry Arthur Jones's *The Hypocrites*, at the Hudson Theatre in New York (2 September 1906, Sec. 4, p. 8, col. 1). *The Beauty of Bath* by Seymour Hicks and Cosmo Hamilton had opened at the Aldwych (London *Times*, 1 September 1906, p. 6), and George R. Sims's "melodrama red"—*The Woman from Gaol*—

Figure 165. Lester Wallack, Judge, *23 February 1884.*

Figure 166. Sheridan Shook and J. W. Collier, Judge, *1 March 1884.*

had been revived in London.[5] Finally, Clyde Fitch had double billing: his *Toddles* was at the Duke of York's in London,[6] and his adaptation of Edith Wharton's *House of Mirth* was playing at the Detroit Opera House (New York *Times,* 18 September 1906, p. 9, col. 4).

Managers like Lester Wallack, Sheridan Shook, and J. W. Collier (figures 165 and 166) were not entirely to blame for the steady outpouring of light-hearted farce; in many cases they and their play-wrights delivered exactly what their audiences demanded. In "The Dramatic Rest-Cure" a typical "tired business man" explains his preference for the kind of cheerful music and slapstick humor common to a George Cohan piece:[7]

When he'd labored all day in his strenuous way
    After dinner he longed for delights
Such as musical chimes and nursery rhymes
    And barber-shop humor in tights.
"Ah, where shall I go for a rest-giving show
    With nothing of brain-fag to view?
Shall I go to see 'Slush' or the drama called
    'Mush,'
    Or the comedy, 'Tittle-Tat-Too?'"

"I long to be smoothed of my troubles and
    soothed
    By a play of pink piffle—don't you?"

He loathed Maeterlinck, for he caused him to
    think;
    He hated Bill Shakespeare, he said;
He scoffed at the hero of Mr. Pinero
    And Shaw gave him pains in the head.
But when from the "drops" two fat
    comedy-cops
    Made music with slapsticks-on-vest,
While the chorus displayed a George Cohan
    brigade,

He cried, "Good! I'm getting a rest."

"There's nothing, in fact, like a knockabout act
To give a poor fellow a rest."

(17 January 1907, p. 100)

The difference between this commentator and the reviewer in *Fun* who dislikes historical dramas is evident; *Life* sought to train its readers to appreciate good drama, while *Fun* was content to enjoy the "pink piffle."

Again, when *Judge* publishes "Playgoer's Memorandum," a versified review like the one in *Fun*, an effort is made to criticize rather than merely to report the offerings of some twenty-seven theaters:

The Miracle—I mean the MADISON
    SQUARE,
Does native drama with such taste and care
That schoolgirl pieces, written just for fun,
Escape contempt, and have a six-months' run.
. . . .
On Fourteenth Street, the "fakirs'" promenade,
The UNION SQUARE succeeds with good
    and bad.
At COLVILLE'S, everything—save risk—is
    run,
And TONY PASTOR'S pleases with a pun.

ACADEMY! where the muses nine resort,
Still shall the war-scarred Colonel hold thy
    fort,
And playful Patti back in triumph bring
The operas of our ancestors to sing!

On Broadway beams a bright particular STAR
Which astronomic agents watch afar;
Modjeska, Irving, Barrett, Booth, McCullough,
Shoot past, and guide the nebulae that follow.
. . . .
The shows the Bowery boy expends his fund
    on
Are the GRAND CENTRAL, NATIONAL,
    and LONDON.
He sees clog-dancing not to be despised,
Hears songs, and penny-dreadfuls dramatized.

******

Playhouses these for all moods, grave or gay,
To waken thought, or charm an hour away.
Like mirrors, they reflect both best and worst,
And show the world what that world shows
    them first.

(5 April 1884, p. 7)

In each case the theater acquires a personality de-pending upon the tenor of its offerings, and certainly the reviewer expects his readers to follow the muses rather than the Bowry boy, to hear the opera star Adelina Patti (managed by the entrepreneur Col. H. Mapleson) rather than to hear popular songs. Clearly *Judge* was not written to appeal to those who read "penny dreadfuls." In the final analysis the humorous reviews, as well as the plays themselves, mirror the "best and worst" of public taste.

As far as some reviewers were concerned, the "worst" was the kind of performance that Lillian Russell made famous. "The Naked Drama" was, says one critic, initiated in 1879 with *The Black Crook*, a "really epochal" operetta that the police hailed for keeping the criminals off the streets and in the theaters.[8] One artist—Otho Cushing—even took a "glimpse into the future" and produced a prophetic drawing of a twentieth-century play that is reminiscent of a scene from *Hair* (*Life*, 23 February 1899, p. 153). The present was, however, sometimes shocking enough:

The drama called "legitimate"
    Might suit a prudish age,
When blushing was not out of date,
    And nakedness the rage;
But now in Nature's simple garb
    Our Thespian nymphs appear,
And, waving handkerchiefs, we rise
    Their lawless legs to cheer.

Melpomene is *en chemise*,
    Thalia's garments dun
Are reefed unseemly at the knees,
    Terpsichore has none!
A most transparent, slender fraud,
    A broad burlesque on dress,
That every night becomes more broad
    Because its width gets less.

So be it—"Beauty unadorned
    Is then adorned the most!"
Let envious skirts be henceforth scorned,
    And bareness be our boast.
Here's—"may each centipedal play
    That's placed the world before
Bear, with bare legs, the palm away
    From brains forevermore."

(*Judge*, 16 January 1884, p. 5)

The critics reacted just as vehemently to overdressing—for the sake of advertising, that is. On 8 December 1880 *Puck* predicted "A Union of Sister

193

Figure 167. "A Union of Sister Arts," Puck, *8 December 1880.*

Arts—Acting and Advertising" (figure 167), giving a scene from *Camille* in which Armand pleads,

"Listen to me, Camille! I am mad with a raging fire, hot as that kindled by Lush's Genuine Old Tom Gin. Beneath the breast of this coat, so elegantly made by Nickle, the famous tailor, beats a heart whose agony is not to be expressed in words. What is this man to me? He is but the shade and shadow of a rival, as unreal as Ochre's picture there on the wall—that size $1.00. Say that you love me still!"

Much of the parodic and illustrative material is, of course, devoted to the theatrical figures themselves, either gathered together in unlikely scenes, such as the wildly improbable Gibson drawing of Salvini, Booth, Gilbert, Bernhardt, Terry, Langtry, and others clowning in a one-ring circus (*Life*, 22 March 1888), or collected in a more complimentary fashion, as in *Puck*'s adulatory "Histrionic and Lyric Firmament" for 1882 (figure 168). Such personalities appeared as a matter of course in innumerable comic series. One of the most impressive collections may be found in *Vanity Fair*, which included over sixty lithographs of actors, managers, and playwrights in its weekly publications. Such well-known names as Bernhardt, Boucicault,

Forbes-Robertson, Ibsen, Irving, Pinero, Shaw, Terry, and Wilde were given curtain calls by the editor Thomas Gibson Bowles, who wrote satirical "biographies" to accompany the illustrations.[9] Less colorful but nonetheless important for an understanding of contemporary opinion were "Mr. Punch's 'Animal Land,'" the "Fancy Portraits" series drawn for *Punch* by Linley Sambourne,[10] Beerbohm's "Personal Remarks" in *Pick-Me-Up*, and the "Gallery of Beauties" and "Growth of Greatness" series in *Life*.

Henry Irving, popular on both sides of the Atlantic, appears prominently in many series. As the first theatrical personality to be included in *Vanity Fair* on 19 December 1874 (figure 169), he was depicted by Carlo Pellegrini "in the harrowing drama of 'The Bells,' of which he left a nightmarelike memory on each one of his audience." He receives praise from the editor Bowles, who notes that while Irving is a "mannerist,' he is still "very superior to the common run of mechanical actors playing solely within the limits of tradition." *Life*'s Henry Guy Carleton agrees with the assessment, although he thoroughly chronicles the actor's mannerisms before he concludes with a paean to his "poetry and charm" and "singular virtues":

194

Figure 168. "Histrionic and Lyric Firmament," Puck, October 1882.

Figure 169. Henry Irving, Vanity Fair, *19 December 1884*.

An aesthetic maiden once said that Mr. Irving's legs were limpid and utter. That is not true. . . . But their sometime scherzo movement I object to. One need not break into a violent schottische in order to cross a stage, and when a pair of legs indulges in that obsolete and extravagant pastime . . . I am inclined to quarrel with them.

. . . For the sepulchral timbre of his voice, nature is no doubt to blame. A crow with a bad cold can not throw himself into the phonetic guise of a canary, be he ever so clever a crow.

(8 November 1883, pp. 238–39)

Irving, Carleton concludes, is "undeniably great" because he appeals directly "to the general heart of man." His talent did not, however, protect him from being criticized for his financial success while on tour. Readers were taken to task for supporting the British economy by paying outrageous prices for tickets, *Life* complaining that Irving was "pelted out of the land" by devalued dollars (11 March 1886, p. 144) and *Judge* that Irving and others like Ellen Terry and Lily Langtry consider America to

Figure 170. "The Showman's Paradise," Judge,
17 November 1883.

*Figure 171. "The Latest Idols of the American Aristo-
crats,"* Judge, *10 November 1883.*

cluded the famous silhouette—bushy hair and spidery legs—in *Punch*'s "Fancy Portraits" series (figure 172). The caption "'Romeo! Romeo! Wherefore art *thou* Romeo!' (But had the Divine WILLIAMS witnessed the performance, he might have been able to satisfy his own query)," suggests that had Shakespeare seen Irving, he would have seen the actor for whom he created the role. *Life*, which not unexpectedly reacted vehemently against the "new drama" of social problems that Ibsen introduced, similarly records its approval of Irving's success in the standard repertory. In his "Biographical Primer" (figure 173) Oliver Herford shows an "odd couple," Irving and Robert Ingersoll (an American lawyer famous for his agnosticism):

> I is for Ibsen, reciting a play,
> While Irving and Ingersoll hasten away.

Finally, the inimitable Max Beerbohm includes Irv-

Figure 172. Henry Irving, "Fancy Portrait," Punch, March 1882.

be a colonial "Harvest Ground," or worse, a circus where a gullible public is willingly hoodwinked by its own anglomania (figures 170 and 171).

Quite aside from providing an excuse for such political and economic commentary, Irving was a boon to caricaturists and humorists alike, all of whom exaggerated his mannerisms and played up his dramatic flair. After Irving appeared as Romeo at the Lyceum in 1882,[11] Linley Sambourne in-

I IS for Ibsen, reciting a play,
While Irving and Ingersoll hasten away.

Figure 173. Henry Irving, "Biographical Primer," Life, 17 August 1889.

ing in his "Personal Remarks" series in the magazine *Pick-Me-Up* (figure 174), to which he contributed regularly in 1894–95.

Another figure who makes frequent appearances on the popular press "stage" is Sarah Bernhardt. Like Irving, she displayed innumerable eccentricities duly exaggerated by most of her caricaturists, except those in *Vanity Fair*, where she is twice portrayed. In one instance Theobald Chartran shows her arrayed in haute couture (5 July 1879); in another an artist as yet unidentified draws her in royal robes, her collar giving her the appearance of a theatrical winged victory (30 October 1912).[12] Others treated her less formally. The caption that accompanies a rarely seen drawing of "The Sarabee" in "Mr. Punch's 'Animal Land'" (figure 175) provides a good summary (in the style of Artemus Ward!) of what attracted the humorists:

This remarkable Animal is the idle of the parizzians. It is very snakey and dramattick. It has the most blood-kerdling little ways of ettracting attenshen. When it travles it takes black tiegers and coffins and skellitens along with it to make people talk and shudder. It has a most lovly serching voise that is ordible in the cheap seats when you cant here a word the June premyier had got to say for himself. It is quite a sculpcher too in its way and has got a stewjo where it paints in trowsers. *That* seems very forwerd and ecentrick but we musnt be to sensurious I suppose. (28 May 1898, p. 250)

Some of the legends about Bernhardt had their basis in fact. An animal lover, she owned every-

Figure 174. Henry Irving, "Personal Remark," Pick-Me-Up, 5 January 1895.

Figure 175. "The Sarabee," Punch, 28 May 1898.

Her originality also extends to other matters and tends to weaken her popularity. Her habit of sleeping in a coffin casts a gloom over the neighborhood in which she lives, and her best-loved pet is a young tiger with an uncontrollable appetite for plump waiters. The proprietors of the hotels she visits do not like to have their best waiters turned into tiger meat, and therefore her patronage is not generally solicited. (12 December 1889, p. 331)

Both magazines comment on her marriage to Jacques Damala, a playboy attaché of the Greek Diplomatic Corps in Paris. As one biographer recounts the affair, Damala became an actor after their marriage and grew increasingly jealous of Bernhardt's success; in December 1882, after nine months, he left her in a fit of pique over her triumph in *Fedora*.[14] *Punch*'s comment was given as part of "The Transit of the Constellation Sara" (figure 177), a "Brilliant Scene in a Circle, or 'Rapid Act,' with which this

Figure 176. Sarah Bernhardt, "Gallery of Beauties," Life, *12 December 1889.*

thing from cheetahs to lizards during her long career. She acquired her coffin as a teenager, when, terrified by a physician's warning about her frail health, she persuaded her mother to buy her a "pretty" memento mori: a rosewood coffin lined with white satin.[13] *Life* similarly kept the popular legend alive by making merry over the "Divine Sara" in its "Gallery of Beauties" (figure 176):

Nature was good to Sarah Bernhardt in fitting her for either of two artistic careers. She chose, however, to be a great actress in preference to dazzling the world as the greatest Living Skeleton of her time. . . .

Figure 177. "The Transit of the Constellation Sara," Punch, *15 August 1882.*

variously gifted *Artiste* has successfully terminated her latest, shortest, and most important Engagement, when she temporarily quitted the Stage for the sake of the Master of the Ring." *Life* would agree with *Punch*'s oblique suggestion that marriage is more important for a woman than a career, as this ironical comment from the "Gallery of Beauties" seems to show: "The French divorce mill grinds so slowly and so exceedingly fine," notes the American publication, "that her transcendent genius could not brook its delays."

Even before her marriage, Bernhardt's first American tour in 1880[15] evoked a spate of commentary about her accent, her histrionics, and her distinctive coffin. The short-lived *Chic* published a diary that purported to be a running account of her astonishment at American manners (October–December 1880). *Puck*'s artists focused on her lankiness, proposing in "The Bernhardt Boom in New York" that a telegraph pole be the proper "advertising medium" for her long and narrow life-sized posters (27 October 1880). *Puck* also published a tribute by "Walt Whitman":

> Sadie!
> Woman of vigorous aspirations and remarkable thinness!
> I hail you. I, Walt, Whitman, son of thunder, child of the ages, I hail you.
> I am the boss poet, and I recognize in you an element of bossness that approximates you to me.
> Blast your impudence!—I like it.
> Your advertising dodges—your bogus sculptures—your painting—your impropriety—your coffin exhibited to all beholders and shown in the newspapers up.
> I like these things. I am these things. I, Walt, the son of a gun, I am all and everyone of these things.
> I am the coffin, and the painting, and the sculptures, and the improprieties—I am all these; I enter into them and become them.
> (27 October 1880, p. 122)

Like *Puck*'s Whitman, the public "liked these things," even if they were done primarily to gain notoriety; given the reaction of the caricaturists and parodists, Bernhardt's "real" life must have seemed as fanciful to the middle-class reading public as that of any character she played on stage.

Figure 178. W. S. Gilbert, "Personal Remark," Pick-Me-Up, *27 October 1894.*

While the popular press amused its readers with accounts of Bernhardt's eccentricities, she was always treated as an outsider, as a creature to be wondered at for her talent and her daring, her foreignness coming less from her French birth than from her actions. William Schwenk Gilbert and Arthur Sullivan, on the other hand, were home-grown, their attractiveness stemming very much from the commonplace nature of what they wrote about. Rather than arousing wonder and admiration about their own personalities, they turned the glass the other way and forced their audience to examine—

200

for the depth of his education and for putting "the calls of Science or the claims of Art" ahead of "the charms of Court favour"; he is "worthy of a foremost place among those who by the assiduous cultivation of God-given gifts have made a name for themselves and for their countries" (14 March 1874).

Punch offered its own brand of humorous praise when it included both in Sambourne's "Fancy Portraits" series. Gilbert is pictured in a nautical setting (figure 181); the accompanying caption plays on the pair's musical triumphs in *The Sorcerer* (1877), *H. M. S. Pinafore* (1878), and *Pirates of Penzance* (1880). Readers were, of course, familiar with the

Figure 179. W. S. Gilbert, "Patience," Vanity Fair, 21 March 1881.

and to know—their own follies and foibles. And because their humor really supported middle-class morality while making fun of manners, their musical and metrical high jinks were adopted wholesale by the popular press. Not that all caricatures are complimentary; Beerbohm's "remark" in *Pick-Me-Up* is a case in point (figure 178). In keeping with the fairly realistic lithographs prepared for *Vanity Fair* by Spy and Ape (figures 179 and 180), Thomas Bowles's comments demonstrate the way in which both composer and librettist became cultural institutions that stood for Britain much in the same way the queen did. Sullivan, for example, is praised

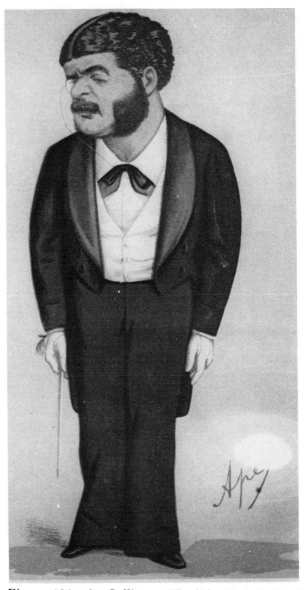

Figure 180. A. Sullivan, "English Music," Vanity Fair, 14 March 1874.

Figure 181. W. S. Gilbert, "Fancy Portrait," Punch, 6 August 1881.

mementos of his musical successes. A capsule biography in verse refers to his attendance at the Royal Academy of Music and the Conservatory at Leipzig, his second collaboration—*Trial by Jury*—with Gilbert (the first, *Thespis* in 1871, four years before), and the rumors that preceded his knighthood:[16]

> As a boy I had such a musical bump,
>   And its size so struck Mr. HELMORE,
> That he said, "Though you sing those songs
>   like a trump,
>   You shall write some yourself that will sell
>   more."
> So I packed off to Leipsic, without *looking back*,
>   And returned in such classical fury,
> That I sat down with HANDEL and
>   HAYDEN and BACH,—
>   And turned out *"Trial by Jury."*
>
> But W. S. G. he jumped for joy
>   As he said, "Though the job dismay you,
> Send Exeter Hall to the deuce, my boy;
>   It's the *haul* with me that'll pay you."
> And we hauled so well, mid jeers and taunts,
>   That we've settled, spite all temptations,
> To stick to our Sisters and our Cousins and our
>   Aunts,—
>   And continue our pleasant relations.
>
> Yet I know a big Duke, and I've written for
>   Leeds,
>   And I think (I don't wish to be snarly),
> If honour's poured out on a chap for his deeds,
>   I'm as good—come, as MONCKTON OR
>   CHARLEY!
> So the next "first night" at the Opera C.,
>   Let's hope, if you're able to find him,
> You'll cry from the pit, "There's W. S. G.
>   In the stalls,—*with a* Knight *behind him*."
>   (30 October 1880, p. 202)

Bab ballads from their publication in *Fun* (1866–71), and avid Savoyards would have recognized the meter in the caption:

> But in spite of some Temptations
> To Translations and Sensations,
>   He remains—
> A *Sorcerer* Young Man,
> A *Pinafore Pirates* Man,
> A brilliant what I call quite idi-yacht-ical
>   Ballady Bab Young Man.
>   (6 August 1881, p. 58)

Sullivan, more elaborately treated (figure 182), is shown dressed in a "pinafore" and surrounded by

Despite its light tone, the poem prefigures the bitterness that Gilbert felt in being passed over for knighthood. Perhaps he would not have agreed with *Vanity Fair* that Sullivan did not seek the "charms of Court favour": royal recognition did not come for Gilbert until 1907, almost a quarter of a century later than for Sullivan. The reason for the delayed recognition of Gilbert's talents is in evidence in *Vanity Fair* and even in the longer treatment in *Punch*. Sullivan, famous for his oratorios and sacred music (including such popular hymns as "Onward Christian Soldiers"), wrote as the British wanted to perceive themselves and to be perceived by posterity; Gilbert, a linguistically clever individual, made them laugh.

In America the two were accepted as an inseparable pair. Much of the reaction is centered around American performances of the operettas; when the *Mikado* appeared in New York, for example, *Life* published no less than seven reviews between 10 July 1885 and 17 December 1885. Not the least of the reaction are the puns, anecdotes, and other ephemeral references to oriental practices that honeycomb the humor columns. Most interesting as a record of changing tastes, however, is the comic essay that appeared in 1911. In this satirical criticism of the New York theatrical scene Channing Pollock creates a scenario in which Gilbert is told that he will never succeed unless he updates his librettos. He must change his title from *Mikado* to "The Girl and the Garter," make the executioner a "rich brewer from St. Louis," plagiarize his jokes

Figure 182. A. Sullivan, "Fancy Portrait," Punch, October 1880.

from the newspapers, and eliminate polysyllabic rhymes. Furthermore, as the manager says,

"Your moon song's up-to-date, but you'll have to can all that 'Tit Willow' and 'Flowers that Bloom in the Spring' stuff. What people want is *numbers*—numbers with girls in 'em, and some kind of stunt like dress-suit cases that turn out to be a battleship flying the American flag." (26 January 1911, p. 206)

Buried in Pollock's commentary is the suggestion that a decline in public taste has consigned the Gilbert and Sullivan productions to a limbo of period pieces; patter songs are not attractive to a public that prefers "pink piffle" and the stagey effects of vaudeville.

British parodists wrote about a decline in taste as well, but pointed to aestheticism as the culprit and used Gilbert's meter and outrageous rhymes in *Patience* as a gloss upon one of Oscar Wilde's statements. After *The Picture of Dorian Gray* appeared in *Lippincott's* in July 1890, *Punch* attacked Wilde's asseveration that " 'Even a colour-sense is more important in the development of the individual than a sense of right and wrong' " by printing a parody of Bunthorne's "high aesthetic song." The parodist objects to the moral laxness which, he says, the aesthetes encourage by insisting that one's reaction to art is primary; he suggests, in fact, that Wilde is like a Satanic snake that needs to be destroyed— preferably by the scorn of his Philistine readers. The poem is quoted in part:

> Then having swamped morality in "intensified
>   personality" (which, of course, must mean
>   your own),
> And the "rational" abolished and "sincerity"
>   demolished, you will find that you have
>   *grown*
> With a "colour-sense" fresh handselled (whilst
>   the moral ditto's cancelled) you'll develop
>   into—well,
> What Philistia's fools malicious might esteem a
>   *vaurien* vicious (alias "hedonic swell").
>   And every one will say
>   As you writhe your sinuous way,
> "If the highest result of the true 'Development'
>   is decomposition, why see
> What a very perfectly developed young man
>   this developed young man must be."
>
> With your perky paradoxes, and your talk of
>   "crinkled ox-eyes," and of books in
>   "Nile-green skin,"

Figure 183. George Bernard Shaw, "Magnetic," Vanity Fair, 28 December 1905.

That show forth unholy histories, and display
    the "deeper mysteries" of strange and
    subtle Sin.
You can squirm, and glose, and hiss on, and
    awake that *nouveau frisson* which is Art's
    best gift to life,
And "develop"—like some cancer (in the
    Art-sphere) whose best answer is the silent
    surgeon's knife!
    And every *man* will say,
    As you wriggle on your way,
"If 'emotion for the sake of emotion is the air of
    Art,' dear me!
What a morbidly muckily emotional young

man the 'developed' young man must be!"
                 (20 September 1890, p. 135)

Given the original patter song, itself satiric instruction in aesthetic posing—

    And every one will say,
      As you walk your mystic way
    "If that's not good enough for him which is
        good enough for *me*,
    Why, what a very cultivated kind of youth this
        kind of youth must be!"

—the poem in *Punch* becomes a doubly strong attack on aestheticism.

George Bernard Shaw is another showman who was made to cavort through the pages of the popular press. Max Beerbohm, signing himself "Ruth," drew the cartoon of Shaw for *Vanity Fair* (figure 183); the playwright also appears in the background of Beerbohm's "Bulbo" drawing of Arthur Wing Pinero, which was published in *Vanity Fair* in 1906. Bowles comments on the "laughing philosopher's" good opinion of himself:

That England is not too hot to hold him illustrates afresh our perfect confidence in our merits, and also our contempt for intellectual ideas. We are neither modest nor clever enough to take Mr. Shaw seriously. But we like a joke; and so, now that he has been discovered, he is very popular. . . . Magnetic, he has the power to infect almost everyone with the delight that he takes in himself. (28 December 1905)

Bowles, of course, is roughly attacking the same middle-class complacency that bothered the playwright himself; Shaw's public does not really understand his principles, he says, and so they think that he is merely humorous, when what he is really proposing is far-reaching social change. That contempt for his ideas did exist is underscored by "The Sufferings of Shaw," *Punch*'s versified objection to a contemporary comparison between Shaw and Socrates. The poem, not worth quoting in full, reviews the course of Socrates' life, then ends on a heavily ironic note:

    Why desecrate the greatest living sage
      By linking him with obsolete barbarians?
    Rather let us with pious zeal engage
      In homage to the Prince of Vegetarians,
    And thank your stars that, as the Huns have
      written,

Figure 184. "Mr. Punch's Christmas Bazaar and Fancy Fair," Punch's Almanack *for 1914.*

One upright man remains in blighted Britain.
(14 April 1915, p. 295)

The "upright man" appears most frequently in *Punch* as an egotistical showman, as in the "King's Georges" series where he—and other "Georges" such as the playwright Sims and the novelist Moore—beats his own drum, singing,

Monarch or peasant, 'tis the same to me:
Counsel for both I've ready—fluent, free.
(7 June 1911, p. 422)

Punning on *Man and Superman* (1903), another *Punch* artist shows Shaw teetering on top of a mountain as "Man and Hinterman; or, John Bull's other adver-

tiser." While he thoughtfully observes, "Yes! The importance of other people *has* been greatly overestimated," his double, or "hinterman," warns that "obituary notices may be too dearly bought" (18 September 1907). Again, he is pictured blowing his own horn in "Mr. Punch's Christmas Bazaar and Fancy Fair" as he and others, among them the novelist Hall Caine and Gilbert and Sullivan, "execute each a modest solo on his favourite instrument" (figure 184).

As a rule, then, *Punch*'s reaction to Shaw was less enlightened than one might have expected, given the caliber of the magazine's readership. Its treatment of the *Blanco Posnet* affair is similarly more a comment on the Shavian view of the world than an

Figure 185. "Church and Stage," Punch, *16 June 1909.*

Figure 186. P. T. Barnum, *"Gallery of Beauties,"* Life,
25 April 1889.

attack on censorship. After the Lord Chamberlain refused to license *The Shewing-Up of Blanco Posnet*, Shaw's play about the sudden conversion to Christianity of a hard-bitten cowboy, Shaw testified to a parliamentary committee and wrote a pamphlet (which became the play's preface) about the dangers of censorship. Bernard Partridge's cartoon shows Shaw standing beside a billboard announcing that "The Bishop of London presents the English Church Pageant." He complains, "Some people have all the luck. I can't get *my* religious play past the censor" (figure 185). The joke seems to be directed against Shaw, who views his play on a par with the established Church. *Blanco Posnet* was ultimately staged by Lady Gregory at the Abbey Theatre in Dublin.[17]

Life, a bastion of the middle-class preconceptions Shaw enjoyed lampooning, was even more un-

friendly than *Punch*, perhaps indicating the more Philistine cast of its readership. Shaw was included, for example, in the column "People I Would Rather not Know" (18 May 1911). The "biography" provided with the comic coat of arms published three years earlier reveals why:

He took up, in turn, every cherished institution, and having clubbed it into insensibility was applauded until he ran out of material. Now he is waiting for more cherished institutions to grow. His favorite flower is the nettle. Principal occupation, praising himself and pooh-poohing Shakespeare. Motto, "The Path of Glory Leads but to the Grave." Address the Suburbs of Westminster Abbey. (Use the knocker.) (25 June 1908, p. 689)

Shaw, of course, was noted for his attack on "Bardolotry," as the pot of mud and splattered "Works of Shakespeare" on the coat of arms suggest. His "triple indictment"—that "Shakespeare's characters do not feel social responsibility; they are seldom great thinkers or artists; and though usually real people, they do not live real lives"[18]—runs counter to *Life*'s fairly conservative theatrical bias.

Tom Masson's Shavian parody of "Old Mother Hubbard" shows further why *Life*, which extolled the cherished institutions of marriage and motherhood, objected to Shaw's iconoclastic humor. Masson implies that Shaw made money by bilking the public and by presenting unpleasant settings, as this excerpt from the scenario shows:

An English home. Horrible furniture, horrible bric-á-brac, horrible books, horrible pictures, horrible everything. In one end of the room is a door. Beyond the door is a cupboard. It is half open, and contains a secret. This secret is known only to one of the two persons occupying the room: a noble dog, and a woman—the unpleasantest work of God. On the whole, it is an extremely nauseating group, only the dog relieving the situation. He is, as usual, half famished. The woman waits her opportunity. (19 October 1905, p. 459)

This survey of major theatrical figures does not, of course, even begin to exhaust the material available. Many other stage personalities are well represented by caricaturists both in the series mentioned

earlier and in individual cuts. P. T. Barnum, for example, remembered for the circus that bears his name, appears frequently. He is shown on the cover of the American *Vanity Fair*, inviting the "confiding public" into his museum to see "the Educated Clam" and "The Abolition Angel Fish" (13 September 1862); he is included in *Life*'s "Gallery of Beauties" (figure 186), where he is described as "proprietor of the great moral show and author of . . . 'The Humbugs of the World'"; he appears in *Puck* as "The Great Temperance Showman" exhibiting a tipsy elephant (figure 187). While Barnum was well known in America, he made his reputation in England by buying Jumbo, an African elephant beloved of children and grownups alike. Even Queen Victoria objected to the sale by the London Zoological Gardens, but to no avail; Jumbo

Figure 187. "The Great Temperance Showman," Puck, 9 April 1882.

Figure 188. P. T. Barnum, "Fancy Portrait," Punch, 9 February 1884.

arrived in New York at Eastertime, 1882, and died three years later in a train accident.[19] Sambourne summed up *Punch*'s sentiment when he depicted Barnum as a sly fox wearing the "almighty dollar" as a watch fob and supported by that portion of human nature phrenologically labeled "credulity" (figure 188).

Others appeared on the popular press "stage" as well. Lily Langtry, launched into society by the Prince of Wales, first appears in *Life* as a sunflower attracting aesthetic "bees" and then as a pastoral beauty with a deceptively innocent expression (figure 189). She frequently attests to the virtues of Pears' Soap; in this example she is one in a quintet of vestal virgins, among them the actress Mary Anderson and the opera singer Adelina Patti, who pose on the steps of "The Temple of Beauty" (figure 190). Arthur Wing Pinero, pegged by Bowles as "the dressiest of contemporary dramatists," is arrayed in a pin-striped outfit and spats by Beerbohm in *Pick-Me-Up* (figure 191) and with bald pate—or "incandescent occiput"—"mistaken by American enthusiasts for the summit of Monte Rosa by sunrise" in *Punch* (18 September 1907, p. 213). Finally, Ibsen, described in *Vanity Fair* as "The Master" to a

Figure 189. Lily Langtry, "Gallery of Beauties," Life, 11 April 1889.

THE SECRET OF A GOOD COMPLEXION.

Figure 190. "The Temple of Beauty," Judge, 28 May 1887.

Figure 191. Arthur Wing Pinero, "Personal Remark,"
Pick-Me-Up, *9 February 1890.*

Figure 192. Henrik Ibsen, "The Master Builder," Vanity Fair, *12 December 1901.*

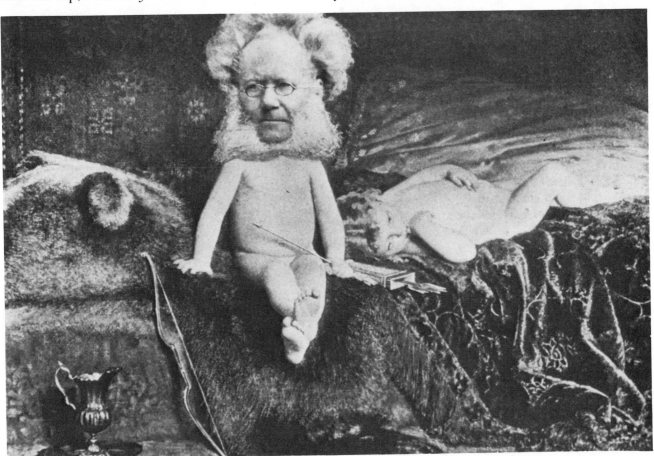

Figure 193. Henrik Ibsen, "The Growth of Greatness,"
Life, *3 January 1895.*

"small band of disciples" (figure 192), is shown in airy garb in *Life* (figure 193).

As a group, then, theatrical figures were frequently caricatured, perhaps because they themselves enjoyed creating drama not just on stage, but everywhere they appeared. The parodic poems, biographies, and reviews that often accompanied the drawings record a lively public interest not only in flamboyant personalities but in the state of the art as well. Of course, much was written primarily to amuse; but the reaction against "pink piffle" and objections to improbable melodramas persistently echoed more serious criticism and, in their own way, helped to educate a less than critical public.

NOTES

1. Allardyce Nicoll gives 29 November 1869 as the first performance date of *Queen Elizabeth of England* in "Appendix B: Hand-List of Plays Produced Between 1850 and 1900," in *A History of Late Nineteenth-Century Drama, 1850–1900*, 2 vols. (Cambridge: Cambridge University Press, 1946), 2:737.

2. An unidentified reviewer with similar tastes published "The Round of the Pantomimes," *Fun*, 11 February 1871, p. 63.

3. *Life* also launched a long and bitter campaign against inadequate fireproofing in theaters and against ticket speculating. See Mott, *History of American Magazines*, 4:564–65, and Flautz, *Gentle Satirist*, pp. 169–71.

4. Both plays are reviewed in the *New York Times*, 1 May 1883, p. 4, col. 6.

5. The play that best fits Coward's description is *The Woman from Gaol;* the first performance date is given as 16 April 1906 in Allardyce Nicoll's *English Drama, 1900–1930* (Cambridge: Cambridge University Press, 1973), p. 952.

6. Nicoll, *English Drama*, p. 646, gives 3 September 1906 as the first performance date for *Toddles*.

7. At the time the poem was published, Cohan had two plays running: *The Governor's Son* (reviewed in the *New York Times*, 5 June 1906, p. 9) and *The Honeymooners* (reviewed in the *New York Times*, 4 June 1907, p. 7).

8. Mott, *History of American Magazines*, 3:206–8.

9. Savory, *Vanity Fair Gallery*, pp. 106–12.

10. For a discussion about the artist, see Leonee Ormond, "*Punch*'s Linley Sambourne," *Nineteenth Century* 4 (1978): 81–87.

11. *Romeo and Juliet* was reviewed in the London *Times*, 9 March 1882, p. 6.

12. Savory, *Vanity Fair Lithographs;* pp. 25, 79, and 112. See pp. xv–xvi for an identification of signatures.

13. Cornelia Otis Skinner, *Madame Sarah* (Boston: Houghton Mifflin, 1967), pp. 20 and 135; the famous coffin is pictured between pp. 168–69.

14. Ibid., pp. 208–13.

15. William Emboden's picture biography, *Sarah Bernhardt* (New York: Macmillan, 1975), gives nine American tours in all.

16. A good account may be found in Christopher Hibbert, *Gilbert and Sullivan and Their Victorian World* (New York: American Heritage, 1976).

17. For a full discussion of the affair, see Archibald Henderson, *Bernard Shaw: Playboy and Prophet* (New York and London: Appleton, 1932).

18. William Irvine, *The Universe of G. B. S.* (New York: McGraw-Hill, 1949), pp. 193–99.

19. The story of Jumbo is told in Irving Wallace's *The Fabulous Showman: The Life and Times of P. T. Barnum* (New York: Knopf, 1959), pp. 289–96.

U IS for Undine, pursuing Ulysses
    And Umberto, who flee her damp, death-dealing
       kisses.

V IS Victoria, most Glorious Queen,
For further particulars, page 17.

9

A Nod to the Novelists

THE YEAR 1870, WHICH MARKED THE END OF Dickens's life, foreshadowed the demise of the Victorian novel as well. As Amy Cruse writes in her analysis of the reading public's taste, by 1880 "the age of the Great Novelists was over."[1] Like other literary changes, this "death" was really a birth fostered by stylistic and thematic experimentation. Novelists were increasingly preoccupied with the way in which the individual coped with a menacing social organism; faced with both scientific and social determinism, they moved from portraying well-knit social structures to exploring the human psyche as realistically as possible. This shift in emphasis from plot to character was not necessarily welcomed by the average magazine reader, who preferred strong, action-filled stories to the more difficult and thought-provoking prose of the psychological novel.

The frustrations and uncertainties of both readers and writers were reflected in the parodic response, which, on the whole, seems self-contradictory. Editors praised such "romantic" writers as Kipling, Stevenson, and Caine, while warning their readers against the ever-popular sensation novel; they bemoaned the death of the "Great Novelists" while satirizing the more philosophical of the new guard. Contributing to the ambiguity of the pattern that emerges is the relative sparsity of references to novelists in the periodicals under consideration. A number of factors seem to be at work. Unlike poems, novels are too lengthy to be parodied in a serial publication; for the same reason, the technique of act-by-act satirical summary that is successful for plays does not work for novels. Moreover, unlike plays, whose genesis is a quasi-religious celebration, novels are not social experiences. The essentially private nature of novel-reading certainly made it difficult for the parodist to gauge the interest of his audience and hence the success of his humor, especially if he suspected that the new realism was not overwhelmingly popular with the general reading public. Finally, to represent both style and content recognizably, the parodist had to master large quantities of material; given the pressure of publication, it is unlikely that he could afford to undertake a lengthy course of reading for the sake of a single weekly column. While some legitimate parodies do occur, of course, much of the material about novelists exists in the form of caricatures, mock interviews, and verses about writing. Like burlesques of popular novelistic styles, most of these approaches sidestepped the necessity for thorough familiarity with an individual author's works.

In the case of the humorous response of the Americans to their British counterparts, *Life* relinquished its normally chauvinistic stance to participate in a "battle of the Ancients and the Moderns."

The editors supported the "Great Novelists" at the expense of American newcomers, invoking Thackeray as a stylistic guide[2] as this cartoon about Howells's and James's small stature illustrates (figure 194). The double-page spread that appeared in 1905 further demonstrates *Life*'s disapproval of current public taste and disregard of the dangers of anglomania (figure 195): Scott, Hawthorne, Balzac, Dickens, Dumas, and Thackeray, dignified in mien, appear as lilliputians when set next to such modern "greats" as the now little-remembered Bertha Rumble and Irving Bacheller, or the better-known—and larger—Hall Caine and Mary Macay (who used "Marie Corelli" as her pen name). In obvious disagreement with *Puck*, which published W. J. Henderson's pleas to heed contemporary works of art rather than blindly honoring old ones,[3] *Life* suggests that the reading public is ignoring the lessons of its dead masters in favor of sensationalism, the novelistic version of drama's "pink piffle."

By 1910 *Life* goes so far as to attack modern journalistic practices for pandering to public taste rather than educating it. In Frank Lovell Nelson's speculation on what would happen "If Thackeray, *et al.*, Came to Park Row," for example, Thackeray's offer of the manuscript of *Vanity Fair* to the editor of a large newspaper brings only derision. The "sermons" and the subplots make the book too long to serialize; furthermore, the characters need modernizing. "Make Becky Sharp a Bowery girl and Lord Steyne a Pittsburgh Millionaire," the editor suggests, foreshadowing in popular terms Dreiser's brilliant treatment of a similar theme in *An American Tragedy;* "let young Osborne be killed in the charge with Roosevelt up San Juan Hill." The real problem, however, is that Thackeray's plot is neither fast-paced nor melodramatic enough for the twentieth-century reader. As the editor says, "What the public wants is an incident in every other line; a villain, a battle, a mystery in every page" (1 December 1910, pp. 1004).

One antidote for the sensationalism that Nelson's satire deplores is precisely what *Life* refuses to countenance: the Jamesian and Howellsian realism which, it complains, *lacks* incident. The solution—nostalgic at best—would seem to be a return to the Victorian frame of mind, a return made impossible by many factors. Modern technology is not the least of these; in fact, a line in *Punch*'s memorial poem to Dickens makes clear exactly why the age of the leisurely Victorian novel could not be reinstated:

Figure 194. "A Literary Combination," Life, 22 February 1883.

Hearing that he has passed beyond the veil,
  Before the Judge who metes to men their
      dues,
Men's cheeks, through English-speaking lands,
    turn pale,
  Far as the speaking wires can bear the
    news—

Blanched at this sudden snapping of a life,
  That seemed of all our lives to hold a share;
So were our memories with his fancies rife,
  So much of *his* thought *our* thoughts seemed
    to bear.

(18 June 1870, p. 244)

The "speaking wires" signify not just the telegraph, but a new age of communication in which life-styles and interests changed radically to keep pace with news flashed instantaneously across the seas. Moreover, people wanted action in the novel to cor-

Figure 195. "Relative Importance of Certain Authors,"
Life, *23 March 1905.*

respond to the action in their own lives or to the action that, for the American of this time, corresponded to a democratic ideal. As Nelson's satire suggests, there is no time either to publish or to read a work the length of Thackeray's.

The public's desire for contemporaneity was not just an American manifestation, however. The British *Fun* laughed at both writers and readers in its demand for wholesome and original works.

Why, in the name of Hygeia, don't some of our novelists turn their attention to sanitation? Instead of grubbing amid the barren and long since exhausted acreage of familiar fiction, with the result of making their "damnable iteration" yet more damnable, and their palpable mediocrity more pronounced, why don't they move with the times? This is an Age of Sanitation. Where, then, is the Sanitary Novel?

Where, indeed, but in *Fun* itself, where it appears as a three-volume, single-page work entitled "Germ-Shadowed: Or, the Kiss that Kills." The piece is facetious and trivial: Chlorinda Delyme, "her infancy and girlhood having been wholly devoted to the absorbing study of sanitary science," becomes engaged to Sandy Soyle, who lives in Hy-

genic Grove. Sandy has invented a double filter for his germ-proof cistern, but fails to protect against floating "microbes," one of which lands in Chlorinda's glass and is transferred from her lips to his. After his death she marries Professor Cesspoole and maintains that their thirteen children have been protected from disease by "their inoculation with the liquefied ashes" of the defunct Soyle (19 October 1892, p. 166)! At one time such a farrago perhaps provided amusement for the general reader; today it shows the drift of public interest. As in the case of *Life*, for whom realism was the unacceptable cure for sensationalism, *Fun*'s mock request for a novel revivified by modern science had its real counterpart in the psychological novels of James and Howells. *Fun*, however, disliked such introspection, as shown by an excerpt from "Fun-Tastic Fictions, An Intro-Spectre," a satirical "instalment of an introspective psychological novelette of the kind that was fashionable in certain circles towards the end of the 19th-century":

"How darest thou wag thy visionary tongue in noise so rude against me! Who the Dickens, or Thackeray; or, to be more up-to-date, who the Blackmore, Hardy, Besant, or Meredith, art thou—"

"Please! . . . I am no other than *thy* INNER EGO!—yea, thy astral Body." (8 March 1893, p. 97)

Fun's sanitary and psychological satires make no reference to specific novels; rather, they are indirect attacks on the direction of the genre itself. Other such attacks mimicked poor style and complained that minor novelists as a group substituted time-worn plots and purple prose for true talent. *Life*'s "Extracts from the Alphabetically Arranged Note-Book of a Popular Novelist" makes the point adequately for modern writers as well. The "dictionary" includes the following suggestions: "*Hotly:* Heroine should flush hotly when she beholds the cloven-foot of the desperado's nature"; "*Curl* of the lips should be scornful when the heroine faces her 'accusers-with-their-short-curt-laugh'"; and "'*Unhand me, Sir!*' is still an appropriate (though moth-eaten) expression in every case where the heroine turns from 'the baffled-villain-with-the-lean-Satanic-face'" (23 October 1890, pp. 222–23). Much more clever is the "Modern Minor Novelist," a parody in *Fun* of Gilbert and Sullivan's "Modern Major General" patter song from *Pinafore*. As in *Life*, "Greats" like Scott and Dickens are held up as standards, and again popular journalism is blamed for misleading the public, this time into an interest in literary gossip rather than in the works themselves.

The Modern Minor Novelist

Look up, O reader! and behold the man 'fore
    whom thou grovellest,
He is the very model of the modern minor
    novelist!
He's teeming with ideas that are weird, and
    strange, and wonderful,
And all his thrilling stories are of lightning and
    of thunder full.

He makes between the critic's brain and
    common-sense a severance,
So that the awe-struck pressmen straightway
    bend the knee in reverence;
They put pars in the papers, ay, and sometimes
    leaders follow,
On Mr. Blank's romances, which beat Scott
    and Dickens hollow!
Next day we're told his genius glows with
    wondrous incandescence,
And all the clubs are eager to be honoured by
    his presence;

Then follow little items, meant to please the
    great man's vanities,
About his house, his love for golf, and other
    like inanities!

We learn he never does a stroke of work before
    eleven,
And spends his time correcting proofs from five
    o'clock till seven;
His output's rather small, but—note the
    log-roller's duplicity!—
He never writes a sentence that is lacking in
    felicity.

He always uses broad-nibbed pens to write his
    stories breezy,
And yet his writing's legible, ev'n comps.
    declare it easy!—
Enough! Such gossip's out of place, devoid of
    rhyme and reason,
Considering this great little man may only last
    a season!
                (4 January 1898, p. 8)

The sensationalism, the ignorance of literary tradition, the concern for lionization: these, *Fun* suggests, are the qualities of the minor novelist, qualities perhaps encouraged by one Professor Machree, who in 1891 set up a "school for novelists" that seems to be the nineteenth-century progenitor of modern writing correspondence courses. In "After this, the Deluge!" *Fun* derides Machree's attempt to circumvent lack of "Genius," "divine inspiration," and "Nature," but nonetheless suggests that the expected torrent of third-rate writing may have a beneficial effect:

Yet the seeming ill-wind may be pregnant of
    good,
    And the "novelists' school" has our best
        benediction,
For soon, should it flourish, its pupils will flood
    Ev'ry market on earth with nonsensical
        fiction.
Then readers of novels will learn to despise
    The contemptible trash they've delighted in
        reading,
And surfeited souls will at last realize
    That on garbage, not meat, they've been
        foolishly feeding.
Yes, worthy's the "novelists' school" of our
    praise

Figure 196. "'A Verray Parfit Nobel Knight,'" Punch, *18 December 1907.*

figures, the periodical did publish "Overheard in Arcady," a homiletic set of parodic novels illustrated by Oliver Herford and others. Both *Once a Week* and *Punch* published memorable sketches, and, of course, *Vanity Fair* included many novelists in its lithograph collection.

When Rudyard Kipling received the Nobel Prize for Literature in 1907, for example, *Punch* pictured him as "'A Verray Parfit Nobel Knight'" receiving a crown of laurel (figure 196). Whether or not he emulated Chaucer's hero is arguable; in fact, this compliment to his gentility is in direct contrast to *Life*'s assessment. In the "Overheard in Arcady" series, Francis Attwood pictures him as a man of the world (figure 197), smoking a cigar and munching on an apple from the tree of knowledge. One of the interlocutors in the accompanying dialogue praises him for being a man of action:

"the critics may call him bumptious, and grotesque, and brutal, and vulgar, and all the other adjectives which they use for what is simply unconventional; but I'll always believe that he has the heart of a man and the voice of a poet. . . . Oh, it is good to read what a strong man has written. Writing is mostly left to the weak who like to talk about their own emotions. Kipling looks at things

Figure 197. Rudyard Kipling, Life, *14 December 1893.*

If the very desirable time it advances
When readers shall lose their unfortunate craze
For the reading of rubbishy, wretched
    romances!

(4 February 1891, p. 45)

To judge by some of the caricatures and parodic novels, however, not all of the readers of popular periodicals demanded "wretched romances." Kipling and Stevenson were not unexpectedly in demand for their adventure tales, but so were Meredith and Trollope. *Fun* published such parodies as "The Adventures of Shylock Tombs" (17 October 1893); the "Strange Case of Mr. Fickll & The O'Hide," by Lorbert Rouis Stevenson (9 January 1894); and "The Bungle Book" by Theyard Kipling (20 September 1898). While most of the pictorial series in *Life* were devoted to American

Figure 198. "Aspects of Current Fiction," Life, *28 January 1897.*

like a man of action, and that's the great thing in life or letters." (14 December 1893, p. 878)

While *Life* may seem to be echoing the Victorian cult of the "manly man" several decades late, it is certainly reflecting its own penchant for strongly plotted works, like those produced by Scott. Its assessment of Kipling is not always so complimentary, however. Four years later what was admirable forthrightness becomes "prolixity," and what was unconventionality is institutionalized as the twentieth-century spirit:

There is but one God of Things as they Are, and R. K. is his prophet. He embodies the spirit of the Age, of which he is a flattering likeness. He has impaled Prolixity on the point of his pen. . . . With the wisdom of Aesop, he combines the pertness of Punch with the imagination of Poe. He wears a kind of magic spectacles through which he sees everything at once on both sides of the street and around the corner; also he has the Inner Vision. He has seen the soul of the machine, and preached the apostleship of Empire—all in the Day's Work; and when twilight fell he has talked with the beasts of the Jungle. (20 June 1907, p. 839)

While *Life* writes tongue-in-cheek here, it clearly prefers Kipling's style to that of such writers as Thomas Hardy, who, it implies, trivialize realism

by overattention to detail. This "Leaf from a Modern Novel (Presumably by Thomas Hardy)" parodies all that Kipling, as a writer of action-packed stories, is not:

She took the sugar-bowl from the tray and sweetened her tea slowly. Not that she did this deliberately or with any special consciousness of the tea. . . . Certain it is that there was a thoughtful expression in her face on this occasion. It was white sugar, she remembered afterwards, nor was there anything either in the tea, or in the sugar, or in the bowl to make this all linger in her memory long after she had completely forgotten other instances when she had taken the sugar-bowl from the tray and sweetened her tea slowly. (18 June 1896, p. 500)

Life actually disparages Hardy on two grounds: quite aside from his diction, his plots were antithetical to *Life*'s perpetual optimism and belief in the efficacy of the individual will.

Not surprisingly, the sensitivity that *Life* rejects as super-subtlety in Hardy it praises in Stevenson. In a parodic dialogue between the doppelgänger Jekyll and Hyde, the humorist Robert Bridges, masquerading as Jekyll, compliments Stevenson on his "grasp" of "a great psychological truth"—the "complexity of our motives and actions." " 'I'll grant that he would like to be only a teller of entrancing tales,' " Jekyll goes on, " 'but he moralizes in spite of himself.'" When Stevenson errs, Bridges implies, is in his "repellant images," all of which accord with "an avowed disciple of idealism, of romance—a votary of beauty." His appeal, nonetheless, lies both in his language and in his breadth of subject matter, "from the purely idyllic to the most complex passions" (22 February 1894, pp. 117–18). Despite the qualifiers, *Life* would seem to prefer Stevenson to Kipling, primarily for the former's moralistic flavor; however, both authors were praised for presenting action rather than intellectualizing it. *Life*'s predilection for Stevenson does not preclude its recognition that the novelist's imitators adopted his worst habits; in a drawing personifying the "aspects of current fiction," Stevenson's "invisible shade" is made to exclaim, "'Good Heavens! What have I let loose?'" (figure 198). What the periodical does not recognize, however, is that the viable alternative to

Figure 200. "'Black' Art," Punch, 26 March 188[...]

Figure 199. "The Author of Shandon Bells," Life, 29 March 1883.

Stevenson's sensational imitators is the very group of realists it castigates.

In contrast to *Life*'s staff, Linley Sambourne of *Punch* made much sport of the "avowed disciples of romance," thus marking an important difference between the readerships and editorial stances of the two periodicals. For the American publication, "romance" was generally equated positively with idealism; for the British, negatively with gothicism or historical escapism. *Life* did, however, join with *Punch* on some occasions, as in this pictorial indictment of the journalist/novelist William Black, pictured by Charles Kendrick in the act of spoonfeeding the reading public with "mush" drawn from *Harper's Monthly* (figure 199). The public's dolls—Madcap Violet, MacLeod of Dare, and the Princess of Thule—are named after some of Black's popular novels, published respectively in 1876, 1879, and 1873. *Punch*'s 1881 reaction is similar, albeit more allusive: Black, having just published *Sunrise*, is pictured as the son of Phoebus, his carriage labeled "The Strange Adventures of a Phaeton" (another title) and piled high with books. He himself is accoutered according to his novels' titles: he has "White Wings" and carries a "Madcap Violet" (figure 200). This "atmospheric novelist," Sambourne implies, may suffer the same fate as the original Phaeton: to be burned out by his own ambition. What *Life* most objected to was Black's unwarranted popularity; what it preferred was the combination of "romance" and realism that produced high values and happy endings leavened by action. Its treatment of Hall Caine, Rossetti's housemate, demonstrates, however, that sensationalism has no part in the definition of what is acceptable. The full-page caricature published on 14 October 1897 (figure 201) is only one of a long series of gibes, many in the form of satirical interviews or reviews. "Caine the Uncanny" is said to have taken a lunatic's letters, written "in her most lurid moments," for his prose (14 August 1902, p. 138); he is pictured as one of "Our Boys," snipping his plots from the Bible and from Shakespeare's works (figure 202); he is described as having "passionate red hair, impulsive ears, bulging brows, throbbing temples, sinewy mouth, prehensile tongue, forty-horse-power lungs, . . . shrinking modesty and complete mastery of the typewriter"

Figure 201. Hall Caine, Life, *14 October 1897.*

Figure 202. "Our Boys," Life, *20 April 1905.*

(20 June 1907, p. 839). Clearly, for *Life*, Caine is as little preferable to the realists as Black is; in neither case does the periodical allow popular opinion to influence what it believed to be its critical (and educative) mission.

Again, both British and Americans join in lampooning the historical novel, but the styles and purport differ. *Life* uses the language of technology to complain primarily about trite plots and characterization, as illustrated by this vignette of a "Historical Novel Factory":

The plot of the novel is a molten steel, the chief dramatic situations dating back to the time of Adam, who no doubt raised Cain with them. The villains are made of scrap brass and pig iron; the heroines, of the best grade of imported sawdust soaked in a strong solution of mush-molly. The composition of the hero is a manufacturers' secret. His sword blade, however, is of the finest tempered steel, villain-proof, and capable of drenching a palatial staircase or a barren winter landscape with the rich life blood of his foes. (6 March 1902, p. 193)

Punch, on the other hand, characteristically focuses not on the genre itself, but on the writers. Sambourne's caricature of William Harrison Ainsworth, for example, shows the novelist holding a quill labeled "Romance" and, dressed in medieval garb, sitting in front of a faintly-sketched effigy of the infamous Jack Shepherd, one of his heroes. The drawing is captioned: "To the greatest Axe-and-Neck-Romancer of our Time, who is quite at the Head of his Profession, we dedicate this Block. *Ad multos Annos!*" (figure 203). The accompanying mock interview, which begins with Ainsworth's claiming that he was born in the Tower of London in 1715, suggests that the novelist's life has been turned into romance. The reporter is greeted by "a retainer handsomely caparisoned in rich Damascus doublet, russet jerkin, and arras trunks, relieved with the heraldic emblazonment of the house, a Tower of London reversed *or*, on a somersault double guevée *gules*"; at the touch of a control handle, "a flood of crimson light pours in through the mullions and trefoils of the great stained oriel window" (24 September 1881, pp. 135–36). While *Punch* seeks to amuse its readers with a potpourri of puns and genealogical quips, it also makes a more serious statement about the artificial nature of the historical novel. *Once a Week* is even more straightforward about its reservations. Along with a drawing of "The Biographer of Jack Sheppard" in doublet and

hose is a brief biography that ends with a paragraph expressing doubts about Ainsworth's effect on the public:

The moral tendency of his writings, and the effect they were likely to produce on the youthful or untrained mind, have often been the subject of criticism. Of these, we think there can be no doubt, the effect must be bad. While we wish Mr. Ainsworth no harm, we wish the cause of morality in fiction well; and we cannot help thinking that if the "fever into which he was thrown" by the recital of the lawless adventures of a highwayman had carried off his passion for writing novels, English literature would have been the gainer. (30 November, 1872, p. 473)

While perhaps not the gainer without Ainsworth, English literature would indeed have been different. By 1882, however, he had died and must be

Figure 203. W. Harrison Ainsworth, Punch, *24 September 1881.*

220

Figure 204. Wilkie Collins, Punch, *14 January 1882.*

Figure 205. "The Novelist Who Invented Sensation," Vanity Fair, *3 February 1872.*

considered more of an influence upon rather than a participant in the popular tradition we seek to sketch.

Wilkie Collins, shown by Sambourne "As the Man in White doing Ink-and-Penance for having Written the *Black Robe*" (figure 204), is a pertinent example in the ongoing reaction to "romantic," "sensation," and "historical" novels, all of which, for the periodicals in question, seem to have been equated. Like Sambourne's caricature of Black, this is an elaborate visual pun on novel titles. Wearing the garb of the heroine in *The Woman in White*, Collins is surrounded by allegorical figures representing his works, including a bird labeled *Poor Miss Finch* (1872), a quarter moon rising over the *Moonstone* (1868), and a doll-like *New Magdalen* (1873). *Vanity Fair*'s contribution to the parodic record of Wilkie Collins emphasizes his romantic bent, to be sure, but finds humor elsewhere in the discrepancy

between his physical size and his powerful literary effects; he is drawn by Andriano Cecioni, looking more like the lawyer he intended to be than the "sensation novelist" the caption proclaims him (figure 205). At least one British periodical reacts to Collins in the way *Life* does to Caine. *Once a Week,* whose biographical commentaries are generally didactic and conservative, presents him as a bill poster for *The Woman in White* (figure 206). While the editors praise his tightly knit plots, they see his sensational themes and suspenseful chapter endings as appropriate for serial publication but detrimental to style. They object to his plots, characters, and diction: "The situations in which these puppets are placed by the wire-puller are often wildly improbable. . . . His English is not drawn from the purest

Figure 206. "He Wrote 'The Woman in White,'" Once
a Week, *24 February 1872.*

fount. . . . He is a manufacturer of interesting
works of fiction, pure and simple" (24 February
1872, p. 197). In 1872 Collins had just published
Poor Miss Finch; to tout him in the caricature for
Woman in White (1860) is certainly to suggest that
his later works are inferior.

Once a Week's objection to Wilkie Collins's melodrama has its mirror image in the same periodical's
treatment of Anthony Trollope's realism. The
sketch of Trollope playing with a clerical puppet
(figure 207) illustrates the biographer's complaint
about the novelist's worldly clergy: he "'to parsons
gave up, what was meant for mankind.'" Other

comments suggest that *Once a Week* shared *Life*'s belief that a good novelist was "an avowed disciple of
idealism, of romance," and was moralistic as well.
For the British publication Collins is too sensational, but Trollope is too down-to-earth. The
"idealist" finds nothing "novel, unselfish, poetic" in
his works; his "point of view is real and perfectly
natural, but it is low." The biographer concludes
that novelists have a "mission" to "educate," not
just to "depict" (1 June 1872, p. 501).

While Trollope was at the height of his powers,
his talent for faithful depiction of manners and
scene seemed to make him, along with Thackeray,
the antidote for the romantic frame of mind. Certainly *Punch* emphasized this quality in "The Bea-
dle! or, the Latest Chronicle of Small Beer-Jester,"
by "Anthony Dollop." In this farrago Mrs. Dowdet
is the petticoat tyrant—" 'Britannia rules the waves;
I rule the See'"—and Mr. Matrix, "tall of stature,
but decidedly Low in his views . . . somewhat
broad-chested, but very narrow-minded," the aspiring Canon (24 July 1880, pp. 27–29). Twenty-
five years later, the qualities that *Punch* parodied in
the Barsetshire series it enshrined in a golden age of
novel writing. Its 1915 poetic tribute to "Father
Anthony" praises the novelist for providing an escape from "the turmoil of these unhappy days."
The poet bewails such modern "inventions" as the
automobile and feminism and longs not just for the
pastoral landscapes that Trollope wrote about but
also for the pastoral attitude of conciliation:

> . . . a wholesome love of England shone bright
> through all your tales—
> Love of her mellow landscape and green
> sequestered vales,
> Love of her ancient homesteads and gray
> ancestral towers,
> Lawns and meadows and gardens bright with
> old-fashioned flowers.
>
> And, though with the fires of passion your
> stories seldom glowed,
> That virtue need not be insipid they very
> clearly showed;
> For life in those placid regions was not all cakes
> and ale,
> And love brought sore disquiet to your
> charming Lily Dale.
>
> Yet, while discreetly checkered with sorrow
> and even crime,
> Your stories mostly ended to the tune of the
> marriage chime,

For you held with good CHARLES DARWIN
    that a novelist worth his salt
Eschewed an unhappy ending as a quite
    incurable fault.

As a satirist of the clergy you served a laudable
    end,
For we recognize that faithful are the wounds
    that are dealt by a friend;
You scarified the pompous and yet delighted to
    paint
In the meek unselfish Warden a thoroughbred
    modern saint.

. . . And your *dramatis personae* had brains of
    every size,
For you loved the simple and stupid as well as
    the witty and wise;
And some of your rarest figures were moulded
    of common clay,
And some of your high-born ladies had the
    meanest parts in the play.

Then, O ye precious penmen, who furiously
    rage
Against the "moral serfdom" of the
    mid-Victorian age,
Lauding your modern idols who make their
    genius plain
In an infinite capacity for giving their readers
    pain—

Go wallow at will in your garbage, mean,
    sinister or smart,
And prate till your jaws are weary of Art for
    the sake of Art,
You cannot abate my freedom to wander far
    and wide
In the pleasant land of Barset by Father
    ANTHONY'S side.

                (21 July 1915, p. 76)

By World War I, then, *Punch* had adopted a view related to the one held by *Life* in its 1905 cartoon (figure 195); the "Great Novelists" have been unjustly replaced by modern idols whose naturalistic or aesthetic outpourings do not measure up to the Victorian novel at its best. Like *Life*'s plea for a return to the Victorian frame of mind, *Punch*'s poem illustrates the nostalgia that permeated the popular view.

For some American publications, at least, George Meredith provided just that attitude of conciliation which proved helpful in coping with modern dislocation. Even though *Puck*'s "Diana of the Knickerbockers," a society poem by Colin Clout, is a banal description of a Gibson girl as a Greek goddess, the title suggests that the underlying classical reference has been borrowed from George Meredith's *Diana of the Crossways:*

> You pace the city: from the groves to you
>   Shepherds, pipes, pastorals, poets have
>   seceded—
> Like Liberty herself, you're *parvenue,*
>   Mistress, which means, like her, you have
>   succeeded.
>
> Leaving what hills, why love you here the
>   flags?

Figure 207. "'To Parsons Gave Up, What Was Meant for Mankind,'" Once a Week, 1 June 1872.

Figure 208. "'That kindly man in grey homespun,'"
Life, *26 November 1893.*

Figure 209. George Meredith, Punch, *28 July 1894.*

> Whence runs your blood, so cold, and yet so
> splendid?
> A huntress, you—to dog-carts and to drags,
> Say, have the hamadryads all descended?
> (1 February 1887, p. 355)

Despite Meredith's sometimes difficult prose (which Clout seems to parody), *Life* wholeheartedly approved of his philosophy. As part of the "Overheard in Arcady" series, Robert Bridges, writing as "Droch," eulogistically presents Meredith as a true humanitarian, a "'kindly man in grey homespun'" (figure 208) whose novels encourage an attitude of individualism and freedom in the reader. In the person of Tom Redworth, Diana's faithful follower, Bridges puts what with *Life*'s emphasis on the cult of womanhood is the highest compliment of all. Claiming that the novelist had comforted him when he thought that his love for Diana was hopeless, Tom quotes Meredith as saying,

"My boy . . . no one can love as you love without eternal profit to your soul—whether in the end you win her or not. It is the strength of Nature in you creating an ideal which has given and will always give a unity and stability to your work. I never see a man successful in the right way (not by luck or selfishness)—a man who is doing strenuously the best that Nature has put in him to do—that I do not begin to look for the *one idea* which is the inspiration of it. . . . Go on, go on, and the very laws of Nature, which are the laws of God, will fight for you!" (26 November 1893, p. 331)

For Tom, the "one idea" that animates him is, of course, Diana herself; for *Life*, the overriding preoccupation was ideal womanhood. Moreover, Meredith's comic spirit was, on one level at least, akin to *Life*'s unfailing optimism and gentle satire. Indeed, Frank Luther Mott points to just this when he notes that the comic spirit, in its "wedding of delicacy and force," was *Life*'s tutelary genius.[4]

Punch's treatment of Meredith was more critical than *Life*'s. As its historiographer explains, *Punch*'s reaction was a function of Burnand's conservative leadership: "In the Sixties, *Punch* had recognized Meredith and Whistler well ahead of the general public, but now [1890s] more and more it reacted to vitality with philistine guffaws."[5] The 1894 parody of *Lord Ormont and his Aminta* may be cited as one example. While not labeled a review, "Lord Ormont's Mate and Matey's Aminta" in fact criticizes Meredith for his innovative technique, as the accompanying sketch makes clear (figure 209): the novelist, portrayed as a frisky bull, is shattering fragile objects such as "Grammar," "Syntax," "Form," and "Construction." The parodist does his best to incorporate references to Meredith's comic spirit, but misses the irony that invigorates Meredith's view:

This was a school. Small wonder if the boys, doubly sensitive under a supercilious head-master of laughter-moving invention, poised for a moment on the to and fro of a needless knockabout jigface with chin and mouth all a-pucker for the inquisitive contest.

And, again, Lord Ormont's sister:

She split sides, convulsed in a take-offish murmur, a roll here, a roll there, rib-tickling with eyes goggling on the forefront of a sentence all rags, tags, and splutters like a jerrybuilder gaping at waste land pegged out in plots, foundations on the dig, and auctioneer prowling hither thither, hammer ready for the "gone" which shall spin a nobody's land into a somebody's money passing over counter or otherwise pocket to pocket, full to empty or almost empty, with a mewling choke-spark of a batter-foot all quills for the bean-feast. (28 July 1894, p. 37)

In contrast, Meredith's death called forth a

Figure 210. George Meredith, Punch, *26 May 1909.*

memorial tribute that, accompanied by a formal drawing, praises the novelist for much of what *Life* enjoyed, his interest in the relationship between man and woman and his humanity (figure 210):

> Yet most we mourn his loss as one who gave
>   The gift of laughter and the boon of tears,
> Interpreter of life, its gay and grave,
>   Its human hopes and fears.
>
> Seer of the soul of things, inspired to know
>   Man's heart and woman's, over all he threw
> The spell of fancy's iridescent glow,
>   The sheen of sunlit dew.
>
> And of the fellowship of that great Age
>   For whose return our eyes have waited long,
> None left so rich a twofold heritage
>   Of high romance and song.
>
> We knew him, fronted like the Olympian gods,
>   Large in his loyalty to land and friend,

Fearless to fight alone with Fortune's odds,
   Fearless to face the end.

And he is dead. And at the parting sign
   We speak, too late, the love he little guessed,
And bid him in the nation's heart for shrine
   Take his eternal rest.

               (26 May 1909, p. 370)

During the period we examine, then, the old "interpreters of life" were passing on to make way for the new. The public reaction to the changing content and styles at the turn of the century is, predictably, a compound of nostalgia for the familiar and humor at the experimentation. While many parodies seem to have been written only for the purpose of amusement, many had a more serious intent as well. By reading only the parodic record, we find that many of the novelists who are remembered today—Collins, Trollope, Stevenson, Kipling, Meredith—received lively presentation; whereas, for the most part, the sentimental novelists whom the parodists seemed to believe were favored by their readers received only indirect notice. If present-day reputation can be called to witness, then certainly the miles of parodic verse and novels have accomplished their homiletic function, for despite *Life*'s fear, even the most poorly prepared undergraduate may have heard of Meredith, but not of Bertha Rumble!

NOTES

1. Cruse, *The Victorians*, p. 285.
2. Flautz, *Gentle Satirist*, p. 119.
3. Henderson wrote *Puck*'s "Unintellectual Life" series in October and November, 1885.
4. Mott, *History*, 4:561.
5. Price, *History of Punch*, p. 131.

W'S for Wagner, who sang and played lots
    For Washington, Wesley, and good Doctor Watts.
His prurient plots pained Wesley and Watts,
But Washington said he " enjoyed them in spots."

X IS Xantippe, who's having her say,
    And frightening the army of Xerxes away.

10
The Amusing Muse Muses: A Mirror on the Magazines

FROM THE THRONE OF VICTORIA TO THE STAGE of Gilbert and Sullivan, the cartoonists and satirists of Victorian comic periodicals had their way with the poets, prophets, and British notables of the day. While we have tried to be broadly representative in our collection, we have by no means exhausted the seemingly limitless treasure that awaits further discovery in these delightful magazines and journals.

Victoria appeared constantly in magazines on both sides of the Atlantic, as did others in the royal family, prime ministers, and prominent parliamentarians. Darwin, probably better known to the public through caricatures and cartoons than through his actual writings or through the more serious debates over them, was so often caricatured that we have had to select only what impressed us as the best of the drawings. He, along with numerous other scientists and inventors, found their ways to the pages of humor journals well into the twentieth century. While Tennyson, Browning and Arnold appeared most frequently during their own lifetimes, Wilde, Swinburne, and the aesthetes lingered longer, perhaps because they and their followers tended to be more vulnerable to potshots from a predominantly philistine press. Thus, a vast gallery of amusing drawings and several volumes of parodies of British poets and prophets still awaits researchers and browsers of the comic periodicals. Our focus has been primarily upon British per-

sonalities, but another similar collection could be assembled by focusing upon prominent Americans, such as Mark Twain, P. T. Barnum, Buffalo Bill Cody, Horace Greeley, and a myriad of presidents, international travelers and socialites, sports and theatrical figures, and other American notables who were victims of the cartoonists and parodists on both sides of the Atlantic.

Our files are thick with examples of all of these, excluded only because of the necessarily limited scope of our purpose in this book. We have picked only those examples we believed would be of interest to the general reader. In some instances, the material may add a new dimension to appreciation of the life and works of those we have treated. In other instances, our selections and explications may serve only to save the reader the necessity of sorting through much doggerel in search of the occasionally clever or amusing pieces. In either case, we offer this book in the spirit of the fun we have had in assembling it.

One final task remains. That task is to comment on the periodicals themselves by illustrating their generally good-natured self-criticism and, occasionally, good-humored attacks on their competitors. While most of the editors and artists of the periodicals are now less well-known than the celebrities they drew and wrote about in their magazines, they are, at least for those of us engaged in the kind of

Figure 211. Punch *editor Shirley Brooks by Frederick Waddy, Once a Week, 20 July 1872.*

research required for this book, nearly as important. Indeed, they were the ones who had their fingers on the pulse of what we now call the "popular culture" of the time. They were the ones who deserve credit for providing us with what a growing number of twentieth-century scholars now recognize as "a clear and very special window into the life and thought of the Victorian age."[1]

Some of the finest caricatures of these editors and artists were produced by *Vanity Fair* in that journal's famous lithograph series and by Frederick Waddy in his 1872 *Once a Week* gallery of notables. Waddy drew *Punch* editor Shirley Brooks (figure 211) shortly after Brooks had taken over, following the death of the founding editor Mark Lemon. The bearded Brooks, wearing the jester's cap arrayed

Figure 212. Thomas Hood, by Waddy, Once a Week, 3 August 1872.

with the titles of his novels, is shown popping out of his Punch and Judy cabinet and carefully clutching his bat of "humour." Waddy's accompanying biographical sketch provides a brief history of *Punch* and some of its distinguished contributors, including Thackeray, Tennyson, Douglas Jerrold, and Thomas Hood. Hood's own face appeared in *Once a Week* in 1872 as the editor of a "rising" new comic journal, *Fun* (figure 212).

Vanity Fair provided readers with drawings of other *Punch* editors, Tom Taylor (figure 213) and

Figure 213. Tom Taylor, by "Spy," Vanity Fair, *11 March 1876.*

Figure 214. George Du Maurier, by "Spy," Vani Fair, *23 January 1896.*

Francis Burnand, the latter of whom made *Punch* "almost readable," according to the rival magazine. *Punch* artists appearing in *Vanity Fair* included John Tenniel and George Du Maurier (figure 214), and *Vanity Fair* offered a pictorial record of two of its own editors, Thomas Gibson Bowles (figures 215 and 216) and Frank Harris, as well as its three most famous artists, Leslie Ward (figure 217), Carlo Pellegrini (figure 218) and Max Beerbohm (see chapter 7, figure 155).

The American *Life*, along with its British cousins *Punch* and *Vanity Fair*, enjoyed occasional jabs at

the rapidly growing publishing industry in America and England. In 1889 *Life* celebrated its sixth birthday with a cartoon spoofing its "less fortunate contemporaries" (figure 219). In varying degrees of destitution, those coming to *Life*'s affluent party include representatives of *Puck, Harper's, The Graphic,* and *Frank Leslie's Magazine!*

Shortly after the turn of the century, *Life* published a drawing by George Parson which, somewhat after the style of Doré's illustrations of Dante's *Inferno*, shows a well-attired gentleman conversing with Satan in what appears to be a lower region of Hell (figure 220). The two stand at the foot of a mountain of bound volumes, and Satan comments to the gentleman, obviously a publisher, "this is the trash you published in the other world." The publisher laments, "And now I suppose I'll have to eat it." Satan responds in a Dantean punishment-to-fit-the-crime manner, "Worse than that; you'll have to read it." One might assume that at least some of the books in *Life*'s underworld scene are bound periodicals!

Earlier, in an 1886 issue, *Life* had burlesqued its own publishing office in an amusingly illustrated piece, "Our Establishment." The text by Carlyle Smith is graced by pictures of "An Exterior View of *Life*'s Office" (figure 221), an "Annex for Aspiring Artists" (figure 222), interior views of the "Inner Office" (figure 223) and "The Dungeon" for such rivals as *Punch* and *Puck* (figure 224), statues of three trustees (figure 225), the business manager, and a contributing poet (figure 226), and *Life*'s own Cunard vessel (figure 227).

Figure 215. Thomas Gibson Bowles, editor of Vanity Fair *and "Jehu Junior" in his regular letterpress biographical sketches of the persons caricatured. By "Spy,"* Vanity Fair, *13 July 1889.*

Figure 216. "Spy's" later cartoon of Bowles after Bowles left the magazine to become a Member of Parliament. From Vanity Fair, *19 October 1905.*

Figure 217. Leslie Ward ("Spy") by Jean de Paleologu ("Pal"), Vanity Fair, 23 November 1889.

Figure 218. Carlo Pellegrini ("Ape") by A. J. Marks Vanity Fair, 27 April 1889.

Our Establishment

As so many of our enterprising contemporaries are advertising the fact that they have new buildings, we can no longer conceal the fact that we too are guilty of a most flagrant degree of prosperity.

It is perhaps not generally known that the proprietors of this journal have recently erected a few dozen edifices to be devoted exclusively to those connected financially or otherwise with our staff. Any words of descriptive praise of our new offices might be deemed fulsome, and with a degree of modesty which we unassumingly though firmly pronounce becoming, we content ourselves with simply offering a few views of this new

edifice of our success, taken on the spots by our artists.

The first plate, with accompanying explanatory notes, represents the general bird's eye view of our establishment. We may say here that a bird's eye is small and unable to grasp as many beauties at one swoop as the more highly endowed orb of mankind, and that our bird omitted many details of our magnificence. Imperfect as the picture is, however, we produce it without a pang.

Among the omitted beauties there are included an Oubliette for the man who forgets to pay his subscription, and a Gallows for the man who hangs around the office and talks all day long. This last helps the man to

Figure 219. Life *remembers "some less fortunate contemporaries" in Charles Dana Gibson's cartoon for the magazine's sixth anniversary, 10 November 1889.*

hang around, but prevents his talking. It is simply a delicate method of ours to keep his feelings from being hurt.

We should likewise like to call attention to the crowd around the subscription door, and to the unusually small number of occupants of our burial ground. As the descriptive note beneath the picture intimates, these mortuary friends of ours were chiefly those who failed to renew and died either from melancholia or some other similar disease immediately after. In justice to our special undertaker, who has charge of our humorous department, we must confess that four of the headstones commemorate Presbyterian Deacons who laughed themselves to death over our pages.

In plate three is given an interior view of our office. Simply calling attention to the very important bulletin in the left foreground, we continue with plate two, which represents a philanthropic venture we have lately entered upon.

It is a little chateau that we use for aspiring artists who want us to tell them how to draw. We take boarders here free of charge, reserving the right to slide them into a dark, dank moat, of which we have a full supply on

Figure 220. George Parson's Doré-like scene of a publisher's "inferno" in Life, *18 July 1901.*

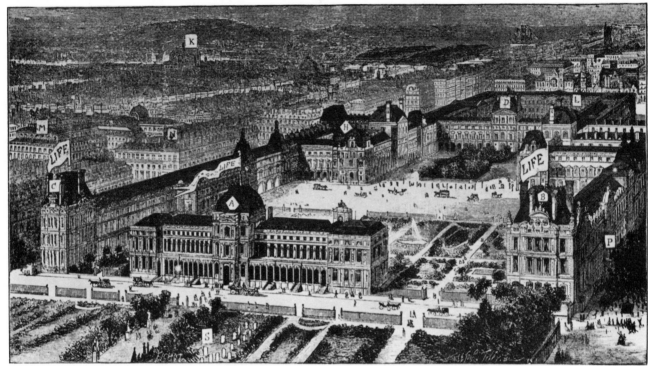

Figure 221. Life *spoofs itself and others in a series of caricatures in an 1886 issue. Here is "An Exterior View of* Life *Offices."*

Figure 222. "Annex for Aspiring Artists," Life *series, 1886.*

Figure 223. "*Inner Office,*" Life *series, 1886.*

Figure 224. Life's "*Dungeon*" *for such rivals as* Punch *and* Puck, Life *series, 1886.*

hand, when they think they have learned the art and begin to contribute.

In the fourth place a really thrilling part of our business is being transacted. It is a formality through which we have to go about four times a day, and consists in filing away youths who try to pass off as original, jokes that *Punch* printed in '49. The last census of our *Punch* dungeon demonstrates the appalling fact that there are 562 poets, 247 artists and 96 "humorists" buried there. This, of course, is exclusive of the editors of *Puck*, whom we have not yet been able to induce to enter.

This particular dungeon is often so crowded that prisoners are taken out in squads of ten and drowned in Central Park. There is a special chamber seventy-seven feet lower down for the accommodation of those heavenly beings who are constantly seeing a sacreligious [*sic*] and indecent meaning in the things they meet in *Life*. Our treatment for these unfortunates is a regular course of the American daily paper. They soon become so familiar with all that is criminal and forbidden that even *Life* seems decently clean and pure.

In extreme cases, when nothing else can sicken him, the *N.Y. Tribune* is placed in his hands—a half hour of that generally "fetches" the most obstinate and callous nature.

As some of our lady friends have expressed a desire to know what the author of our delicate verses looks like, and as several of our creditors would find it convenient to become familiar with the lineaments of our business manager, we have reproduced two accurate photographs of them also.

It frequently happens to the editorial constitution that a trip to Europe is necessary. Of course such necessity must be considered, and we are pleased to announce that

Figure 226. Statues of Life's business manager and a contributing poet, Life series, 1886.

236

Figure 227. Life's own Cunard vessel, Life *series, 1886.*

Figure 228. Whitelaw Reid (left) and W. R. Hearst (right) in Life's vaudeville act of editors. "Power of the Press," Life, 26 September 1901.

we have recently built a magnificently appointed vessel for this purpose. Time in editorial work being an inseparable adjunct to success, it is impossible for the editor to do as ordinary mortals do and walk to the steamer with his wardrobe in his pocket. Appreciating this fact, a special engineer, at the request of the United States Government, has laid a surface road from the pier to our main entrance, from which the editor embarks. The only transatlantic lines now passing our door are the Cunard and White Star. There is, however, a sharp competition among other lines for this business.

The vessel is frequently handy, too, in crossing Broadway when our Street Commissioners are transacting private business. Lack of space alone prevents our saying more in this regard. Enough has been said, however, to convince the public that we are at least even with the age, if not one or two cycles ahead. We cannot help mentioning here our unparalleled collection of art treasures, among which will be found a brazen group representing three metropolitan trustees wrestling with the truth.

In conclusion, we have only to say that in spite of all this magnificence and enterprise, sample copies may still be had at the old stand. Price, ten cents.

Another *Life* "serio-comedy" is set at three A.M. in Printing House Square and parodies five leading journalists of the day. James Gordon Bennett, Paul Dana, Whitelaw Reid, E. L. Godkin, and W. R. Hearst appear as a troupe of vaudeville performers in a review, "The Power of the Press" (figures 228 and 229). As magazines and newspapers assaulted the newstands of America and Britain with ever-increasing numbers, publishers themselves were bombarded by unsolicited manuscripts from aspiring amateur bards. Thus, in what is probably history's first song dedicated to all who have ever received rejection notices, *Life* offered a poem, "Declined With Thanks," complete with a collage of some twenty fellow-publishers' letterheads, all with notes beginning with varying forms of "We regret that the enclosed MS is not quite suitable for our purposes" (figure 230).

Like *Life*, *Punch* also had its fun with the rapid rise, and often equally rapid fall, of periodicals. Eight that managed to survive are victims of puns in an 1887 illustration, "Magazine Explosions," by one "D. Crambo, Junior" (figure 231), and numerous of the lesser-known that found their ways into *Punch* cartoons included *Lancet* (figure 232), *Roseleaves* (figure 233), *The Knacker*, *The Gadfly* (figure 234) and

Figure 229. James Gordon Bennett (left) and Paul Dana (right) in Life's *vaudeville act of editors. "Power of the Press,"* Life, *26 September 1901.*

Figure 230. "Declined with Thanks," in Life, 14 November 1901.

Century. (Scent Sherry—ahem!)   Quart early.

Fought Knightly.   Corn-'ill.

Black woo'd.   "Ill us trated!"

Harpers and Phrasers.   "Temple! Bah!"

Figure 231. "Magazine Explosions," Punch, 16 April 1887.

The Daily Neator (figure 235). Along with such visual satire, Punch also delighted in verbal, usually in the form of comic poems "dedicated" to such as Nineteenth Century, Sporting Times, Police Court News, and The Illustrated London News.

Thanks to the Modern Language Association's 1978 publication of Victorian Periodicals: A Guide to Research, those of us who engage in periodicals research can do so with increased enthusiasm. Our "cause" is well stated in the preface to that volume:

The time is long past when it was necessary either to defend or to justify research and study of British Victorian periodicals. In the last fifteen years they have emerged as a major source of information for students of the nineteenth century. It is well recognized by scholars across the disciplines, in history, literature, economics, art history, social history, politics, the sciences, and many other fields, that periodicals offer a clear and very special window into the life and thought of the Victorian age. . . . Those who have been at work in the periodical field over the past twenty or so years are convinced that

DEPRESSING!

Griggles. "HULLO, DUMPLEY! WHAT ARE YOU READING! 'CHRISTMAS NUMBER OF THE *LANCET!* PUT IT DOWN, AND COME AND HAVE A GAME O' PYRAMIDS!"

Figure 232. "Depressing!" Punch, 27 January 1883.

ALL IN THE DAY'S WORK.

Critic. "HOW'S THE *BOOK* GOING, OLD MAN!"

Author. "OH—ALL RIGHT, I FANCY. THE PRESS HAS NOTIC[ED] ALREADY. YESTERDAY'S *ROSELEAVES* HAILS ME AS THE C[?] *THACKERAY!*"

Critic. "AH, *I* WROTE THAT!"

Author. "DID YOU REALLY! HOW CAN I THANK YOU! O[?] OTHER HAND, THIS WEEK'S *KNACKER* SAYS THAT I'VE BEEN FORTUN[?] ARRESTED BY MADNESS ON THE ROAD TO IDIOTCY!"

Critic. "AH, I WROTE THAT TOO!"

Figure 233. "All in the Day's Work," Punch, 16 December 1893.

UNSIGNED MAGAZINE ARTICLES.

Keats-Jones. "I SAY, JUST LOOK WHAT SOME ANONYMOUS ASS IN *THE KNACKER* SAYS ABOUT THOSE SONNETS OF MINE, WHICH YOU TOLD ME YOU CONSIDERED AS GOOD AS WORDSWORTH'S!"

Shelley-Brown. "MY DEAR FELLOW, WE'RE IN THE SAME BOAT! YOU KNOW THAT LAST BOOK OF MINE THAT YOU SAID YOU LIKED SO MUCH! WELL, JUST SEE WHAT'S SAID OF IT IN *THE GADFLY!* I WONDER WHO THE FOOL IS!"

[*Keats-Jones is the Author of the "Gadfly" review of Brown's book, and Shelley-Brown writes all the literary notices in the "Knacker."*]

Figure 234. "Unsigned Magazine Articles," Punch, 21 December 1895.

Figure 235. "He Had Succeeded," Punch, 29 February 1896.

HE HAD SUCCEEDED.

A. "OH, I SAY, THAT SKETCH YOU DID OF ME IN THE *DAILY NEATOR*
DE ME LOOK THE SORT OF CONCEITED ASS ONE WOULD LIKE TO KICK!"
B. "YOU THINK SO! AND I WAS AFRAID I HAD QUITE FAILED TO
CH THE CHARACTER!"

Figure 237. "The Modern Headsman. Celebrities begging for mercy of the caricaturist. Heads taken off while you wait." Punch, 14 September 1889.

Figure 236. "The Publisher: You say this is your first novel. A Chinese romance. Never been abroad, hey? Just made it up as you went along. Well, this is a find! (To clerk) James, order fifty thousand copies printed at once, advertise whole edition of two hundred thousand sold before publication, and get out lithographs of the young lady." Life, 26 September 1901.

study of untapped information in periodicals represents one of the great breakthroughs in modern Victorian scholarship.[2]

In his chapter "The Rationale—Why Read Victorian Periodicals," John S. North adds;

Periodical literature is the largest single source of Victorian material available to us, and the most comprehensive. . . . Needless to say, much trivia will inevitably be uncovered in the files of obscure periodicals. In passing through the listings of titles, searching for a single magazine, the student will certainly be oppressed by irrelevant material. When the laborious task of turning page after page of hundreds of issues is begun, the patience of even the most single-minded scholar will be tried as the dust accumulates on hands, face, and clothing.[3]

After the dust has settled from the flurry of page-turning, one begins to suspect that he has been sprinkled with magic dust, or at least with some kind of strange narcotic that lures him back to the seemingly inexhaustible supply of unexamined pages in the mountain of magazines, journals, and newspapers that await further scanning.

NOTES

1. J. Don Vann and Rosemary T. Van Arsdel, eds., *Victorian Periodicals: A Guide to Research* (New York: Modern Language Association, 1978), p. ix.
2. Ibid., pp. ix and x.
3. Ibid., pp. 3 and 20.

Mr. Punch bids farewell, Punch, *27 June 1900.*

Y IS for Young, the great Mormon saint,
   Who thinks little Yum Yum and Yvette so quaint
He has to be instantly held in restraint.

Z IS for Zola, presenting La Terre
   To Zenobia the brave and Zuleika the fair,
Whose blushes they artfully conceal with their hair.

Bibliography

Aronson, Theo. *Grandmama of Europe: The Crowned Descendants of Queen Victoria*. Indianapolis and New York: Bobbs-Merrill, 1973.

Beckson, Karl, ed. *Oscar Wilde, The Critical Heritage*. New York: Barnes & Noble, 1970.

Brough, James. *The Prince and the Lily*. New York: Coward, McCann, & Geoghegan, 1975.

Broughton, Northup and Pearsall. *Robert Browning: A Bibliography, 1830–1950*. Ithaca, N.Y.: Cornell University Press, 1953.

Coe, Brian. *The Birth of Photography: The Story of the Formative Years, 1800–1900*. New York: Taplinger, 1977.

Coupe, Charles. "Tennysonian Sea-Echoes." *American Catholic Quarterly Review* 28 (1903): 455–63.

Crane, Walter. *An Artist's Reminiscences*. New York: Macmillan, 1907.

Cruse, Amy. *The Victorians and Their Reading*. Boston: Houghton Mifflin, 1935.

Duff, David. *Victoria in the Highlands*. London: Frederick Muller, 1970.

———. *Victoria Travels*. London: Frederick Muller, 1970.

Edel, Leon. *Henry James*. 5 vols. Philadelphia: Lippincott, 1955–72.

Eidson, John. "Tennyson's *The Foresters* on the American Stage." *Philological Quarterly* 43 (1964): 549–57.

Ellegard, Alvar. "The Readership of the Periodical Press in Mid-Victorian Britain, Part II." *Victorian Periodicals Newsletter*, no. 13 (1971): 22.

Emboden, William. *Sarah Bernhardt*. New York: Macmillan, 1975.

Everitt, Graham. *English Caricaturists and Graphic Humorists of the Nineteenth Century*. London: Swan Sonnenschein, 1893.

Ewbank, David R. "Kidding the Victorian Poets: A Collection of Parodies." *Victorian Poetry* 15, no. 1 (Spring 1977): 66–73.

Flautz, John. *Life: The Gentle Satirist*. Bowling Green, Ohio: Bowling Green University Popular Press, 1972.

Gaunt, William. *The Restless Century, Paintings in Britain 1800–1900*. London: Phaidon Press, 1972.

Gilder, Richard Watson. "Newspaper, the Magazine, and the Public." *Outlook*, 4 February 1899, pp. 316–21.

Graves, Charles L. *Mr. Punch's History of Modern England*. 4 vols. London: Cassell, 1921–22.

Gray, Donald. "A List of Comic Periodicals Published in Great Britain, 1800–1900, with a Prefatory Essay." *Victorian Periodicals Newsletter*, no. 15 (1972): 2–79.

Griffin, W. Hall. *The Life of Robert Browning*. London: Methuen and Co., 1938.

Gohdes, Clarence. *American Literature in Nineteenth-Century England*. Carbondale, Ill.: Southern Illinois University Press, 1944.

Hamilton, Walter. *Parodies of the Works of English and American Authors*. 6 vols. London: Reeves & Turner, 1884–89.

Hancher, Michael. "The Beerbohm Caricature of Browning and the Browning Society." *The Browning Newsletter*, 9 (Fall 1972): 23–33.

Harris, Eileen. *Vanity Fair: An Exhibition of Original Cartoons*. London: National Portrait Gallery, 1976.

Henderson, Archibald. *Bernard Shaw: Playboy and Prophet*. New York and London: Appleton, 1932.

Hess, Stephen, and Kaplan, Milton. *The Ungentlemanly Art: A History of American Political Cartoons*. Rev. ed. New York: Macmillan, 1974.

Hibbard, Christopher. *Gilbert and Sullivan and Their Vic-*

torian World. New York: American Heritage, 1976.

Hilton, Timothy. *The Pre-Raphaelites.* New York: Abrams, 1970.

Holloway, John. *The Victorian Sage.* New York: Norton, 1965.

Holman, Harriet. "Matthew Arnold's Elocution Lessons." *New England Quarterly* 18 (1945): 480.

Honan, Park. *Matthew Arnold.* New York: McGraw-Hill, 1981.

Hyde, H. Montgomery. *Oscar Wilde.* New York: Farrar, Straus, & Giroux, 1975.

Irvine, William. *The Universe of G. B. S.* New York: McGraw-Hill, 1949.

Jerrold, Walter, and Leonard, R. M. *A Century of Parody and Imitation.* London: Oxford University Press, 1913.

Keating, P. J. "Robert Browning: A Reader's Guide." In *Robert Browning,* edited by Isobel Armstrong. Writers and Their Background series. Athens: Ohio University Press, 1974.

Lauterbach, Edward Stewart. "*Fun* and its Contributors: The Literary History of a Victorian Humor Magazine." Ph. D. dissertation, University of Illinois, 1961; Ann Arbor: University Microfilms 61-1636, 1961.

Lee, Sidney. *King Edward VII, a Biography.* 2 vols. New York: Macmillan, 1925–27.

Leonard, Chilson. "Arnold in America: A Study of Matthew Arnold's Literary Relations with America and of his Visits to this Country in 1883 and 1886." Ph. D. dissertation, Yale University, 1932.

Lewis, Lloyd, and Smith, Henry Justin. *Oscar Wilde Discovers America (1882).* New York: Benjamin Blom, 1936.

Longford, Elizabeth. *Queen Victoria: Born to Succeed.* New York: Harper and Row, 1964.

Lott, John Bertrand. "Matthew Arnold as Satirist." Ph. D. dissertation, Harvard University, 1961; Ann Arbor: University Microfilms 61-2317, 1961.

Lynch, Bohun. *Max Beerbohm in Perspective: With a Prefatory Letter by M. B.* London: William Heinemann, 1921.

McCallum, James Dow. "The Apostle of Culture Meets America." *New England Quarterly* 2 (1929): 374–75.

Madden, Lionel, and Dixon, Diana. *The Periodical Press in Britain: A Bibliography of Modern Studies.* New York: Garland, 1976.

Magnus, Philip. *King Edward the Seventh.* New York: E. P. Dutton, 1964.

Marshall, George O., Jr. *Tennyson in Parody and Jest: An Essay and a Selection.* Lincoln, England: Tennyson Research Centre, 1975.

Maurice, Arthur Bartlett, and Cooper, Frederick Taber. *The History of the Nineteenth Century in Caricature.* New York: Cooper Square, 1970.

Mitchell, John Ames. "How *Life* Began." *Life* (Jubilee Number), January 1883, pp. 17–18.

Mott, Frank Luther. *A History of American Magazines.* 5 vols. Cambridge, Mass.: Harvard University Press, 1938–68.

Naylor, Leonard E. *The Irrepressible Victorian: The Story of Thomas Gibson Bowles.* London: Macdonald and Co., 1965.

Neiman, Fraser, ed. *Essays, Letters, and Reviews by Matthew Arnold.* Cambridge, Mass.: Harvard University Press, 1960.

Newhall, Beaumont. *The History of Photography from 1839 to the Present Day* New York: The Museum of Modern Art, 1964.

Nicoll, Allardyce. *English Drama, 1900–1930.* Cambridge: Cambridge University Press, 1973.

———. *A History of Late Nineteenth-Century Drama, 1850–1900.* 2 vols. Cambridge: Cambridge University Press, 1946.

North, John S. "The Rationale—Why Read Victorian Periodicals?" In *Victorian Periodicals: A Guide to Research,* edited by J. Don Vann and Rosemary T. VanArsdel. New York: Modern Language Association, 1978.

Ormond, Leonee. "*Punch's* Linley Sambourne." *Nineteenth Century* 4 (1978): 81–87.

Pearson, John. *Edward the Rake.* New York and London: Harcourt, 1975.

Postma, Jelle. *Tennyson as Seen by his Parodists.* 1926. Reprint. New York: Haskell, 1966.

Prager, Arthur. *The Mahogany Tree: An Informal History of Punch.* New York: Hawthorne Books, 1979.

Price, R. G. G. *A History of Punch.* London: Collins, 1957.

Qualls, Barry V. "W. H. Mallock's *Every Man His Own Poet.*" *Victorian Poetry* 16 (1978): 184.

Riewald, J. G. *Beerbohm's Literary Caricatures from Homer to Huxley.* Hamden, Conn.: Archon Books, 1977.

Robbins, William. *The Ethical Idealism of Matthew Arnold: A Study of the Nature and Sources of his Moral and Religious Ideas.* London: William Heinemann, 1959.

Sanderson, Edgar, and Melville, Lewis. *King Edward VII.* 6 vols. London: Gresham, 1910.

Sansom, William. *Victorian Life in Photographs.* London: Thames and Hudson, 1974.

Savory, Jerold J. *Other Likenesses of Robert Browning: The Poet in Caricature, Cartoon and Comic Commentary.* Browning Interests series, no. 26. Waco, Texas: Baylor University Armstrong Browning Library, 1981.

———, ed. *The Vanity Fair Gallery: A Collector's Guide to the Caricatures.* New Jersey and London: A. S. Barnes & Co., 1979.

———. *The Vanity Fair Lithographs: An Illustrated Checklist.* New York: Garland, 1978.

Skinner, Cornelia Otis. *Madame Sarah.* Boston: Houghton Mifflin, 1967.

Spielmann, M. H. *The History of Punch.* London: Cassell, 1895.

Super, R. H., ed. *The Complete Prose Works of Matthew*

Arnold. 11 vols. Ann Arbor: University of Michigan Press, 1960–77.

————. *The Time-Spirit of Matthew Arnold*. Ann Arbor: University of Michigan Press, 1970.

Van, J. Don, and VanArsdel, Rosemary T., eds. *Victorian Periodicals: A Guide to Research*. New York: Modern Language Association, 1978.

Waddy, Frederick. *Cartoon Portraits and Biographical Sketches of Men of the Day*. London: 1873.

Wallace, Irving. *The Fabulous Showman: The Life and Times of P. T. Barnum*. New York: Knopf, 1959.

Ward, Leslie. *Forty Years of "Spy."* London: Chatto and Windus, 1915.

Weygandt, Cornelius. *The Time of Tennyson: English Victorian Poetry as It Affected America*. 1926. Reprint. London: Hogarth, 1973.

Wilson, Elizabeth. *Robert Browning's Portraits, Photographs and Other Likenesses*. Browning Interests series. Waco, Texas: Baylor University Armstrong Browning Library, 1943.

Index

This index includes only proper names that appear in the text.